THE COMPLETE BOOK OF
LONG-DISTANCE
CYCLING

THE COMPLETE BOOK OF
LONG-DISTANCE
CYCLING

Build the **Strength, Skills, and Confidence** to **Ride** as **Far** as You Want

by Edmund R. **Burke,** Ph.D., and Ed **Pavelka**

RODALE

NOTICE

The information in this book is meant to supplement, not replace, proper cycling training. Like any sport involving speed, equipment, balance, and environmental factors, cycling poses some inherent risk. The authors and publisher advise readers to take full responsibility for their safety and know their limits. Before following the advice in this book, be sure that your equipment is well-maintained, and do not take risks beyond your level of experience, aptitude, training, and comfort.

Cover and Interior Designer: Susan P. Eugster

Library of Congress Cataloging-in-Publication Data
Burke, Ed.
    The complete book of long-distance cycling : build the strength, skills, and confidence to ride as far as you want / Edmund R. Burke and Ed Pavelka.
       p.   cm.
    Includes index.
    ISBN 1–57954–199–2 paperback
    1. Cycling—Training.   I. Pavelka, Ed.   II. Title.
    GV1048 .B873   2000
    613.7'11—dc21   00–009615

Distributed to the book trade by St. Martin's Press

2 4 6 8 10 9 7 5 3 1   paperback

Visit us on the Web at www.rodalesportsandfitness.com, or call us toll-free at (800) 848-4735.

WE **INSPIRE** AND **ENABLE** PEOPLE TO IMPROVE
THEIR LIVES AND THE WORLD AROUND THEM

Contents

Acknowledgments. . .vii
Foreword. . .ix

1 START SMART

1 Ride Long, Ride Strong. . .**3**
2 Tame Time. . .**22**
3 Get Fit to Ride. . .**30**
4 Better Bike Handling. . .**43**
5 Gear That Goes and Goes. . .**59**
6 Food for the Long Haul. . .**90**
7 The Mental Edge. . .**108**

2 THE RIDES

8 Long Rides: Up to 100 Miles. . .**121**
9 Longer Rides: 100 to 200 Miles. . .**137**
10 Longest Rides: 200 Miles . . . and Beyond. . .**154**

3 COMFORT and HEALTH

11 Danger Zones. . .**167**
12 End Saddle Sores. . .**185**
13 Body Shop. . .**190**
14 Aches and Pains. . .**198**
15 Battling Your Body and the Elements. . .**216**
16 Women's Issues. . .**233**
17 Stay Loose. . .**242**
18 Year-Round Fitness. . .**252**

Glossary. . .269
About the Authors. . .275
Photo Credits. . .277
Index. . .279

ACKNOWLEDGMENTS

I am indebted to many people for the information, ideas, and concepts that make up this book. Most of all, I appreciate the athletes and coaches with whom I have worked over the last 20 years—in particular, I mention Eddie Borysewicz, who first showed me the meaning of hard work and a true love of cycling.

My gratitude also goes out to the many friends who provided me with the push I needed when I returned to active riding as an "adult-onset cyclist." Here, I refer especially to Bob Anderson, Harvey Newton, Jay T. Kearney, Ron Wisner, and all the cyclists with whom I have ridden at various PAC Tour and Carpenter-Phinney camps. I am grateful to all who believed in me and let me participate in this great sport with them.

A big thank-you for their support also goes to the various cycling companies out there, and to all of the publishers and editors who continue to help me speak to the needs of cyclists of all abilities and aspirations. Also, I am obliged to the University of Colorado at Colorado Springs for its continuing support of my teaching, research, writing, and travel to speak at workshops and seminars around the world.

Of course, I give special thanks to Ed Pavelka, who first helped me with my writing in 1977 while he was editor at *VeloNews*. He made those struggling articles better than I ever dreamed they could be. As my coauthor and editor, he has again taken my words and honed them, this time into a book of which I am very proud.

Finally, to my wife, Kathleen, go my most heartfelt appreciation and gratitude. She continues to put up with my long hours at the computer, my busy travel schedule, my renewed life of training, and my constant refrains of, "I'm almost finished" and "I'll be back in a few hours from my bike ride." Thanks, Kathleen, for your unselfish support of everything I do. Without you, none of this would be possible.

—Ed Burke

As usual, Burke has left almost no room to say anything! So I will limit this to five people who have made a huge difference in my cycling and my life: Fred Matheny, Pete Penseyres, Skip Hamilton, Jeff Linder, and Lon Haldeman. Thanks, guys! I'll ride with you anytime.

—Ed Pavelka

Challenges for Each of Us

By Lon Haldeman

More than a century ago, bicycles rolled side by side with horses and wagons. Thousands of patents for cycling equipment were issued, and bicycle designs were a high priority among companies and consumers. Cyclists began riding greater distances for transportation, competition, and personal satisfaction. For the first time in history, a person on a bicycle on a good road could travel farther in one day than with any other mode of land transportation. A cyclist had the ability to go more than a hundred miles and enjoy it at the same time.

In my opinion, long-distance cycling is the most important part of our sport. You can ride for fitness or transportation, but if you don't enjoy it, you will find other ways to get a workout or get to work. On the other hand, if you like riding in order to view the countryside and see the scenery over the next hill, you will naturally want to ride longer distances. Your fitness will improve, and so will your confidence in your ability. You will want to see new places and challenge yourself with faster times and longer miles. Endurance cycling becomes the result of enjoyment.

Growing up in Illinois, I was fortunate to have parents who let me travel far away by bike, and now I have a wife who lets me keep traveling. My mom and dad, Mary Jane and Ed, had to listen to the constant whir of my indoor trainer all winter when I was in high school. They supported me during my first record attempts and in all of my Race Across America adventures. They helped make long-distance riding enjoyable, and they made it easy for me to pursue a career in cycling.

I met my future wife, Susan Notorangelo, by chance at the Bicycle Across Missouri ride in 1980. We never talked or said hello—just shared a glance during the preride breakfast at a Denny's restaurant. After several months of writing letters, we finally met the next summer. Two years later, we were married, and the next week rode a tandem across America in 10 days. Since then, we have bicycled across the country together more than 50 times in races, tours, and record attempts. Our personal goals have changed over the years, but we still have a passion for long-distance cycling and the people we meet through the sport.

When I think back over my cycling career, it's hard to decide when my enthusiasm started. I remember my parents buying me a gold coaster-brake Hiawatha bike from the local hardware store when I was 10. It had chrome fenders and a built-in headlight. Those were the days of learning to ride in the backyard on grass. After a while, I was able to venture onto the parking lots and streets around our house. Then I went a little farther, several blocks from home. I felt like a long-distance cyclist.

I bought my first 10-speed in the eighth grade—a white AMF Scorcher that came unassembled in a box for $69. The water towers across the Illinois prairie became my new cycling destinations. I rode to all of the towns within 10 miles. With my cable-driven speedometer, I measured and mapped every farm road in the area. After mastering a 12-mile ride, I increased my distance to 15 miles. As my endurance and confidence grew, so did my definition of a long-distance cyclist. I was beginning to understand that long distances were something just beyond what I had already done.

Being an endurance cyclist became more than just riding miles, however. I was learning the importance of equipment, diet, and training. My next bicycles were a combination of customized parts that didn't quite match. There was always something to fix by improvising. Brake pads were fabricated from pieces of wood; worn tires were lined on the inside with duct tape; broken derailleurs were shimmed with sticks and rocks. My first cycling shorts were cutoffs made from black double-knit dress slacks. My tennis shoes were stiffened with insoles made from sheet aluminum. I was happy to be riding anything, so this cobbled-together equipment was fine as long as it let me reach new places.

The anticipation of attempting a new goal is one of the best rewards of riding long distances. Not being 100 percent sure you are going to succeed is part of the challenge and adds to the excitement. I felt this way on my first 10-mile ride, and I had the same feeling the night before my first Race Across America. I think this is why riders find so much personal satisfaction in endurance cycling. Setting new goals that take you farther and faster . . . sometimes failing in those goals

. . . finding a way to succeed . . . always looking for improvement.

In *The Complete Book of Long-Distance Cycling,* Ed Pavelka and Ed Burke give you an education that took me 30 years to learn. Read it, remember it, and ride it. By adding your own cycling experiences, you can make this book more than a reference for technical knowledge. Our sport has challenges that begin as easily as exploring a new road or going past the point you know. Have fun, and fill up your personal pages with a lifetime of cycling satisfaction.

Lon Haldeman is a leader in ultramarathon cycling. Following a competitive career in which he won the first two Races Across America, he founded PAC Tour to help other cyclists experience the achievement of riding long distances rapidly. PAC Tour offers endurance training camps and fully supported west-to-east and south-to-north transcontinental tours that take about 3 weeks at an average of 110 to 140 miles per day. For details, log on to www.pactour.com.

PART 1
Start
Smart

Ride Long, Ride Strong

One of the classic stories in cycling comes from a press interview with Fausto Coppi, the legendary Italian road racer of the 1940s and 1950s. "Please tell us, sir," ventured a wide-eyed reporter, "what it takes to become such a great champion." Coppi looked at the trembling young man, thought for a long moment, and then agreed to reveal the secret. A hush swept over the room. "You must do three things," Coppi said. "Ride your bike"—everyone leaned in to hear—"ride your bike, ride your bike."

Not to be outdone, Eddy Merckx, the greatest cyclist of the next generation (and we say of all time), had a succinct two-word formula for success: "Ride lots." So, you get the point. To get good on your bike, you have to get on your bike. Nothing can substitute. And the more you ride, the closer you'll come to your full potential as a cyclist.

Ride with a Plan

That said, there are more and less effective ways to "ride lots." This chapter is dedicated to making sure that you get the most from every hour spent on your bike. A systematic approach to training is the key to the steady progress that makes you as good as you can be. No matter what your ultimate goal, the basic principles of training always apply. There are just two main variables: quantity and quality. In combination, they produce all of the different ways to "ride your bike."

A cyclist training for an ultimate test such as the Tour de France or Race Across America might ride 35 hours per week with a mix of intervals, lactate threshold training (explained a little later in this chapter), hill work, and long miles for endurance. A cyclist looking to improve his century time might do similar training but for fewer than half the hours. An older rider might do less of the intense work. Ditto for a touring cyclist, who will benefit more by emphasizing steady distance and climbing.

If you've been on your bike at all, we don't need to remind you of how challenging it is to ride longer distances. Challenge is the reason that so many riders gravitate to endurance events. There's always a satisfying sense of achievement in going farther on the bike than once seemed possible. Ed Pavelka clearly remembers when 15 miles was his limit; how he bonked so badly on his first attempt at 50 miles that he couldn't ride again for a week (and didn't want to, either); how his first century was delayed for half an hour at the 80-mile mark while he sprawled on the floor of a convenience store trying to summon enough energy to finish. He thought about these things during Paris-Brest-Paris '99 while he was riding the last 500 miles straight through—and finishing with strength to spare. You'll have examples like this, too, as you train and ride events year after year, building your ability to go where few other cyclists can follow.

How does it happen? Adaptation. This is a key concept in all training, but it's especially meaningful for long-distance cyclists. You've probably already felt how tired you become when reaching your limit of endurance. Everything complains. Your legs hurt, your feet throb, your upper body aches—and your butt is filing a formal complaint against cruel and unusual punishment. But flesh heals, and the mind grows stronger. The next time you ride this distance, it's not quite as tough. Not a cakewalk, but you're closer to the finish before the difficulties rise up. Your body is adapting. So you feel confident about adding a few miles. And on and on the process goes, until once-distant goals are being achieved.

Be Yourself

Perhaps the worst thing any cyclist can do is try to duplicate the training of superior riders. This is a shortcut to disaster, not success. Training must be structured around your personality and physical capabilities. It must be realistic about the time you have for cycling, and then it must use that time effectively.

There is no disputing that some people have greater natural talent than others, but more failures occur from incorrect training than from lack of ability. Motivation, determination, and a real passion for cycling are vital, too. The sport is rife with examples of people who have special physical gifts but quit riding or doing anything else physical once past their so-called prime. They hang up their bikes and live on

The excitement of a journey through many challenges awaits everyone who wants to ride long distances. If you have the desire, this book will show you the way.

memories. Meanwhile, an average person who sticks with a consistent cycling program often achieves his or her greatest success later in life, thanks to years of fitness, experience, and love for riding a bike.

The most important ingredient in anyone's training is desire. The amount that you feel goes a long way toward determining how much progress you make. But, as with just about everything else in life, you need to keep desire in perspective by having moderation. Too much desire can make your training even less effective than if you have too little. We'll be discussing this dangerous phenomenon, known as over-training, in a moment.

Build the Base

New Zealand's Peter Snell was one of the greatest middle-distance runners of all time. He trained under renowned running coach Arthur Lydiard, a proponent of large volumes of endurance work. Peter once said, "What people didn't understand about Lydiard's program was that it wasn't the high mileage that made the runners great. Rather, it was the training they were able to do because they had done the mileage."

Putting in the miles is like building the foundation. It's the base on which every other part of a training program depends. It allows you to feel comfortable on the bike for longer periods. It prepares your body for the demands of interval training and speedwork. (Yes, folks, there's a lot more to endurance training than simply riding long distances, as we'll soon see.) You gain the stamina required for advanced training techniques by slowly but steadily increasing your aerobic fitness. This comes from staying on the bike for longer and longer periods. Your body adapts. It works more efficiently.

Contrary to popular belief, endurance training is not used specifically in cycling to increase maximal aerobic capacity, or max VO2. The intensity is too low to have a major effect on the ability to use oxygen (though it certainly has some). In fact, one of the greatest disservices perpetrated on cyclists in recent times is the concept of long, slow distance (LSD) training. This promises that lots of low-effort miles will improve aerobic capacity enough to allow effective performance in conditions, such as road races, that require anaerobic efforts. Nope. Long, steady rides only give you the base upon which to do the kind of training that much harder efforts require. That's what Peter Snell was saying.

If you only do endurance training, you won't have the anaerobic power to push on steep hills or take your pulls in a fast paceline. To the contrary, endurance rides are by definition aerobic. They're done at an effort below which lactic acid (lactate) begins to accumulate in the blood—the sign that anaerobic metabolism is being used to produce energy. Think of long-distance training as having two main purposes: to stress and strengthen the aerobic energy system, and to provide the learning experiences that come only from being on the bike for extended periods.

Long, steady cycling stimulates your slow-twitch muscle fibers because they are more responsive to lower intensity than fast-twitch fibers. Each of us has both fiber types in a unique ratio that helps determine whether we will be better at making short, intense efforts such as sprinting (fast-twitch) or at making extended aerobic efforts (slow-twitch). Endurance training causes adaptations to the muscle cells and cardiovascular system that allow slow-twitch fibers to work longer at low intensities with less fatigue.

Research by physiologist Edward Coyle, Ph.D., at the University of Texas has shown well-trained slow-twitch fibers to be more efficient at converting chemical energy within the muscle into the mechanical work of pedaling. This means two very good things: Fewer muscle fibers are needed to maintain a given pace, and those that are activated don't need to work as hard. Your energy economy improves, thanks to the reduction in muscle activity and oxygen consumption. Pedaling seems to take less effort.

Proof of these benefits comes from research on national-class road racers by David Costill, Ph.D., and his coworkers at Ball State University in Muncie, Indiana. They found that when the cyclists significantly increased their mileage, there was little change in the maximum amount of oxygen they were able to consume (max VO2). Instead, the riders' improved performance was attributable to their muscle fibers using oxygen more economically.

Energy Sources

Dr. Costill's team also confirmed that endurance training improves the ability to use the carbohydrate energy that's stored as glycogen in the muscles and liver. This is important because glycogen is the preferred fuel for muscles during cycling and other physical activities. However, if you ride at high intensity, glycogen stores can be depleted in as little as 2 hours. Then you "hit the wall" or, as we say in cycling, you "bonk."

Well-trained cyclists can store from 300 to 500 grams of carbohydrate (1,200 to 2,000 calories) as glycogen in their muscles. This reserve can be prolonged by eating and drinking carbohydrate during rides, and by using fat for fuel. The latter is another key benefit of endurance training. Long-distance specialists such as Danny Chew, a Race Across America champion, are incredibly adept at burning fat. In fact, a couple of months after winning the 1999 RAAM, Danny rode the hilly 170 miles from his home in Pittsburgh to State College, Pennsylvania, without eating or drinking a thing. Why? Just to set another of the eccentric personal records for which he's famous. Don't try that at home. (Danny's lifetime goal, by the way, is to ride one million miles. Presumably, he'll eat something along the way.)

A primary objective in long-distance training is to become so good at using fat and sparing glycogen that you rarely, if ever, deplete your glycogen stores. In chapter 6, we'll tell you lots more about the role that nutrition plays in achieving top performance.

The Electronic Cyclist

To get the most benefit from the time you spend training, you need to join the computer age. Two pieces of equipment are all but essential: a cyclecomputer and a heart rate monitor (HRM). Sometimes they come in the same unit, but it's more common to buy them separately. Multifunction cyclecomputers are very affordable ($30 and up), and it's likely that you already have one. You may not be as familiar with HRMs, which generally cost around $100 for a model with the basic features you need for the training we're going to recommend.

In the view of Lance Armstrong's coach, Chris Carmichael, "A heart rate monitor and a cyclecomputer bring more precision to your training. They help you avoid riding too intensely on recovery days and too easily when you should be pushing the limits."

In recent years, Chris has used heart rate monitoring to help Lance and other Europe-based pro road racers structure their programs. The guys train and race with high-end Polar monitors that record heart rate for download to a PC. Then they fax or e-mail the data to Chris in the States so he can analyze it and prescribe the next few workouts.

Wouldn't you love guidance like that? Well, you could hire Chris, or you can do a pretty good job of coaching yourself when you use an HRM. Downloadability isn't essential, but you do need to know exactly how hard or easy you are working during your training and events. It's not possible to be accurate the old-fashioned way, using perceived exertion.

Max Heart Rate

For objective training to work, you must know your maximum heart rate. This is vital because, as we'll see, all training intensities are based on it. The easiest—but most inaccurate—way to find max HR is with a formula that's been around for years: subtract your age from 220. If this gives you the correct number, it's purely by chance. The error is often on the low side. For example, when Ed Pavelka's lab-tested max was 178 beats per minute (bpm), the formula said it should have been 167. If he based his training on the lower number, he'd be riding even slower than he already does.

A much better method is with something called a "graduated stress test" that pushes you to max HR on the bike, either indoors or out. Like most tests, this one isn't fun, but it doesn't last too long, and you need to do it just once each season. Here are two ways.

Caution: We urge you to inform your doctor and obtain his or her permission before you undergo this extreme exertion.

Wearing your HRM, warm up well on your way to a long, fairly steep hill. Start the climb at a brisk pace, using a gear that would be a bit too big in normal circumstances. Get out of the saddle and

Chris Carmichael has based a business (Carmichael Training Systems) on successfully helping Lance Armstrong and other pros reach their potential. Chris says heart rate monitoring is the key to training.

push, push, push, till you're burning like a marshmallow too close to the coals. Then sprint as if the world championship were depending on it. Just as you slump into a quivering heap, the number you see through the black spots is your max HR. This is when it's helpful to have a monitor that memorizes the highest heart rate attained.

Don't have a suitable hill? Then do a series of progressively harder efforts either on the road or on your indoor trainer. While maintaining a cadence of 90 to 100 revolutions per minute (rpm), increase your gears as necessary to boost your speed by ½ mile per hour (mph) every 30 seconds. Keep ramping up till you're making an extreme effort and your heart rate is redlining. Indoors, it helps to have a sadistic friend who will shout encouragement or threats into your ear.

Once you have your max HR, training becomes a matter of percentages. These define your heart rate zones. Workouts are then structured to keep you riding within specific ranges. Here's how it works.

Zone 1—less than 65% of maximum heart rate, to promote recovery and use fat stores as the primary fuel source.

Zone 2—65% to 84%, to build aerobic endurance.

Zone 3—85% to 94%, to reach lactate threshold (LT), the point at which the greatest aerobic improvement occurs.

Zone 4—95% to 100%, to develop the anaerobic system for short bursts of max effort in sprinting or all-out climbing (not something that's essential to train for in endurance cycling, thank goodness).

Note: The border between zones 2 and 3 should not be considered exact, because there is such a range of individual differences. For example, an untrained cyclist might reach his LT at about 75 percent of max heart rate, while someone highly trained might not get there till 85 percent or higher. It's better to miss on the low side till your training gives you reason to adjust upward.

When selecting a heart rate monitor, look for one that lets you set zones defined by a flashing display or audible signal when your pulse goes above or below the limits. Consider this an essential feature. See chapter 5 for additional advice. The ultimate tool is the computer interface we've mentioned, allowing you to transfer, store, graph, and analyze your heart rate during training and events. Many coaches and racing cyclists use this type because they want every edge. We won't discourage you from going this route if it suits your mentality. Don't feel that it's necessary, though. An accurate monitor that lets you set zones is what's most important.

Workout Intensity

We're often asked, "How fast should I ride during endurance training?" Now you understand why this is the wrong question. Forget miles per hour and think about the *intensity* of your efforts. Speed is unimportant, because it's so dependent on things you can't control, such as the terrain and the environment. There's no sense in comparing your average miles per hour on a hot, hilly, windy ride with your pace in perfect weather on flat ground. The same goes when riding solo versus riding in a group, or riding your mountain bike versus your road bike.

Instead, use intensity as your guide. Your HRM, not your cycle-computer, is the best speedometer. When your program calls for an easy recovery day, an HRM will keep you from unwittingly increasing the effort, as we all tend to do. Conversely, when the ride is supposed to be intense, the HRM will insist that you keep your effort high. Without an objective number to use as a guide, you'll likely migrate to the halfway effort that Chris Carmichael spoke of—too hard for recovery and teaching your body to burn fat for fuel, but too easy to fully develop your aerobic power.

Here's the big problem with always riding at a steady effort: Following a period of fairly rapid improvement as you get in shape, there is almost always a plateau. Progress slows or even stalls. However, you may be enjoying cycling so much that it's hard to recognize that the

Endurance and intensity aren't mutually exclusive. Pete Penseyres averaged 23 mph for 750 miles to help set the senior record of 5½ days in the Team Race Across America.

training benefits are lagging behind the time you're spending on the bike.

What's missing at this point? Intensity. The training is purely aerobic. More and more steady miles have no consequence other than gobbling up a bigger part of each day. Then you enter an event in which the pace or terrain demands an effort that's beyond what you've experienced in training, and you struggle. You get dropped by cyclists who you know are riding less than you. The reason is that your training has rarely, if ever, exposed you to your lactate threshold (also called the anaerobic threshold). It hasn't prepared you to ride at your anaerobic edge, recover, and do it over and over like you might when riding a hilly event or doing your part in a strong paceline. The immortal football coach Pop Warner probably didn't ride a bike very much, but his famous credo pertains to cyclists as well as tailbacks: "You play the way you practice."

LT Testing

In order to train most effectively, you need to know your lactate threshold heart rate so that you can pinpoint the line between zones 2 and 3—where the change from aerobic to anaerobic energy production takes place. The most accurate way you can determine this is with a max VO2 test at a hospital or exercise physiology lab. But there also are do-it-yourself methods that can give you a number very close to the lab result.

(continued on page 14)

Riding with Father Time

Attend your 25th high school reunion, and you'll see that the passing years have been a lot kinder to some former classmates than to others. We'll bet that you, a dedicated cyclist, will be in the top percentile in terms of health and fitness.

But even among cyclists there can be big differences. Some riders suffer a significant decline in performance in their early thirties, while others, such as mountain biking legend Ned Overend (who won his second consecutive Xterra off-road triathlon world championship at age 44), remain near their best much longer. Some even ride better than ever at age 50, as Ed Pavelka, Fred Matheny, Pete Penseyres, and Skip Hamilton did in 1996. The same summer they broke the senior record in Team RAAM, they each achieved a personal best in their state's 40-kilometer (km) time trial, beating times they'd posted as spry youngsters in their thirties.

How is this possible? Let's look at several factors that bear on cycling performance as we age.

Endurance. There's no question that regular endurance exercise can maintain aerobic capacity well into middle age. In studies, competitive runners in the 40–49, 50–59, and 60–69 age groups were found to have nearly identical abilities to use oxygen. Twenty-four of these runners were retested 10 years later. Those who had continued training showed no significant reduction in maximum oxygen uptake (max VO2). This tells us that establishing and maintaining a relatively high level of endurance may nearly nullify the decline in aerobic capacity that normally comes with growing older. And it's never too late to start.

Strength. Other studies have found that strength training can preserve musculoskeletal fitness well into middle age. In fact, most people can gain muscle mass and strength no matter how old they are. The alternative is not good—sedentary people lose muscle tissue three times as fast as people who maintain fitness. In fact, an inactive adult male will lose about half a pound of muscle annually, and probably won't realize a weight loss because fat is being added at an even faster rate.

Bone mass. After age 35, there is a decline in total bone mass. This can be as much as 1 percent per year in men, and 3 percent per year in women, beginning with menopause. With low density comes an increased risk of broken bones and osteoporosis, that insidious disease that makes bones porous and brittle, and results in skeletal deformities. Although osteoporosis is often associated with women, it claims male victims, too.

Exercise is the key to building maximum bone mass, as well as to retarding the gradual loss that typically begins at around age 35. For women, estrogen replacement therapy and other treatments also can be a great help.

Flexibility. How smoothly do you rise from a chair? As we age, we begin moving more slowly and stiffly. You can see this in others and feel it in yourself.

Flying at 50 in Team RAAM '96. From left: Jeff Linder, Ed Pavelka, Skip Hamilton, Pete Penseyres, Fred Matheny, sponsored by *Bicycling* **magazine.**

We can't bounce around like children forever, but consistent physical activity will lessen the amount of muscle inflexibility, joint degeneration, and orthopedic injury.

About 80 percent of all lower back pain results from inflexible, poorly conditioned muscles. Cycling, combined with daily stretching, can work wonders in just a few weeks. As muscles and joints are strengthened, the door reopens to other activities that can be enjoyed with a low risk of discomfort or injury.

The bottom line. The bad news is what we already know. As we age, we experience a gradual decline in our cardiovascular endurance, muscular strength, and metabolic function, among other things. These changes increase our risk of cardiovascular disease, musculoskeletal injury, and various degenerative disorders. The older we get, the weaker and sicker we may become.

The good news is that regular endurance exercise and strength training can delay the debilitating effects of aging. The message is clear: Considering the relatively low investment in time and the high dividends of physical fitness, a consistent exercise program that revolves around cycling will improve your life like nothing else.

Will you ride as strongly in your sixties as you did in your thirties? Probably not. Then again, let's see what Ed, Fred, Pete, and Skip do in 2006, when they race in Team RAAM as 60-year-olds. Their slogan is "Under 6 in '06," which, if accomplished, could get them across the country nearly as fast as they went in 1996: 5 days, 11 hours, and 21 minutes.

Perform the following test soon so your training efforts are on target. It was developed by Rob Sleamaker, author of *Serious Training for Serious Athletes*. After a good warmup, ride an 8- to 10-mile flat time trial or a long, steady climb at a pace that you would describe as "moderately hard." This should be the fastest speed that you can sustain for the distance without tailing off near the end. Wear your HRM, use a stopwatch or your cyclecomputer's timer, and have a small notebook in your pocket for recording the date, distance ridden, elapsed time, and average heart rate.

Once you're underway with the test, your heart rate should stabilize in about 5 minutes. Then start your timer. Stop it when you've completed the course or climb, and record the elapsed time. Assume that the heart rate you sustained is your LT heart rate.

Repeat this test every 6 weeks during the season. You can do it in place of an interval training session or hill workout. As you become fitter, the point at which lactic acid starts to accumulate will occur at a higher heart rate. In other words, you'll be able to ride faster and do it longer. Elite cyclists typically don't reach their LT until they're at about 85 percent of their maximum heart rate.

Want a way to confirm your LT on any ride? According to coach Chris Carmichael's rule of thumb, "You are usually at your lactate threshold heart rate when you're breathing hard and it's difficult to carry on a conversation with your riding partners. Before long, your leg muscles will start telling you, too."

LT Training

Ask any cycling coach how to improve power and average speed, and you'll likely be advised to spend at least one ride each week working at your LT. This intensity is often described as "pushing too hard" by the person doing it. It's not the most fun type of riding you'll ever experience, but it may very well be the most productive. It increases the effort you can make before crossing into the anaerobic realm of lactic acid accumulation. That's when cycling gets really hard—heavy breathing, burning muscles, quickly increasing fatigue. By systematically reaching and slightly exceeding this point in training, you'll experience an adaptation that improves your cycling in impressive ways. You'll be able to sustain high-intensity work at a lower heart rate, as well as push the intensity even higher before crossing the line where lactic acid accumulation forces you to slow down.

Threshold training has traditionally been done by racers, not en-

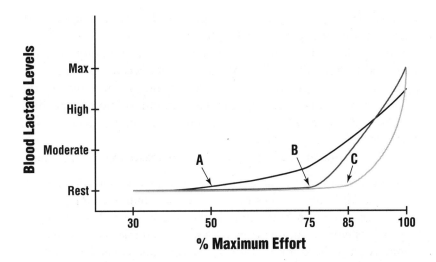

Faster riding is related to higher lactate thresholds. Training at LT moves the lactic acid accumulation point to the right—that is, toward greater speeds. Everything else being equal, the higher your LT, the faster the pace you can sustain over long distances, up extended climbs, and into strong headwinds. Simply put, you can ride at a higher percentage of your potential.
Point A = without training.
Point B = after moderate training.
Point C = after full training.

durance riders. In recent years, however, the distinction has been melted away by cyclists who compete in long-distance events ranging from centuries to RAAM. They've proven that whether the goal is personal records or finishing at the front of the field, the addition of intense training brings significantly better results than simply riding more miles. This is the guiding principle for the specific training programs that you'll find in part 2.

Adding Distance

Don't continuously increase your mileage (or time on the bike, if that's the way you keep track) week after week. Enthusiasm can inspire you to overachieve, but reality is always lurking just down the road in the form of an overuse injury, overtraining, or burnout. Remember, too, that you need to do what's right for you, not what other riders are doing. The fastest and yet safest progress will come by sticking with your own well-thought-out program.

After steady mileage increases to the limit of your ability to adapt, you need to hold steady for a week or more. Periodic self-imposed plateaus let you regenerate physically and mentally before making the next increase. A plateau could even last a month or more, depending on your age, your years in cycling, and the amount of training you need for the events you want to ride.

Use these four tips to help manage the increases in your training.

- Measure workouts in miles or time. Miles work well for road riding, while time makes more sense for mountain biking. If you participate in both, time is the better choice because it provides more accurate comparisons. For example, let's say one day you ride hard for an hour on the road and cover 20 miles, while on another day you cover only 8 miles in an hour on technical singletrack. These rides are equal in time and effort, but mileage won't tell you that.

- Alternate longer weeks with shorter weeks. This is likely to give you more energy. By setting monthly mileage goals, you can be more flexible with weekly mileages.

- Don't become a slave to your training diary. A sure tip-off is trying to reach a certain mileage total on the last day of the week or month, no matter what it takes. Remember, successful training depends on the proper blend of intensity and rest, not simply on the total miles ridden.

- If injury or illness causes you to miss days or even weeks of riding, don't try to make it up quickly. Instead, build back up gradually until you regain your former level. Rushing it only invites a relapse that will set you back even further.

The Danger of Overtraining

In *The Lore of Running*, Tim Noakes, M.D., gives examples of several nationally ranked athletes who had symptoms of training too much. One complained that he was lethargic and sleeping poorly. He also had less enthusiasm for training, and particularly for competition. He said his legs felt "sore" and "heavy," and that these sensations persisted for several training sessions. It would be hard to find a better example of the syndrome known as overtraining.

The bad things that result from overtraining are very real for long-distance cyclists. In training, it's difficult but essential to find the ideal level that's defined by the point just short of where you exceed your body's ability to adapt and grow stronger. If you blow it like this runner, all of the effort that should be making you better will only make you worse.

Overtraining is a threat to everyone who wants to excel. The desire to ride longer and stronger carries with it the drive to train more frequently or more intensely or both. At first, there's usually significant improvement, which has a predictable effect: Hey, if this much is making me better, more will make me great! But instead of a straight line to astounding performances, you find yourself dwelling on a plateau well below your projected goals. The solution seems obvious—you need to train more. When this results in zero improvement or even deterioration, a sense of inadequacy and frustration develops. Now there are changes in behavior and personality. As chronic fatigue sets in, you lose confidence and purpose, a symptom that can impact your social and professional life as well as your cycling.

What a mess! Thankfully, avoiding overtraining is easy if you keep an eye peeled for these warning signs. There are two components—physical and emotional.

PHYSICAL

- Tiredness that persists

- Heavy feeling in legs

- Muscle soreness

- Inability to complete training rides as scheduled

- Steady weight loss

- Sleep disturbances

- Elevated morning heart rate

- Lack of appetite

- Swelling in lymph nodes

- Flulike symptoms, including fever, chills, and aches

- Constipation or diarrhea

EMOTIONAL

- Anxiety

- Depression

- Desire to quit or shorten rides

- Inability to concentrate

- Irritability

- Loss of enthusiasm

In the early 1980s, Dick Brown, then administrator and physiologist for a world-class running club called Athletics West, decided to find some measurable warning signs of overtraining. Each day, he asked his runners to record their morning body weight, morning heart rate, and hours of sleep. His analysis showed that if an athlete's morning pulse is 10 percent or more higher than normal, if his weight is down 3 percent or more, or if he sleeps 10 percent less than usual, then he hasn't recovered from the previous day's workout.

Dick's advice to someone who exhibits any two of these signals is to train short and easy till the numbers are normal again. If all three are out of bounds, it means a day off is in order—no training at all.

To help keep your door closed to overtraining, follow these tips.

- Sleep at least 8 hours per night when you are riding long or hard. Studies have shown that athletes who are overtraining go to bed later, sleep less soundly, and wake up tired.

- Eat a well-balanced diet.

- Down a carbohydrate/protein recovery drink as soon as possible after each ride.

- Do at least 8 weeks of steady foundation riding before doing intervals or hill training.

- Limit mileage increases to 10 percent per week so that physical and mental strain is manageable.

- Try to nap for 15 to 30 minutes before an afternoon ride, especially on a day that calls for distance or intensity.

- Follow a program that's right for your ability and goals, not those of a local hotshot or someone you read about in a magazine.

- Use a training diary to record your morning heart rate, morning body weight (after emptying bladder), sleep patterns, and level of enthusiasm. This will help you spot negative patterns emerging.

To count your pulse, use the carotid artery (beside your Adam's apple) for 15 seconds and multiply by four for the beats per minute. An increase of more than five or six bpm from one morning to the next indicates that you may not be recovered from the previous day's training or you are getting sick. Don't train hard that day. A persistent elevation of five to 10 beats per minute indicates a more serious level of overtraining. You should take a few days off until your pulse returns to normal. If your morning weight is down several pounds from the day before, you are dehydrated and need to drink plenty before training again. Steady weight loss for several weeks is an ominous sign of overtraining.

Remember that rest is as essential as work. Muscles must be allowed to recover if they're to grow stronger. Regularly scheduled rest days allow you to train as long and hard as necessary to reach your goals, while minimizing the risk of overtraining.

Training Diary

The value of keeping a training log was proven once again when Ed Burke caught himself wondering why his legs didn't seem to have any snap during hard efforts, why he wasn't recovering very well between rides, and why, coming into the most important part of the season, he simply wasn't feeling on top of his game. Ed, a guy who occasionally practices what he preaches, had kept good records of his rides, making it easy for him to take an objective look at his blossoming dilemma. It became clear that he had been riding quite a few miles, some of them strenuously, and recent down time for business travel had added more stress instead of more recovery. Looking deeper, he saw that for two consecutive months he had trained more hours than was planned, producing a 20 percent increase made even riskier by the boost in intensity. The answer was now obvious: Ed was in the early stages of chronic fatigue. He knew exactly why, which was the key to making effective changes.

Ed's mistake is typical of riders in a serious program. But he didn't compound it by failing to keep a daily record of his training. He reviewed his diary to get the hard numbers and subjective impressions he needed in order to alter his program and derail overtraining. Let's see how you, too, can write the most valuable book on your cycling bookshelf.

By the Numbers

The basis of a diary is the daily entry. The categories that you fill in should be customized to your training program and the descriptive narrative that you may want to add. Consider items such as these.

- Waking heart rate

- Morning weight

- Hours and quality of sleep (including naps)

- Diet on and off the bike (especially anything unusual)

- A rating from A to F or 1 to 5 that indicates your enthusiasm for training and life itself

Each ride can be captured with the following:

- Time of day

- Temperature and wind

- Type of training (steady distance, intervals, climbing, etc.)

- Heart rate zones and time spent in them

- Course

- Elapsed time

- Mileage

- Average speed

- Gears used

- Riding partners

- Vertical feet (if your cyclecomputer has an altitude function)

- A subjective rating of how you felt

Also note any equipment or position changes. This is important for finding the source of soreness or injuries that may crop up days later. End each week by totaling the miles or hours (or both). Do the same for the month and year to date. Beware of increases beyond a safe and sane 10 percent.

You can record all of this in a commercial training diary with categories for these things, or you can fashion your own log with a blank notebook or loose-leaf binder. You might want to include a special section for your mental training, described in chapter 7.

Note: Don't make your diary so extensive that it takes more than 3 or 4 minutes to fill in. Otherwise, it may start feeling like a chore. Once you begin skipping days, the diary's value for tracking effort and spotting trends (other than laziness) is gone. To help you stay up to date, keep your diary where you park your bike so that it's right there to fill in after each ride.

Thanks for the Memories

Remember that ride you thought you'd never forget? Probably not. Besides the cold, hard facts, a diary contains words and phrases that can instantly transport you back to rides that form the fabric of your cycling life. Sights, sounds, friends, strangers, flat tires, thunderstorms, and killer hills—notes can jog your memory and let you ride a ride all over again. This benefit may not seem important early on, but take it from your authors: The value grows as the years pass. Ed Pavelka has diaries dating to 1976 (and is annoyed with himself for not writing down much from his start 5 years before that). Pulling one out to look up a fact—Hey, didn't that brevet in Maryland go right through Burkittsville, later made famous by *The Blair Witch Project?*—always results in several minutes of slow page turning and reminiscing. For a long-distance rider who covers so much ground in a variety of places, a diary is all the more valuable.

❷

Tame Time

Albert Einstein was known for a couple of things besides riding a bike. But the greatest mind of the twentieth century really got a kick out of cycling. You can see it in one old photo that shows him in his typically disheveled clothes, pedaling a clunky one-speed at what looks like about 3 miles per hour. The smile on his face says it all. Maybe this was even the instant he hit on the Theory of Relativity. "I thought of that while riding my bike," he once revealed.

One thing Einstein might also tell us is that he wished he'd had more time to ride. Relatively speaking, finding enough time is the chief challenge among cyclists no matter what their aspirations in the sport. It always ranks at the top of *Bicycling* magazine's surveys of its readers—the dedicated recreational cyclists who ride for fitness and often aspire to at least one century each season. As you'll see, training to ride 100 miles takes a definite time commitment, and this commitment must grow if your goals become even bigger.

When you factor in a family, a career, and all of life's many responsibilities, finding the time to be a long-distance cyclist may very well be the biggest challenge you'll face. But always remember: You're not disadvantaged because you can't ride as much as you'd like—you're normal. The trick is to know effective strategies, and then use your creativity to adapt them to your unique circumstances. When you really want to find the time, you will.

What follows are ways that work. Not every one will fit your life, but many will jump-start your imagination. Some are tips for finding more riding time, while others will help you make the most of the time you have. The result easily could be enough extra time to double your cycling. Remember, though, that having the time to ride doesn't always mean that you should ride. You must complement training with sufficient recovery in order to make progress—something we'll be harping on throughout this book.

Time Management

Set goals. When you have the date of an important event circled on the calendar, you won't have difficulty motivating yourself to find riding opportunities. As the crucial day nears, you can justify arranging other parts of your life around cycling for a change. Afterward, reduce your cycling to recover, restore balance, and take care of things you ignored. Then, identify another goal to build toward. There's nothing like seeing progress to keep you interested in training.

Know your needs. Let's say your goal is the club century. You may assume that you need to be doing time-consuming 80-mile rides to train for it. Not true, as you'll see in chapter 8's training programs. In fact, most cyclists find that they can handle about three times the duration of their average training ride, as long as they maintain a sensible pace, keep eating and drinking, and take an occasional short break. So, if you find the time to average 35 miles every other day for several months, you should be capable of a 100-miler. For beginners who have a half-century or metric century as their goal, a 15- to 20-mile daily average is sufficient. Remember that we're talking average ride, so longer outings on Saturday and Sunday can balance shorter rides on busy weekdays.

Ride early or late. With good planning, it may be possible to ride before or after your core work hours, however long they might be. Schedule weekday rides in your appointment calendar so that they become as important as any other responsibility.

Riding at dawn has several advantages. It sets the tone for a confident day. You'll feel good about having your workout safely behind you no matter what else happens. In summer, the air at daybreak is cooler and cleaner. There's usually less traffic and less wind, and you avoid the risk of afternoon thunderstorms. In winter, a bright, reliable lighting system makes it possible to be on the road despite late sunrises. Because morning training can cut into your sleep, you may need to go to bed earlier to avoid fatigue that could undermine both cycling and job performance.

Riding in the evening is possible thanks to modern lighting systems. They expand cycling potential past sunset, ridding you of anxiety about getting home in time to squeeze in a ride before dark. And there are other advantages. By not saddling up until twilight, you can miss rush-hour traffic, the air will be cooler, and you can enjoy a beautiful sight that your unlit counterparts are sprinting home to avoid: sunset. Use a taillight, wear reflective clothing, and decorate your bike with reflective tape. You'll be such a sight that most drivers will give you more room than they ever do in daylight.

Ride at noon. Many companies now accept midday recreation by employees. Some even encourage it with flextime. When you're forced to fit your ride into an hour during the workday, you have the impetus to push yourself. The result should be lots of improvement for the time spent. Riding at lunchtime can work if you have suitable roads near your job (a park may be available if you work in a city), a way to clean up afterward, and a safe place to keep your bike. Make up for the missed meal by snacking on wholesome foods at your desk an hour before and after riding.

Commute by bike. The oldest advice for creating training time is still the best: Ride your bike to your daily destination and back. Let's say you live 10 miles from your job. Driving that distance in stop-and-go rush-hour traffic takes 30 minutes. By using a 12-mile route that keeps you off the busy roads, you can ride there in about 50 minutes. So, you get 24 miles of round-trip cycling per day, and it takes only 40 minutes more than sitting behind the steering wheel, wondering how you'll find the time to squeeze in a ride.

Commuting miles aren't likely to be top quality, given the stop-and-go nature of riding in town, but you can improve them with some ingenuity. The simplest way is to find a longer route home and do some real training while you blow away the day's work stress. You'll get a decent workout and free your evening for other activities.

Long-distance cycling has numerous examples of how well commuting can be turned into effective training. At the very top of the sport, Pete Penseyres and Seana Hogan trained during their commutes to win seven Races Across America between them. Seana even supplemented her rides to and from work with lunchtime training. Ed Pavelka commuted for years while working for *Bicycling* magazine, using hilly routes to ride 35 to 55 miles each day. With this year-round base, he was able to step up training for events all the way up to Paris-Brest-Paris and RAAM.

Commuting may seem rife with difficulties as you contemplate trying it, but take it from Pete, Seana, Ed, and about three million other cyclists who do it and love it: It's much easier to fit into your lifestyle than you imagine. As we often say, the only thing that can stop you from commuting is that you simply won't give it a try.

Ride for transportation. You want to do things with your spouse and kids on the weekends, but you also want to ride. Do both by pedaling to the lake while the rest of the family drives. If you depart early

If you want to make the most of limited time, head for the hills.

you'll all arrive at the same time, then you can enjoy the rest of the day knowing you got your miles. Throw the bike on the car rack and return with the family (unless you can talk them into letting you ride back, too).

Some long-distance specialists take this method to a very productive extreme. Pete Penseyres, for example, rode the 800-mile round-trip when he needed to visit his RAAM sponsors. His wife, Joanne, drove support, helping Pete turn a potential interruption in his schedule into some valuable endurance training. When Ed Pavelka wanted to make a weekend round-trip between Syracuse, New York, and Allentown, Pennsylvania, he covered the 515 miles by bike to turn it into a dress rehearsal for Paris-Brest-Paris. And then there's Danny Chew, who is famous for riding long distances to get to long-distance events. In 1999, after reaching the finish in Savannah, Georgia, to win his second RAAM, he then rode home—to Pittsburgh.

Emphasize quality. Get maximum results from each minute on the bike by riding with a purpose. For example, if you're going with a group, practice your paceline skills. If you're solo, do low-gear sprints to work on your spin or climb hills to develop power. On a recovery ride practice cornering, riding with no hands, or other skills that don't tax your cardiovascular system. Beginning in chapter 8, we're going to give you several training schedules for advancing to a century and beyond. You'll see how each day requires a different type of riding for maximum improvement.

Ride hills. Minute for minute, it's hard to beat the benefits of time spent climbing. Take it from three-time Tour de France champion Greg LeMond, who says, "There's no better training than riding hills.

For me it was the easiest way to get in shape." It improves every-thing—strength, power, stamina, cardiovascular conditioning. As op-posed to a flat 90-minute ride, one that includes a couple of thousand vertical feet will leave you feeling happily hammered, satisfied that you got a lot for your precious on-bike time.

Be organized. Keep your riding gear in the same place so that you don't waste time hunting for something while your cycling clock is ticking. Lay out your clothes and food, and mix your drinks the night before. After the ride, put your sweaty clothes in the washer while you're in the shower. When you're clean, they're clean, and you can hang them to dry for the next ride. Routine means efficiency.

Drink your food. You want to go for a ride but you're famished. It'll pare pedaling time to fix a meal and eat it, plus the load in your stomach will make you feel like the human equivalent of a flat tire. The solution is to use a commercial drink that contains a calorie-rich

Efficient Equipment

Cycling time is precious enough without losing any to equipment shortcomings. Use these tips to prevent mechanical problems and have what it takes to ride despite inclement weather.

Prevent punctures. For most of us, a flat tire costs about 10 minutes, a hefty chunk of time when you have only an hour to ride. Make punctures a thing of the past by using tires with a protective belt in their tread or installing an impenetrable liner. You can also use thorn-resistant tubes or add fluids that make tubes self-sealing. To save time when a flat does happen, use a CO_2 cartridge rather than a hand pump to inflate your spare.

Avoid frequent inflation. Some butyl inner tubes hold air pressure better than others, and all are superior to latex. By using less-porous tubes, you can save time by adding air once every week or two rather than before every ride.

Own a beater bike. How does an old-but-reliable bike save time? Because you can ride it on wet days and not feel like you have to detail it afterwards. In fact, it can save rides by getting you out the door in iffy weather. Install fenders, reflective tape, and a rack trunk to carry your rain jacket.

Own harsh-weather gear. Just as a lighting system can create time for cycling, so can rainwear and winter clothing. Don't let a little moisture or windchill cancel any opportunities. If you have the right protection, you'll find mix of carbohydrate and protein. Scoop the powder into the blender with some skim milk and a banana for a nutritious and satisfying liquid meal. It takes less than 5 minutes and digests nearly as fast.

Ride inside. Sweating for an hour or so on an indoor trainer isn't something you want to do often during the season, but it will keep you pedaling when a real ride gets ruined by bad weather or life's frustrating interruptions. Make the experience as interesting as possible by listening to fast music and/or watching cycling videos. Make it more productive by wearing your heart rate monitor and varying your pace with several hard efforts. Strive for the same intensity you get on the road.

Merge one weekly ride. If you ride four times a week for 80 total miles, you can save time and probably improve your fitness by covering the same distance in three rides. The saving occurs because you have one less day of bike prep, dressing, warming up, cooling down, undressing, cleaning up, and so on. More on-bike time will be at a pro-

that some very gratifying rides occur on days when you could easily have stayed home to moan about the weather.

Become a mechanic. If you have the work space, basic tools, and know-how to take care of your bike's common mechanical needs, you can save lots of time. In just minutes, you'll be able to fix a problem that would otherwise require two trips to the bike shop sandwiched around the several days your machine waits in line. Most problems are easy to remedy if you have a good manual. We're partial to two from Rodale, the exhaustive *Bicycling Magazine's Complete Guide to Bicycle Maintenance and Repair* and the more elementary *Bicycling Magazine's Basic Maintenance and Repair*.

Be an instant fixer. Let's say you're on a ride and notice that the brakes need adjusting, a wheel is out of true, or the chain lacks lube. Service your bike immediately upon returning. You won't have to make time for it later or delay the start of your next ride (or realize in the midst of it that the problem slipped your mind).

Use a dry chain lube. If you live in an area that isn't overly wet or humid, use a lube that goes on wet but dries to the touch. This saves time because you'll rarely if ever need to clean the chain or drivetrain to keep your bike working smoothly.

ductive pace, and the longer outings will improve your endurance, too.

Ride less. If your attempts to wedge more cycling into your life result mainly in stress and frustration during certain periods, relieve the strain by making rides 10 percent shorter. The pressure will disappear, but your fitness won't if you increase ride quality. In the same vein, plan *not* to ride some days so you don't feel like you're being deprived. Use these days to recover from a tough workout or rest up for the next one. Take care of life's other responsibilities so that time for cycling is both created and protected.

Attend a camp or tour. Want to pack a week of pure cycling into your life? Do it on vacation. Camps are great because you ride every day and learn so much about training and techniques from experienced coaches. Each March, for example, former RAAM champion Lon Haldeman holds two 1-week camps in southern Arizona, giving more than a hundred long-distance enthusiasts a head start on the season. Your authors usually serve on the coaching staff, along with endurance experts such as John Hughes, Fred Matheny, and Lon himself. In addition, organized rides like Lon's PAC Tours give cyclists a chance to average as much as 140 miles per day for a week or more on some of North America's most scenic roads.

Get a coach. If you want maximum motivation to schedule rides and squeeze the most out of each one, hire a coach. Check at your local bike shop or club to see if there's one in your area. A great resource for coaches who specialize in long-distance riding is the UltraMarathon Cycling Association (www.ultracycling.com). Most coaches will work with riders anywhere in the country through the mail or Internet. Another option is training software, such as the Lance Armstrong Cycling Plan from PC Coach (www.pccoach.com). Codeveloped by Ed Burke, it can easily be adapted to training for endurance events.

Ride a tandem. A bike built for two doesn't actually create time, but it does create time together. It's the solution if your riding is reduced by concerns about leaving your significant other behind (either at home or way down the road). A tandem keeps two riders of unequal ability together, and it makes chatting easier. You can push the pedals as hard as you want while your partner does the same, allowing each of you to find the right intensity.

Tow your toddler. Rather than feel like a hostage to your youngster, put the little bugger into a bike trailer made for the purpose and take a ride. Besides creating training time when you'd otherwise be babysitting, you'll get a great power workout on hills. Look for a trailer that's weatherproof and has an anti-tip-over hitch. If your spouse isn't as

Put Lon Haldeman on a bike (even indoors) and he's a happy man. In his RAAM championship years, Lon merged training with work by commuting up to 100 miles a day.

strong but wants to ride, too, the trailer behind your bike will help equalize your speeds.

Oh, and one last thing: Keep it fun! For most of us, cycling is so enjoyable that we can't do enough. Make sure it stays that way. Don't feel pressured to ride at any cost, and never let training become monotonous. Above all, don't get down when something in your busy life stymies your plans. Be flexible and keep your perspective. When cycling is fun, you'll always be finding ways to fit it in.

3

Get Fit to Ride

Endurance cycling is full of prodigious numbers—the distances ridden, the calories consumed, the tires trashed. Another statistic that can seem astounding is the number of pedal strokes made. Let's suppose that it takes you 6 hours to ride a century, and you pedal at the rate of 90 revolutions per minute throughout. As you cross the finish line, you will be making your 64,800th pedal stroke. Wow, that's a lot! But it barely registers on the scale of what happens during a full season. For example, Ed Pavelka figures that during the year in which he had his biggest mileage total, he got there by pushing the pedals around approximately 13,340,000 times!

Can you say "repetitive use injury"? You can see why long-distance cyclists are prime candidates for these, especially if they aren't pedaling from a perfect position. Your body and bike must fit together and work together in sweet harmony for you to be efficient, comfortable, and injury-free. The more you ride, the more essential this is. If even one position parameter is amiss, it could result in anything from a nagging ache to a troublesome pain to a debilitating injury as you repeat your pedal stroke thousands of times.

Road Bike

Fortunately, it isn't difficult to arrive at an excellent riding position. But it does take time and attention. You have to be careful with your initial bike setup, and then conscientiously stay aware of your body's response and the need for occasional refinements. As time goes by, your position will stabilize and you'll be in a smooth groove—until, that is, you decide to switch bikes, shoes, pedals, saddles, or any other component that affects your body/bike relationship. Then it's time to begin again, though this time you'll have the help of experience and measurements recorded from your old position.

What follows are guidelines developed by former *Bicycling* magazine editors Geoff Drake and Fred Matheny from the advice of several coaches and medical experts. It also includes tips from
long-distance specialists John Hughes and Lon Haldeman, as well as
Andrew Pruitt, Ed.D. Andy, director of the Boulder Center for Sports
Medicine in Boulder, Colorado, has probably solved more position
problems than anyone during his years of work with elite road and
off-road cyclists, including a number of endurance specialists. His
Rule #1 is well worth remembering: "Adjust your bike to fit your
body—don't force your body to fit the bike."

Note: If you've been riding long enough to be set in your current
position, don't make big changes should you discover that something
is out of bounds. There's less chance of injury if you make adjustments
in small increments over several weeks so your body can adapt. On
the other hand, if you're a new cyclist or have been off the bike for a
while, go ahead and set everything according to these guidelines before you start riding.

1. **Arms.** Beware of cyclist's rigor mortis. Keep your elbows bent
   and relaxed to absorb shock and prevent veering when you hit
   a bump. Hold your arms in line with your body, not splayed to
   the side, to make a more compact, aerodynamic package.

2. **Upper body and shoulders.** The operative words: Be still.
   Imagine the calories wasted by rocking side to side with every
   pedal stroke on a long ride. Also, beware of creeping forward
   on the saddle and hunching your back when tired. Shift to a
   higher gear and periodically stand to pedal to prevent stiffness
   in your hips and back, as well as to relieve saddle pressure.

3. **Head and neck.** Avoid letting your head droop, especially
   when you're tired. You'll lose sight of what's ahead on the
   road, and on a very long ride it could even allow you to doze
   off. Periodically change your hand location to alter your upper
   body's position and the angle of your neck. Tilt your head
   from side to side to stretch and relax neck muscles. Neck
   discomfort is a problem for quite a few long-distance cyclists,
   so it's helpful to do strengthening exercises.

4. **Hands.** Change your hand position frequently to prevent
   finger numbness and upper-body stiffness. A white-knuckle
   hold on the handlebar is unnecessary and will produce energy-
   sapping muscle tension throughout your arms and shoulders.

(continued on page 34)

Road Bike Position

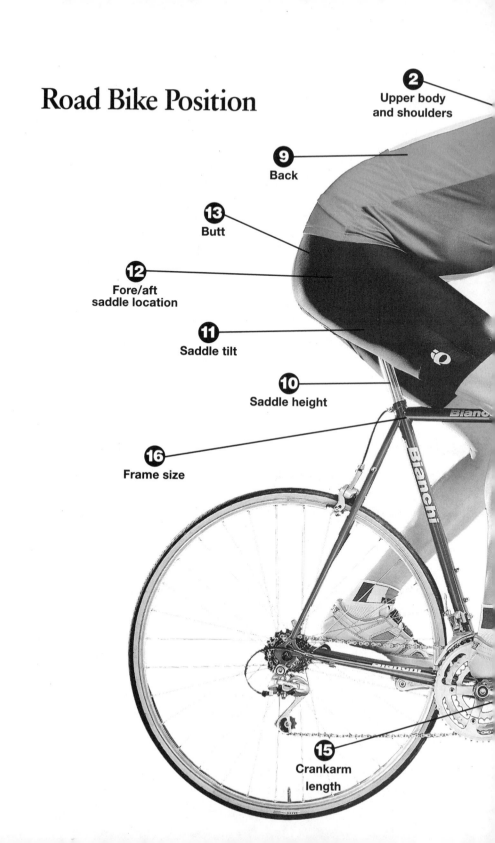

2 Upper body and shoulders

9 Back

13 Butt

12 Fore/aft saddle location

11 Saddle tilt

10 Saddle height

16 Frame size

15 Crankarm length

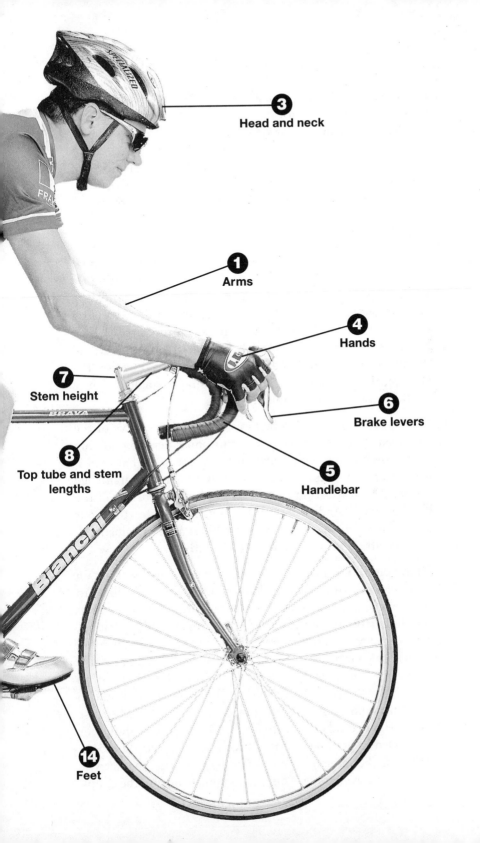

3 Head and neck

1 Arms

4 Hands

7 Stem height

6 Brake levers

8 Top tube and stem lengths

5 Handlebar

14 Feet

Flutter your fingers occasionally as a reminder to loosen your grip. Grasp the drops for descents or high-speed riding, and the brake lever hoods for relaxed cruising. On long climbs, hold the top of the bar to sit upright and open your chest for easier breathing. When standing, grasp the hoods lightly and gently sway the bike from side to side in sync with your pedal strokes. Always keep each thumb and a finger closed around the lever hood or bar to prevent losing hold on an unexpected bump.

5. **Handlebar.** In general, the width of a drop bar should equal your shoulder width. But for long-distance cycling, slightly wider is better because it provides more room for a handlebar bag and opens your chest for breathing. It also slows steering response just a bit. Quick steering isn't necessary or even advantageous. Some bar models have a large drop (vertical distance) to help big hands fit into the hooks. Position the bottom, flat portion of the bar horizontal or angled slightly down (toward the rear brake).

6. **Brake levers.** Levers can be moved around the curve of the handlebar to give you the best compromise between holding the hoods and braking when your hands are in the bar hooks. Most riders do best if the lever tips touch a straightedge extended forward from under the flat, bottom portion of the bar. Remember Andy Pruitt's rule, though. If you feel that your body will be more comfortable if the levers aren't symmetrical, don't be afraid to position them differently.

7. **Stem height.** With the stem high enough (normally about an inch below the top of the saddle), you'll be more inclined to use the entire handlebar, including the drops. This is key to avoiding stiffness by altering your upper body position. Putting the bar lower can improve aerodynamics, but it could also cause your back to become uncomfortably tight as a ride wears on. When using aero bars, position them initially so that your elbows are at saddle height (being careful not to raise the stem above its maximum extension line, because your weight could cause it to break). The armrests should be positioned to put your elbows directly under your shoulders. Strive for the same back and shoulder position whether you are on the aero bars or riding with your hands on the drops.

As time goes by, gradually lower your aero bar position to a point where your aerodynamics are improved but your comfort isn't compromised. Flexibility helps make this possible, so increase it with stretching.

8. **Top tube and stem lengths.** These combined dimensions, which determine your "reach," vary according to your flexibility and anatomy. There is no ultimate prescription, but there is a good starting point: When you're comfortably seated with elbows slightly bent and hands on the brake lever hoods, look down. The front hub will be obscured by the handlebar if your reach is in the ballpark. This is a relatively upright position that should work well for most endurance cycling. However, if your goal is fast, competitive centuries, you may benefit from a longer stem extension to improve aerodynamics by making you lower and flatter.

9. **Back.** When sitting with your hands on the brake lever hoods and your elbows slightly bent, your back should be at about a 45-degree angle to the top tube. This will decrease to about 30 degrees when you ride on the drops or on aero bars. At any angle, a straight ("flat") back is the defining mark of a well-positioned road rider. The correct stem and top-tube combination is crucial for this, but so is hip flexibility. Concentrate on rotating the top of your hips forward. If you think of trying to touch the top tube with your belly button, it will help stop you from rounding your back. That said, don't be concerned if your unique anatomical makeup prevents you from obtaining a perfect profile. Some great riders (Lance Armstrong, for instance) have a more rounded back that no positioning tricks can change. It seems to make no difference, as long as all of the correct position dimensions are met.

10. **Saddle height.** There are various formulas for this, but you needn't be a mathematician to know what the correct height looks like. Your knees should be slightly bent (25 to 35 degrees) at the bottom of the pedal stroke, and your hips shouldn't rock on the saddle (when viewed from behind). Here's a method that works well for many riders. It was popularized by Greg LeMond during his heyday as a professional road racer. Begin by facing a wall with your bare feet 6 inches apart. Put a large

hardcover book square against the wall and pull it firmly into
your crotch. Mark the wall at the top of the book, then
measure up from the floor. This is your inseam length.
Multiply it by 0.883. The result is your saddle height, the
distance from the top of the saddle to the center of the crank
axle, measured in line with the bike's seat tube.

11. **Saddle tilt.** The saddle should be level, which you can check
by laying a yardstick along its length and comparing it to
something horizontal like a tabletop or windowsill. A slight
downward tilt (one or two degrees) may be more comfortable
if you're using an aero bar and leaning far forward. More tilt
than this will cause you to slide forward and put excessive
weight on your hands and arms.

12. **Fore/aft saddle location.** Sit comfortably in the center of the
saddle with the crankarms horizontal. Drop a plumb line from
the front of your forward kneecap. It should touch the end of
the crankarm. This is the neutral position, and you should be
able to achieve it by loosening the seatpost clamp and sliding
the saddle fore or aft. To increase leverage for climbing or
pushing big gears, you can set the saddle so that the line falls
a centimeter or more behind the end of the crankarm like the
rider in the photo. (Conversely, a more forward position
improves leg speed, which is not a need in endurance cycling.)
Remember, if your reach to the handlebar is wrong, change
your stem length to correct it—not your fore/aft saddle
position.

13. **Butt.** By sliding backward or forward on the saddle, you can
accentuate different muscle groups. This can be useful on a
long climb. Moving forward emphasizes the quadriceps
muscle on the front of the thigh, while moving back brings the
opposite side hamstrings and glutes into play.

14. **Feet.** Notice your footprints as you walk from a swimming
pool. Some of us are pigeon-toed and others are duck-footed.
To prevent knee injury, strive for a cleat position that
accommodates your natural foot angle. Make cleat
adjustments on rides until you feel right, or pay a shop to do
it using a fitting device. Better still, use a clipless pedal system
that allows your feet to pivot freely ("float") to their natural
orientation, thus making precise adjustment unnecessary.

Conventional advice says to position cleats fore/aft so that the ball of each foot is directly above the pedal axle. However, Lon Haldeman recommends a different setup for long-distance cycling, based on his personal experience and working with many of his PAC Tour riders. To reduce the risk of numbing pressure and pain, Lon moves cleats backward so that the ball of the foot is as much as 2 centimeters (cm) in front of the pedal axle. This works, and doesn't seem to have any negative effect on pedaling. (The saddle may need to be lowered a bit, and its fore/aft position may need to be changed.) One problem here is that many shoes won't allow cleats to be positioned far enough rearward unless new holes are drilled. Some models won't allow it at all because of their sole design.

Other Bikes

Hybrids (also known as cross-bikes) generally have 700C wheels like road bikes but a flat handlebar like mountain bikes. They are close to road bikes for most dimensions. However, you may wish to select a frame size at the small end of your acceptable range if you'll be riding it off road, for greater crotch clearance.

Some hybrids have a higher bottom bracket than road bikes, which means that their stand-over height will be less for the identical-size frame. You want at least 2 inches of clearance between your crotch and the top tube.

Many hybrids come with a short, high-rise stem, supplying an upright position for casual riding. In time, you may wish to purchase a longer stem with less rise to get closer to the ideal 45-degree back angle described in the advice for fitting a mountain bike.

Touring bikes are road bikes, but with several special design features. These include a longer wheelbase, greater frame clearances around the wheels, and numerous frame fittings ("braze-ons"). Together, these provide the means to attach fenders, racks, panniers, extra bottle cages, a lighting system—everything necessary for long, self-supported rides. In addition, the frame geometry of touring bikes gives them sure and stable handling, particularly when carrying a load. Follow the road bike instructions for setting your riding position.

15. **Crankarm length.** Longer crankarms add leverage for stronger climbing, but they may inhibit pedaling speed. This is not a bad trade-off for long-distance cycling, where cadences above 90 to 100 revolutions per minute are unnecessary. In general, if your inseam is less than 29 inches, use 165-mm crankarms; 29 to 32 inches, 170-mm; 33 or 34 inches, 172.5-mm; and more than 34 inches, 175-mm. You might want to experiment with the next longer length.

16. **Frame.** Measure your inseam using the LeMond method described earlier, and then multiply by 0.67. This equals your road frame size, measured along the seat tube from the center of the crank axle to the center of the top tube. As a double check, this should produce 4 to 5 inches of exposed seatpost when your saddle height is correct. (The post's maximum extension line shouldn't show, of course.)

Mountain Bike

Unlike road riding, mountain biking is chock-full of variety—your position is constantly changing as you pedal over undulating terrain and ride around or over obstacles. Even so, there are several important setup dimensions and riding techniques that will improve your performance. Spend a few minutes going through these guidelines. If you find something that should be changed, do it gradually over time so that you won't create more problems than you solve.

1. **Saddle height.** Seatpost lengths of 350 millimeters are common, so a lot of post can be out of the frame before the maximum extension line shows. For efficient pedaling, your knee should remain slightly bent at the bottom of the pedal stroke (the same as on a road bike). It's a good idea to lower the saddle slightly for rough terrain, enabling you to rise up so that the bike can float beneath you without pounding your crotch. On steep descents, some riders drop the saddle even farther to keep their weight low and rearward, but others just slide their butt off the back.

2. **Saddle tilt.** Most off-road riders prefer a level saddle, but some (including many women) find that a slight nose-down tilt avoids pressure and irritation. Others go slightly nose-up, which helps them sit back and lessen strain on their arms.

3. **Fore/aft saddle location.** This variable is for finding the correct pedaling position, not for adjusting your reach to the handlebar—that's why stems come with different extensions. To adjust it, use the same procedure described for roadies.

4. **Stem.** Mountain bike stems come in a huge variety of extensions (from 60 to 150 millimeters) and rises (from −5 to +25 degrees). For good control, the stem should place the handlebar an inch or two below the top of the saddle. This helps put weight on the front wheel so that it's easier to steer on climbs and less likely to pop up. Never exceed the stem's maximum height line, lest it break and cause a nasty crash. The forward extension should allow comfortably bent arms and a straight back. A longer and lower reach works for fast cruising, but a higher, closer hand position is more comfortable for the long haul. It also affords more control on difficult trails.

5. **Handlebar width.** An end-to-end measurement of 21 to 24 inches is common. If the bar seems too wide, trim it with a hacksaw or pipe cutter. First, though, move your controls inward and take a ride to make sure you'll like the new width. And remember to leave a bit extra at each end if you use bar-ends. In general, the narrower the bar, the quicker the steering and the more attention you must pay. Wider bars slow down steering inputs and provide more control at slow speed.

6. **Handlebar sweep.** Flat bars can be straight or have around five degrees of rearward bend per side. The choice is strictly one of arm and wrist comfort. Be aware that changing the sweep also changes your reach to the grips and could require a different stem length. Also available are "riser" bars with an upward bend. These allow a lower stem position. They're typically wider to improve control.

7. **Bar-ends.** These short, forward extensions are great for climbing leverage and achieving a longer, lower position on flat fire roads or pavement. Angle them slightly upward. Models that curve inward help protect your hands, and they're less likely to snag brush on tight singletrack. If you're thinking of installing bar-ends, first be sure that your handlebar can accept them. Some ultralight bars can't.

(continued on page 42)

Mountain Bike Position

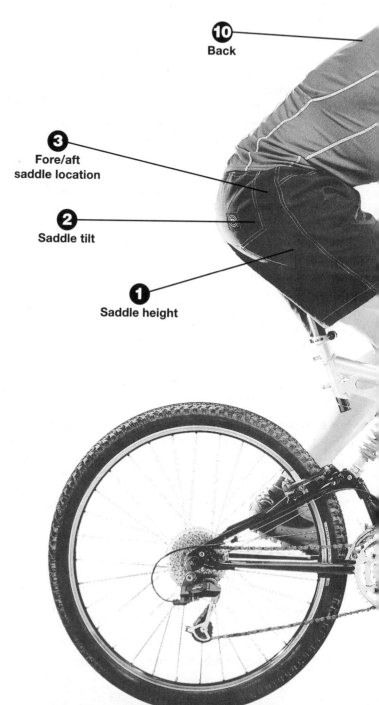

11 Upper Body

10 Back

3 Fore/aft saddle location

2 Saddle tilt

1 Saddle height

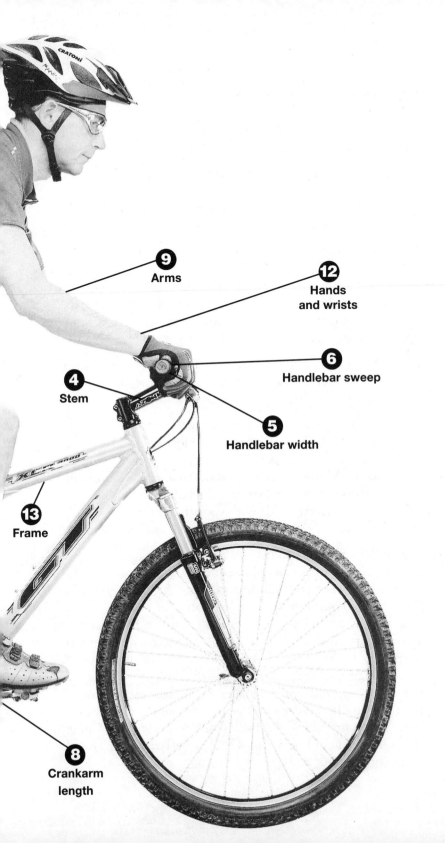

9 Arms

12 Hands and wrists

6 Handlebar sweep

4 Stem

5 Handlebar width

13 Frame

8 Crankarm length

8. **Crankarm length.** Manufacturers usually vary this with frame size. For greater leverage on steep climbs, mountain bikes typically come with crankarms 5 millimeters longer than would a road bike for the same-size rider.

9. **Arms.** Slightly bent arms act as shock absorbers. If you can reach the bar only with straight elbows, you probably need a shorter stem. Stretching can help you gain the hip flexibility to rotate farther forward.

10. **Back.** When your top-tube/stem-length combo is correct, you should have a forward lean of about 45 degrees during normal riding. This is an efficient angle because the strong gluteus muscles of the butt don't contribute much to pedaling when you're sitting more upright. Plus, a forward lean shifts some weight to the arms, so your butt doesn't get as sore.

11. **Upper body.** Don't hunch your shoulders, and you'll avoid muscle soreness and fatigue. Tilt or rotate your head every few minutes to stave off tight neck muscles.

12. **Hands and wrists.** Grasp the bar just firmly enough to maintain control. Set the brake levers close to the grips, and angle them so you can operate each with a finger or two and still hold the handlebar comfortably. Your wrists should be straight when you're standing over the saddle and braking, as on a downhill. Always ride with your thumbs under the bar (not resting on top), so your hands can't slip off on a bump.

13. **Frame.** Spontaneous (sometimes unwanted) dismounts are a part of riding off road. Consequently, you need lots of clearance between you and the top tube. The ideal mountain bike size is about 4 inches smaller than your road bike size. This isn't as critical if you'll be riding only on pavement or smooth dirt roads, but there's no advantage to having a frame any larger than the smallest size that allows enough saddle height and reach to the handlebar. Smaller frames are lighter, stiffer, and more maneuverable. Because manufacturers specify frame size in different ways, use the stand-over test. When straddling the bike while wearing your riding shoes, there should be about 4 inches between your crotch and the top tube.

4

Better Bike Handling

Good riding techniques are good
riding techniques—the same basic cycling skills apply to a 10-mile
commute to work or your club's annual century ride. Even so, there
are certain techniques that come into play much more in long-distance
events than in shorter jaunts. Included are eating and drinking while
riding, on-bike stretching, and tricks for maintaining saddle comfort.
You'll find these and other techniques, such as night riding and dealing
with heat or cold, in various chapters. Here, we're taking a deeper
look into several other skills that deserve special attention, including
drafting, climbing, riding on windy days, riding in the rain, and riding
a loaded bike.

Drafting

You will use more energy in events than you need to if you don't share
the effort with other riders. Drafting is a technique worth learning and
then using to your advantage. The companionship and collective effort make long distances more fun, too.

For safety and efficiency, you and the others should be compatible
in terms of pace and skills. Joining a paceline with riders who are too
fast can push you into risky heart rate territory when it's your turn at
the front. On the other hand, joining a relatively slow group isn't an
advantage if your goal is a strong personal performance. It can help
you recover for a few minutes or even survive when things aren't going
well for some reason, but keep an eye peeled for a better opportunity.
One will probably roll past before long.

When joining a paceline, always announce your presence. Everyone
needs to realize that you're in the rotation. Otherwise, a cyclist who
has been pulling off and dropping in behind the guy in the red jersey,
for example, may automatically do it again without realizing that now

you're behind that rider. We've seen close calls and even crashes because of this. The risk goes up late in a ride, when people are physically and mentally tired—and paying less attention.

Drafting has two advantages. Compared with riding solo, it allows you to ride at any given speed with less effort, or to ride faster using the same effort. In a landmark study at the University of Florida, James Hagberg, Ph.D., found that the energy cost (oxygen consumed) at 20 miles per hour is 18 percent less for a drafting rider. Interestingly, Jim also determined that the number of riders has no effect—the savings is the same whether you are drafting one rider or a line of four riders. At 23 miles per hour, the cost savings increases to 27 percent. Of course, at any given speed, the front cyclist uses the same energy as when riding solo. But by alternating turns in the lead, two or more equally matched cyclists can ride from 1 to 3 miles per hour faster than a single rider who is expending the same energy.

A tandem is about 10 percent faster than a single bike because the rear rider is, in effect, drafting close behind the front rider. For an even greater advantage, consider a low-slung recumbent. Because of the wide range of designs for these, it's hard to put an exact number on the drag reduction, but it's on the order of 25 percent at 20 miles per hour.

Paceline Pointers

In Jim Hagberg's study, the space between riders was kept to between 8 and 20 inches. Half a foot requires lots of attention and leaves very little room for error. A gap of about 2 feet is both effective and safe. It lets you ride nearly as relaxed as when solo, but you'll be using only about 85 percent of the energy required to go the same speed. In addition, use these tips to reap the benefits of paceline riding while reducing the risks.

Don't stare at the rear wheel of the bike you're following. Let your peripheral vision keep tabs while you look a couple of riders ahead to see what they're doing. Then you'll be prepared if something happens to make them veer or change speed. Remember, a paceline is like a Slinky. What happens at the front quickly flows to the back.

Don't overlap someone's rear wheel. If that rider should veer and hit your front wheel even lightly, you'll likely lose control and crash.

Don't brake. Doing so will slow you too much, open a gap, and possibly cause a dangerous chain reaction. Instead, if you begin to overtake the rider you're following, ease your pedal pressure (but don't coast), sit up to catch more wind, or move out to the side a bit.

When in a paceline during a long event such as California's Davis Double, you can relax like you do when riding solo and still get lots of draft if you allow a couple of feet between bikes.

Once you've lost enough speed, tuck back into line and smoothly resume normal pedaling.

When taking the lead, don't accelerate. Glance at your cyclecomputer and maintain the same speed as when drafting so that you don't cause gaps to open between other riders. You take the front because the other rider slows to drop back, not because you increase speed.

When you're leading up a hill, stay seated and keep your cadence and pedal pressure constant by shifting to a lower gear. If you must get out of the saddle, announce, "Standing!" a couple of strokes before you actually do it. Then avoid decelerating and striking the front wheel of the following rider by rising just as your right leg (or left, if that's the one you favor) is beginning the downstroke. Push your bike slightly forward as you make this move. Even some good cyclists do this incorrectly, so try to notice who they are. Then, when you're behind one and come to a hill, create a safety margin by dropping back half a length or moving to the side.

When your turn at the front is over, glance behind before pulling off. Make sure there isn't a rider there or traffic coming. This glance also lets the following rider know that you're about to relinquish the lead. Accelerate slightly to get clear as you move over, and then immediately reduce pedal pressure to begin dropping back. Stay close to the line as you do. When the last rider begins passing you, pick up speed so that you can slide behind his wheel without letting a gap open.

Eat and drink when you're the last person in line. In this position, you can sit up and reach for your food and bottle. An inadvertent swerve won't cause a problem for anyone.

Headwinds and Tailwinds

Do you ever get the feeling that the wind is always blowing against you? It actually is, more often than not. According to the laws of physics, only those winds within the trailing 160 degrees of an imaginary circle drawn around you provide assistance. Wind from anywhere in the other 200 degrees works to slow you. In other words, even a pure crosswind raises the drag. It must shift another 10 degrees to the rear before it begins to offer any help.

If you're riding on an out-and-back or circular course, any steady wind is bad no matter what the direction, and a pure crosswind is the worst. Unfortunately, the time you gain with the wind never equals the time you lose against it, so your average speed is bound to be slower. The objective on a ride like this should be to consume the same energy no matter in which direction you're traveling. Do your best to keep your heart rate steady. Avoid the mistake of pushing hard into a headwind and then resting with a tailwind. This usually produces a slower average speed even while using more energy. Gear down when going against the wind, and use a low, aero position. Sit up with a tailwind to make yourself more like a sail.

Beware of a crosswind from the left. You'll naturally lean into it in order to ride a straight line. Then, when traffic passes and momentarily blocks the wind, you may veer left into the lane. Reduce this effect by expecting it. Keep your elbows and grip relaxed to enable quick responses to changing forces.

Aerodynamics

We used to think that aerodynamics mattered only for a time trialist or a pursuiter pounding along at 30 miles per hour. But now we know better. Anything you can do to improve how well you, your equipment, or your clothing moves through the air can put you miles ahead on a long ride, even at half the speed a racer travels.

Wind is unavoidable in cycling, whether it's occurring naturally or we create it by our movement. While riding at 15 to 20 miles per hour on a calm day, the air accounts for 70 to 80 percent of the resistance you must overcome. In fact, the retarding force of air resistance increases as the square of the velocity. In simple terms, if you double your speed, you'll collide with twice as many air molecules that strike you twice as fast. This results in four times the drag.

It gets worse. The power required to overcome this resistance is even greater, equaling drag times velocity. This means that the energy needed to defeat air resistance increases proportionally to the cube of velocity. In order to double your speed, you have to use nearly eight times more energy. Looked at another way, if you're riding at 20 miles per hour and then double your power output, your speed will increase only about 6 miles per hour.

Obviously, anything you can do to decrease air resistance will improve your speed. Besides drafting, you can cheat the wind by reducing your frontal area and streamlining your bicycle, components, and clothing. Aero wheels may help or hinder, depending on crosswind conditions. A deep, V-shape rim or wide composite spokes in a front wheel can make a bike hard to control on a gusty day. Otherwise, lightweight aero wheels should be an advantage in centuries and for other fast, unloaded riding. Exactly how much is hard to say. Tests are typically conducted at time trial speeds of around 30 miles per hour, but it stands to reason that there is a helpful drag reduction in the area of 20 to 24 miles per hour as well.

FRONTAL AREA

The biggest advance in streamlining has been aero bars that allow a downhill-skier cycling position. Using them lowers a typical rider's frontal area from 4.2 square feet in the upright touring posture to about 3.6 square feet (versus 3.9 square feet when riding low on the drops). At typical long-distance riding speeds of 15 to 25 miles per hour, the improvement can mean a 1- to 2-miles-per-hour increase for the same power output. Aero bars may also be the most economical way to boost speed, costing only a tenth of the tab for a pair of aerodynamic wheels. On most rides, you can use an aero bar at least half the time—enough for it to make a significant improvement in your performance.

Be ready for quicker handling and oversteer (more steering reaction than expected) when you're laid out on an aero bar. This happens because the position puts your hands in front of the handlebar and adds weight to the front wheel. Practice steering around patches in the road to get the hang of it. For actual cornering, it's safest to sit up in a normal position for better balance and braking.

When you need to carry extra clothing, food, or equipment, pack it on top of a rear rack rather than in side-mounted panniers. An expandable rack trunk can hold lots of stuff, and it sits behind your body where it catches little air. If you also use a handlebar bag, make it the smallest one that meets your needs. Some are more streamlined than others. Don't use a bar-mounted mirror when a much smaller one that attaches to your helmet or glasses will work just as well. Position your cyclecomputer, heart rate monitor, and cue sheet in line with the air flow. Don't use bottles and cages if a streamlined hydration system on your back holds enough to get you safely between fuel stops. Several small reductions in frontal area can add up to a measurable amount of speed.

CLOTHING

In addition to lowering your frontal area, be sure to streamline what you wear. Comfort is paramount in long-distance cycling, but there's no reason that clothes have to be baggy to be comfortable. Wear a jersey that's form-fitting so that it won't flap in the wind or billow like a drag chute when it's unzipped for ventilation. The fabric should have a smooth texture, such as CoolMax or Lycra. Even vests, jackets, and rainwear should fit as snug as possible without compromising comfort. All vented helmets are about equally streamlined and create no more air resistance than an unhelmeted head.

Climbing

Don't go anaerobic. That's the best advice we can give you for climbing in events (not for training, though, where occasionally pushing past the point of lactic acid accumulation has important benefits). In events, however, your best overall performances will come if you climb strongly but avoid the glycogen-gobbling consequences of switching to anaerobic metabolism. You'll read more about your energy systems in other chapters. Here, we concentrate on techniques that will maximize your climbing efficiency.

At cycling camps, the first question we hear about riding uphill is always the same: Is it better to sit or stand? There is no absolute answer. It depends on the terrain and personal preference—what feels better to you. That said, most riders will find that sitting uses less energy because body weight is supported by the bike. For the majority of cyclists, going from the saddle to standing causes an increase in heart rate in the range of three to five beats per minute. Not a lot, but it adds up. And remember, the exertion of climbing may already have you near your lactate threshold. A slight increase can put you into dangerous territory. The best way to learn your body's reaction to any climbing technique is to take your heart rate monitor for a hilly ride.

The rule of thumb is to climb long, steady hills in the saddle to conserve energy. Even so, it's good to stand occasionally for a couple of dozen pedal strokes. This increases comfort by changing body position and altering the muscles that are bearing the strain. Before rising, shift to the next higher gear (smaller cog) so you won't lose speed. Cadence tends to drop when you stand. Move fluidly as you go in and out of the saddle, so momentum isn't interrupted.

Long, undulating climbs give you natural intervals for sitting (shallow sections) and standing (steeper pitches). Short rollers are best taken by standing and jamming to keep your momentum. Here are some other tips.

Don't lean too far forward when standing. This slows you by grinding the front tire into the pavement, or causing the rear wheel to lose traction on a trail. Keep your body centered, grip the brake lever hoods or bar-ends, and let the bike sway several inches to each side in sync with your pedal stokes. Don't exaggerate this motion and waste energy—just establish a rhythm.

Use the right gear. The correct ratio when you're standing will make it feel like you're walking up stairs. The gear is too low if you're bouncing and feeling little pedal pressure, causing you to drive the pedals through their power stroke too quickly. On the other hand, if you must work the bike from side to side with a grinding cadence, the gear is too high.

Go low. The recently retired Ron Kiefel, who is macho enough to have ridden seven Tours de France, now uses a little 39x26 low gear for the climbs near his home on Colorado's Front Range. Your authors gear down like this, too. We recommend triple-chainring cranksets on road bikes for bail-out gears that can save the day on hilly ultra rides.

Keep your cadence up. On extended climbs, use a gear that you can pedal at about 70 to 80 rpm. This will be a relatively low gear that helps control your heart rate for the entire hill.

Pedal in circles. Concentrate on pedaling across the stroke, rather than simply up and down. The idea is to apply some power horizontally, especially through the bottom. This recruits more leg muscles and enhances momentum.

Shift just before you need to. Anticipate shifts to lower gears, such as when starting a climb. Don't shift too soon and waste precious momentum, but do shift before you're forced to apply heavy pressure to keep the crankset turning. Should you misjudge, reduce pressure for one revolution the instant you make the shift, allowing the chain to move with less delay and grinding.

Start easy. To climb faster, begin in a lower gear than you need and shift up as you ascend. Coach Chris Carmichael says to imagine yourself as a carpet unrolling. It's the way pro road racers do it. The alternative—starting a long climb in the biggest gear you can handle—is likely to have you slogging away and searching for lower (and slower) gears well before the top. Be conservative early, and then you'll have the option of stepping up your pace.

Sit up. Most roadies find they can't breathe as well if they grip the handlebar drops when climbing. Besides, the aerodynamic advantage of a low position isn't important at climbing speeds. Instead, grip the bar top or the brake lever hoods to sit up and help your diaphragm expand. Mountain bikers may use bar-ends to get the same open position as well as better leverage during frequent changes from sitting to standing.

Breathe deeply and rhythmically. To prevent shallow panting, concentrate on expelling air forcefully and completely, letting your lungs refill passively. Do this in sync with your pedal strokes. If a climb eases briefly, maintain your deep breathing to recover and be ready for the next pitch.

Slide on the saddle. On long, gradual climbs, move forward on the seat to emphasize the quadriceps muscles on the front of your thighs. After pedaling in this position for a while, slide back to relieve the quads and accentuate the gluteus muscles in your buttocks. These shifts help fend off muscle fatigue and extend your energy.

Relax your upper body. During the strain of climbing, you may find yourself clenching your jaw, tensing your hands and arms, and hunching your shoulders. To fight these energy-sapping tendencies, grip the bar lightly and bend your elbows slightly, whether you're sitting or standing. Keep your back flat and your shoulders back so that your chest is open for full, deep breathing. You'll be supple, able to move smoothly with the pedaling motion.

Bob a bit. Rocking your upper body helps establish a rhythm that aids climbing. Don't intentionally exaggerate this, but also don't try to prevent it. Do what feels natural.

Train with weights. Gain climbing power with squats or leg presses. These exercises build the quadriceps, calf, and gluteus (butt) muscles. For the upper body, rowing exercises develop the strength to pull on the handlebar and balance the force exerted by the legs.

Finish every hill. It's natural to let up near the top of a climb when the crest finally comes into view. Whew, I made it, you think, as you ease pedal pressure to reduce the strain. Then your pace slows to a crawl, and it takes forever to finally reach the top. Instead, make time on every hill by not reducing your effort until gravity is pulling you the other way. You might even shift up and stand across the crest to stretch your legs and build extra momentum for the descent. It takes mental discipline to climb this way, but the rewards are significant in a hilly event. Make it a habit by finishing every hill you ride in training.

Finally, here's a smart tactic from Pete Penseyres, one of ultra cycling's best antigravity riders:

Climb as fast as possible without going anaerobic, then rest on the descent, rather than climb easily and push on the descent. Here's an example of how this works. Let's assume that you have a 5-mile climb followed by a 5-mile descent. You might think that it's better to go up easy, then blast down the other side with gravity's help. But if you climb the hill at 10 miles per hour and then pedal hard to descend at 40 miles per hour, it will take you 37:30 to cover the 10 miles. If you climb harder (but not anaerobically) at 12 miles per hour and then tuck and coast down at 35 miles per hour, it will take you only 33:36. This savings of almost 4 minutes is worth 1.2 miles if you're averaging 18 miles per hour on the ride. As you rest on long descents, turn the pedals slowly so your legs don't stiffen.

Riding in the Rain

As a long-distance cyclist, you can count on quite a few miles in inclement weather. On some rides, you'll experience everything from dazzling sun to a drenching downpour. It pays to gain experience by training in the rain once in a while. You'll find that once you're in it, a rainy day is never as bad as it appears through the window of your cozy home. In fact, if you have the raingear we describe in chapter 5, it can be quite comfortable and a lot of fun. Let's check several technique tips that will make it safe, too.

Fast cornering on a wet road isn't a skill that we need in long-distance cycling. It's much safer to reduce speed. Don't be embarrassed—even European pros are known to ride through corners at walking speed in rainy races. To make any wet corner less treacherous, make it more shallow by approaching wide, steering straight through the turn, and then exiting wide. In effect, this transforms one tight turn into two shallow ones. As you coast through, the outside pedal should be down with your weight on it. Of course, be sure traffic is clear before using the whole lane this way.

When you expect wet or soft surfaces, slightly deflate your tires to

Dogs

As long-distance riders, we're bound to encounter a nuisance dog now and then, the kind that loves to hassle cyclists. In almost every case, the cur is merely defending its well-defined territory. So, when a mean dog is running out to get you, usually the best tactic is to sprint like crazy to get a lead and benefit from a dog's instinct to come up from behind. This helps you keep it away from your front wheel. Then maintain your effort for the few seconds it takes to ride past the magic boundary. We've seen dogs come to a four-paw screeching halt when there seemed to be nothing to stop them but their own sense of turf-defending victory.

If a dog is gaining ground and coming up alongside, buy time by squirting your bottle at it, raising your pump menacingly and swinging it if you have to (won't work with a mini pump), or using a commercial dog repellent such as Halt. Often, simply raising a hand like you're about to throw something will make it flinch away. So might shouts of "No!" or "Git!" or "Go home!" Repeated several times in a strong voice, these commands mimic the dog's owner and may put an end to the chase.

If nothing works and you're cornered, get off your bike. The lack of motion may end the threat. Keep your bike between you and the dog until it either wanders off or help arrives. If a dog is a continual nuisance, don't hesitate to report it to the authorities. You have a right to use public roads (and favorite training routes) without being attacked.

increase the size of their contact patch. For example, instead of using the full recommended pressure of about 110 pounds per square inch (psi) in your road tires, reduce them to about 90. Bleed just enough air so that the tires deform slightly under your weight, but not so much that they squash like radial car tires. You don't want them squirming or allowing pinch flats. The same goes for the knobbies on a mountain bike. Reduce pressure proportionally, say, from 45 to 35 pounds per square inch.

Be especially cautious on the road when rain begins, particularly if it's been dry for a few days. Oil and dust will float to the surface, making the pavement surprisingly slick. But as rain continues and washes this slippery film away, your traction may become almost as secure as on a dry road. Nevertheless, painted lines, steel surfaces (manhole covers, grates, railroad tracks, bridge decks), and leaves are always slick when wet. Never ride through a puddle if you can avoid it. There could be a gaping hole hidden under what looks like shallow water.

When you're braking in the rain or any time your rims are wet, remember that the first few wheel revolutions will do nothing to slow you. They only wipe moisture from the rims and brake pads. Anticipate this, and allow considerably more stopping distance. Once the rims are squeegeed dry, the brakes may suddenly take hold. Be ready to loosen your grip on the levers as soon as you feel the grab, or you could lock a wheel and skid.

Normally, applying the front brake harder than the rear is the most effective way to stop. On slick surfaces, however, braking hard up front invites a front-wheel skid, which will almost always cause a fall. Emphasize the rear brake instead. It's much easier to maintain control if it's the rear wheel that momentarily locks.

It can be tough to see through rain or the spray sent up from other bikes. Protect your vision with clear or yellow lenses, but avoid dark tints, which will lessen details on a gloomy day. You also can keep rain out of your eyes by wearing a brimmed cap under your helmet or a helmet visor. Make yourself more visible to motorists by using a brightly colored rain jacket with reflective stripes or piping.

When you get home after a rainy ride, hose down your bike while it's still wet. Most of the crud will rinse right off. Then dry it with an old towel. Wipe the chain well. Lube it and the pivot points of derailleurs and brakes, as well as each place that cables slide in and out of guides or housing. Voilà! In 10 minutes, your bike may be cleaner than it was before the ride.

Loaded Touring

For many cyclists, the idea of bike touring sparks an urge to travel the road or trail in search of adventure, discovery, excitement, and friendships. These worthy objectives will only come true, however, if you avoid common mistakes that can snare touring cyclists. The following list was compiled from several veteran tour guides. Combine these tips with the general endurance-cycling advice throughout this book, and you'll have the know-how to pack up and ride anywhere.

Train before the tour, not during it. Some people figure that they can ride themselves into shape during the first week of the tour. A much smarter approach is to start training about 3 months before the trip. If you're beginning from ground zero, ride 15 miles a day, three times a week. Raise this to 20 miles after the fifth time. Keep gradually increasing the distance. As your form improves, check your trip itinerary and find your longest day. If it's 90 miles, you should work up to about 70 miles in training. Full-distance rides aren't necessary. At a touring pace with occasional breaks, you should be able to ride about twice as far in a day as the average of your longest training rides.

Be mentally prepared. Some people quit their tour because they let things get to them. It's not a physical problem, it's a mental one. You must be prepared to face difficult times and work through them. You must convince yourself that things will improve as you continue, because they will.

Practice getting loaded. The trick to mounting, dismounting, and walking with a loaded bike is to keep it vertical so that its weight stays centered over the wheels. Otherwise, it takes lots of strength to keep it from toppling over. If you're going on a camping trip, do at least two training rides with your bike fully loaded, especially if you're new to riding with panniers. The extra weight changes your bike's stability and handling, which means that your riding techniques must also change.

You need to brake earlier, for example, because your bike is so much heavier. Turning also is affected, and you need to be cautious on rough roads to reduce impact on your wheels. You may not be able to climb well when standing, so get used to sitting and spinning your lowest "granny" gear. Descending on a loaded bike can lead to a scary condition called shimmy or speed wobble. The bike begins to shake, and it might quickly become uncontrollable. To stop shimmy, accelerate or decelerate from the speed at which it occurs. It also helps to lean forward, putting more weight on the front wheel. Often, the quickest solution is to clamp the top tube between your knees.

Protect your points of contact. Make sure that your saddle is the most comfortable you can find. Lots of padding isn't the answer, because during hours of pedaling it can cause chafing and pressure points. Never install a different saddle shortly before a tour. Always give yourself several weeks to adapt to it. If you're renting a bike, take your own saddle. Wear clean shorts every day, and use a chamois lubricant to reduce chafing. As for hands, padded gloves help prevent finger numbness and raw skin, but it's still essential to change your grip on the handlebar frequently. For more hand positions, consider an aero bar for your road bike and bar-ends for your mountain bike. Feet must have protection from pedal pressure, so a good choice for road or off-road touring is a mountain bike shoe/pedal system that works with recessed cleats. The shoes have a semirigid sole that allows comfortable walking as well as riding.

Pack only the essentials. On a 2-week self-contained trip, you shouldn't need more than 40 pounds of gear. Think of it like this: Once you're packed for 2 weeks, you're packed for 3 months. You just recycle stuff. A common mistake is taking too many clothes, trying to cover all conditions. With advances in fabrics, especially in sweat-wicking and insulating underwear, you can layer and carry a lot less.

Eat well. You'll be burning several thousand calories each day, so you must keep replenishing your fuel. This is not the time to try to lose a few pounds by restricting your diet. You'll only run low on energy. We've seen vegetarians ride strongly, and we've seen people who eat total garbage ride strongly. A lot of it is mental. If you're convinced your diet will affect your riding, it probably will. You need plenty of carbohydrate for daily energy, but you also need some fat and protein and lots of liquids.

Distribute your weight. On rough surfaces, level the pedals and rise several inches off the seat. Bend your elbows and knees to absorb impact and save your butt and hands. For descents, move back on the saddle to get your weight over the rear wheel. This is especially important off road. On steep descents, you may have to slide completely off the back, with the seat under your stomach.

Avoid crunching the gears. Lighten your pedal pressure just as you shift, especially if you're going uphill. Don't expect the gears to change very well (or at all) when you're straining to keep moving. The best tactic when riding loaded is to shift to a lower gear just before the hill begins, not after.

Use the front brake. It supplies the majority of your stopping

Perfect packing! The front panniers are centered on the axle to allow neutral steering. Train on your loaded bike occasionally, so you'll know how it will behave on tour.

power. Off road, it's not true that you shouldn't use the front brake going downhill. In fact, your rear wheel will do little but skid when your weight is forward on a descent. Just make sure your weight is rearward, to prevent the bike from tipping forward. An exception to front braking comes in a corner with a loose surface. Ease up so that the front wheel doesn't dig into the soil and throw you.

Practice uphill starts. When you're stopped in the midst of a climb with a loaded bike, it's a real challenge to start pedaling again. Walk the bike to a spot that's more level, squeeze the rear brake to prevent it from rolling backward, swing a leg over, and then put one pedal into the power position (between top center and horizontal). Simultaneously release the brake and apply pedal pressure moderately—not with a jab—so you won't veer. Don't worry about clicking in the other foot until you're well underway.

Here's a potpourri of advice about loading up for a tour. A great way to learn more about all aspects of long-distance cycling is by joining the nonprofit Adventure Cycling Association and receiving its magazine, *Adventure Cyclist,* plus its catalogs of tours, maps, and products. For information, check its Web site: www.adv-cycling.org. Likewise, the nonprofit League of American Bicyclists (LAB) has a touring as well as advocacy orientation. To see what LAB offers go to www.bikeleague.org. Here's the list.

- You don't need to pack an extensive wardrobe, even on an extended tour, if you choose clothes that dry quickly after washing.

- Tightly roll your clothes. They'll take less space than when folded. Put them in clear, zip-shut plastic bags to keep them clean, dry, and organized.

- Pack heavy items and things you don't use frequently, such as tools, in the bottom of your panniers to keep the center of gravity low.

- For optimum bike handling with loads of 20 pounds or more, put approximately 60 percent of the cargo in the rear panniers, 35 percent in the front panniers, and 5 percent in a handlebar bag. Balance the load from side to side to ensure a stable ride.

- Put your most frequently used items in your handlebar bag. For example, these might include your camera, notebook, map, sunscreen, and puncture repair kit.

- Front panniers, which are usually one-third smaller than rear ones, are best mounted on a low rack that centers them on the front axle. The farther away from the axle a front load is carried, the more difficult steering becomes.

- If you take a cooking kit, use the pot to store your spices, scouring pads, and other small items. To save space, remove food from bulky packages and put it into plastic bags.

- Never start a tour with full panniers. If you've stuffed in all of your gear and strained the zippers shut, what happens the first time you buy an item? You're almost certain to add to your belongings as the adventure progresses.

- Reserve one rear pannier for soiled items such as shoes, dirty clothes, or a ground cloth. Similarly, wet items should be kept from dry ones.

- Pack the bulkiest items, such as a sleeping bag and pad, atop the rear rack.

- Although some panniers may claim to be waterproof, don't take chances. Put everything into sturdy plastic bags with tight closures. Remember, if it's worth having, it's probably worth having dry.

- Check your packing list, then check it again. Cross off anything that isn't absolutely necessary. You want to be comfortable, but a large part of your comfort will be determined by the amount of weight that you carry.

- A 1:1 low-gear ratio (for example, 28-tooth chainring and 28-tooth cog) is necessary if you'll be hauling your load up hills. Even lower gearing, created by a larger cog or smaller ring, may be necessary for mountainous terrain.

- Schedule each day of a tour so that you'll reach your destination by early afternoon. This provides a buffer against unexpected delays. It also gives you time to remove your panniers and explore the area unencumbered.

5

Gear That Goes and Goes

Do you love cycling because of the
equipment, or in spite of the equipment? Your authors are enthusiasti-
cally in the first category. We admit to a fascination with the interplay
of the human body and cycling's machinery. When you think about it,
what other device can amplify physical ability as effectively as a bicycle? Imagine a person pedaling across America in 7 days and 23
hours, as Michael Secrest has, or totaling 354 off-road miles in 24
hours, as John Stamstad has. Beyond the bike itself, there are dozens of
products that can improve speed, efficiency, durability, safety, carrying
capacity, or that often-elusive quality that every cyclist seeks: comfort.
When it comes to riding long distances, each of these is important.

In this chapter, we share our insights about a wide range of products that you may want to use, depending on which variety of endurance cycling is calling your name. It's always risky to write about
specific brands and models because cycling technology is constantly
evolving, with new or revamped products being introduced all the
time. With this in mind, we'll give you a few specific name recommendations but lots of generic advice that you can use when shopping
in the current marketplace.

First, of course, you need a bike that's suited to the type of long-
distance cycling you plan to do. Use this overview to pigeonhole the
category, and then select the model with the price and features that
you prefer.

Racing/Sport Bikes

Recreational one-day rides include everything up to a double century,
but they top out at around a hundred miles for many cyclists. Organized events almost always have well-stocked rest stops, making it unnecessary to carry much extra food or fluid. This means that almost

A light and agile sport bike is ideal for long one-day rides when it's equipped with a triple crankset. Using the smallest chainring makes climbing easier, conserving energy that can be used for endurance.

any type of bicycle can work. Look around at the starting line of a century ride and you're likely to see everything from criterium bikes to hybrids to mountain bikes.

A great tool for one-day rides is what could be called a road sport bike. You don't need to buy a true road racing machine unless you have several thousand dollars to burn, simply want to own top-line equipment, or your goal is to ride events competitively. In general, an investment of between $800 and $1,200 will get you a bike that not only looks like a pure racer but also performs nearly as well for long recreational rides.

Or, it might even perform better. If you ride in hilly terrain, you'll be smart to avoid a racing bike's traditional two-chainring crankset and get a sport bike's triple-chainring one. Numerous models in the price range just mentioned are equipped this way. The third chainring gives you an entire range of low gears that no racing bike has. You'll climb with less effort, and the bike will be more suitable if your horizons expand to longer events. A triple gives you the pulling power to handle hills when the bike is loaded with the extra equipment and supplies that you need for multiday events or tours. Unloaded, a triple's weight penalty is so slight that it won't drag down your performance when your goal is a fast time.

Four frame materials are commonly found. Steel and aluminum prevail in the target price range, with titanium and carbon fiber becoming available as you move up the scale. Don't drive yourself crazy about this choice. In the opinion of Lon Haldeman, it's a frame's design as much as what it's made of that determines the ride. As he puts it, "I've ridden all types of frame materials in the Race Across America, and couldn't tell the difference on a dark night." Lon recommends judging a bike by how it feels in the last half of a long ride. If you can't wait to finish and get off, the bike or your position on it certainly isn't comfortable. Any of the four materials can result in a smooth ride or a harsh one, depending on tube dimensions and the angles at which they're assembled.

Lightness is important, and not only for the usual reason. Less weight probably means a more compliant frame, helping it soak up more shock on rough surfaces, not just climb easier. Lon notes that some of the best frames he's ridden in ultramarathon events would probably be criticized as too flexible by many riders. To Lon, a tall and strong cyclist of around 200 pounds, these frames were comfortable and efficient because they didn't subject him to harsh road shock day after day.

In working with the hundreds of cyclists who've participated in his PAC Tours and endurance camps, Lon has devised this simple formula to calculate how much a given rider's bike should weigh: no more than 12 percent of body weight. Thus, if you weigh 200 pounds, your bike should be 24 pounds or less. If you weigh 150 pounds, you should be riding an 18-pound bike. Admittedly, lighter riders are going to have a harder time finding a bike that fits this formula, especially on a modest budget. In this case, they should buy the lightest bike they can afford. Weight equals drag, so lighter is always better, as long as durability isn't compromised.

Touring Bikes

A triple crankset is mandatory, and the bike should be designed for extra carrying capacity and long-distance comfort. A touring frame will have a long wheelbase and relaxed angles for stability and comfort. Longer chainstays will create additional clearance between the wheels and frame so that fenders and wider tires fit easily, and your heels don't hit rear panniers. Most models will have cantilever brakes, another way to allow more room between the frame and wheels. Dropout eyelets and other fittings will make the installation of racks

(continued on page 64)

Equipment for Women

Women aren't shaped like men, but you wouldn't have known this from decades' worth of cycling equipment. Thankfully, the industry has woken up to the fact and now produces everything from bikes to gloves in women-specific designs.

According to Andrew Pruitt, Ed.D., director of the Boulder Center for Sports Medicine in Boulder, Colorado, most women have a proportionately shorter torso and longer legs than men, plus a wider pelvis and less upper-body strength. Andy Pruitt knows the problems women have in fitting typical bikes because he has worked for years with U.S. National Team riders at the Olympic Training Center in Colorado Springs. Even if a bike fits a woman's leg length, its top tube, stem, or crankarms might be too long, and its saddle could be too narrow.

So what happens if a woman's bike doesn't fit right?

If you toodle only a couple of miles around the neighborhood, probably nothing. But when you're a long-distance cyclist, you'll experience back, neck, hip, or butt pain that can range from mild to incapacitating. And your pedaling efficiency may suffer just as much. Fortunately, these problems are now well understood, and more manufacturers are answering the need for bikes that fit women better. Sara Henry, who has written extensively on this topic, comments, "Not every woman needs a women's bike, but every woman needs a bike that fits, particularly in the critical distance between the seat and handlebar. A woman's bike may be the best place to start looking." Sara highlights the key considerations below.

Frame. Because of their proportionately shorter torsos, women usually need a shorter top tube. But if the rider is quite small—say, under 5 feet 4 inches— the top tube can be so short that it brings the front wheel too close. This causes feet to overlap the wheel when either one is fully forward in the pedal stroke. The result can be contact and a crash during slow riding when the wheel might be turned sharply. Some manufacturers resolve this problem by using a smaller-diameter front wheel.

Georgena Terry, founder of Terry Precision Cycling for Women, is a leader in this area. Her company makes its smaller road bikes with a 24-inch front wheel and a standard 700C wheel in back. This trick also allows these bikes to retain a relatively normal head-tube angle for proper steering behavior. No matter how tall a woman is, Georgena notes, "her muscles are not only generally smaller than a man's but are distributed differently, resulting in more force on joints. A slightly more upright riding position eases those forces."

Stem. The simplest fix for an overly long top tube is to install a stem with a shorter forward extension, bringing the bar closer to the seat. Several manufacturers make very short stems. Order one at your local bike shop.

Handlebar. Women's shoulders tend to be narrower then men's. A bar that's too wide may cause pain in the upper back and neck. Terry offers 36- and 38-centimeter drop bars to more precisely correspond to a woman's shoulder width (measured from bony end to bony end). The flat bars found on mountain bikes and hybrids can easily be shortened with a pipe cutter at a bike shop.

Crankarms. Arm lengths of 160 or 165 millimeters, rather than the standard 170 millimeters, are a better fit for women (and men) who have an inseam of less than 29½ inches (measured from crotch to floor in bare feet). Keep in mind that mountain bike crankarms should be 5 millimeters longer than those on road bikes, for better leverage on steep climbs and in slow-speed maneuvers.

Saddle. Because women's pelvises are slightly wider than men's, their sit bones are farther apart. To support these bones and keep weight from resting solely on the tender tissue between them, women may need a saddle that's wider in the rear. In addition, comfort may be helped by cutouts or specially padded sections.

Anatomical saddles for women have slightly more width for full support, and cutouts to reduce uncomfortable crotch contact.

Brake levers. With smaller hands and shorter fingers, many women can benefit from short-reach brake levers for their road bike. Check at a shop for the models currently available. Usually, mountain bike levers have adjustment screws for shortening their distance to the bar.

As with equipment, the day is gone when women cyclists have no choice but to wear clothes made for men. Most cycling apparel companies now offer garments cut specifically for women. Other companies extend this concept to shoes and helmets. Performance, the country's largest cycling retailer, has a wide selection of women's clothing and products in its shops, catalog, and Web site (www.performancebike.com). Terry is another good source.

and fenders simple and secure. Unloaded and stripped of accessories, a touring bike won't hold you back in recreational centuries. Loaded, it becomes a two-wheel RV, ideal for self-contained excursions that could last for weeks.

Most major bike manufacturers have at least one model that fits the touring definition. In addition, there are small specialty companies, such as Rivendell, Bruce Gordon, and numerous custom frame-builders, who produce this type of bike. Compared to a sport bike with triple chainrings, a true touring bike does a better job of accommodating all of the gear and then giving you a stable ride. You'll be especially thankful on descents, where high-speed shimmy is a threat to any loaded bike.

Because of their frame geometry, touring bikes are less nimble than more compact sport or racing models. Their handling is greatly affected, too, when weight is being carried. Get used to this behavior by occasionally loading the bike for training rides with the same equipment and weight that you'll be carrying for tours or multiday events. These dry runs also let you check the operation of your bags and racks, and determine the best fore/aft weight distribution (normally around 40/60).

Mountain Bikes

The day has come when a dual-suspension bike is the right type for long-distance mountain biking. This wasn't the case until recently, because rear-suspension weight was high and performance was inefficient. Now, however, these deficiencies have largely been solved, and engineering continues to improve with each new model year.

Compared to hardtail mountain bikes with front suspension only, a dualie's comfort is well worth the extra pound or two. You can stay seated on almost anything your wheels encounter, saving the energy required to lift your body out of the saddle hundreds of times on a long ride. In addition, rear suspension helps the wheel stay in contact with the ground instead of hopping and chattering, a big benefit on descents. Unlike a suspension seatpost or beam, it works when you're standing, too. And it helps leverage your rear wheel into the ground on climbs. The new designs greatly reduce or eliminate the funky, out-of-round pedaling sensation that plagued early rear suspensions.

Sold? So are a growing number of top racers, including Ned Overend, who in 1999 won his second Xterra off-road world triathlon championship using a dual-suspension bike, the 24-pound Specialized

You can't beat the comfort of dual suspension when riding long distances off road. The benefits are well worth the slight weight penalty.

S-Works FSRxc. In fact, Ned had been riding a dualie for three seasons, seeing no downside that comes close to negating the advantages. Comfort alone makes a dualie the right bike for rugged off-road ultra rides, as well as for the growing number of 24-hour races.

It's possible to tour on a mountain bike, and some riders prefer one because it allows the use of dirt or gravel roads and jeep trails. Barends are a must for the alternate hand position they provide. Aero bars also can be installed. Many hardtails will accept standard rear racks and bags, but dualies can't. For them, use a cantilever-style, shelflike rack that attaches to the seatpost and extends over the rear wheel. See below for more information about racks.

Tandems

Most long-distance events, from centuries to Paris-Brest-Paris to RAAM, have tandem categories—male/male, female/female, and mixed. Tandems are terrific for long distances because they're fast and efficient, and they keep you and your partner together throughout. This last point is why tandems are favored by cyclists of different abilities. They're the ultimate equalizer, allowing each rider to exert at his or her own level but never become separated. During a long day of cycling, the companionship and teamwork adds yet another dimension to the sense of accomplishment.

Like single bikes, tandems come in various designs and materials. More than two dozen North American companies offer at least one model. If you intend to do some unsupported events or light touring, make sure the frame has dropout eyelets and other fittings for attaching racks, bags, and fenders. For fully loaded touring, a tandem can't actually carry double the gear for two riders. A good way to expand capacity is with a pull-behind trailer such as the B.O.B. Yak, which has a single wheel to make it nearly as narrow as the bike. A trailer also helps keep weight off the tandem's wheels—usually the most troublesome equipment (though all components take a harder beating than when just one cyclist is using them). Tandem builders compensate by using rims, spokes, and spoking patterns that increase strength and durability. In addition, there are hybrid tandems that use

A tandem with rear suspension is a godsend for the stoker, who can't easily see upcoming bumps in the road. It helps the captain, too, because he doesn't have to warn about every surface irregularity that could cause saddle pain.

beefy 26-inch wheels like a mountain bike. These allow routes that include poor pavement and dirt or gravel roads.

For the comfort of the rear rider, consider rear suspension. This could be in the form of a shock-absorbing seatpost or a flexible Softride carbon-fiber beam (see photo to left). Depending on the size of the cyclists, the stoker may not have a good view of the road. He or she can get hammered by bumps unless the captain is constantly calling a warning. A shock post will fit any conventional tandem, and the captain may well want one, too, so that there's less need to stand over rough stuff. Tandem frames that incorporate the Softride beam are made by at least three companies—Burley, Co-Motion, and Longbikes. Co-Motion also builds a tandem with a beam for the captain, too. A different solution is a recumbent tandem, which puts both riders in a relaxed, laid-back position, enjoying better visibility and the other recumbent features we discuss next.

Recumbents

These chaise lounges on wheels are fun to ride any distance, but they seem particularly suited to endurance cycling. Comfort is the key reason. Your upper body is reclined and supported by the seat, taking strain off your back, neck, arms, and shoulders. This position also gives you great views all around without having to crane your neck. There is no weight on your hands, so numbing pressure is eliminated.

But the biggest advantage for many recumbent fans is sitting on a broad cushion instead of a firm, narrow saddle. Besides more overall comfort, this removes a typical saddle's pressure on the nerves and blood vessels that run through the crotch. No more genital numbness. For men, this also eliminates the conditions that some doctors suspect can contribute to erectile dysfunction.

All isn't perfect, though. A recumbent rider sits on the gluteus muscles used in pedaling, which can cause their own version of discomfort on a long ride. Also, without air circulation, solid seats make your butt and back wet with sweat. (Mesh seats reduce this problem.) Recumbents don't climb well on long or steep hills because you can't stand and use body weight for extra power. This makes climbing purely a matter of leg strength, except on short rollers where momentum helps a recumbent move as fast as any bike. Most recumbents are equipped with triple cranksets, providing very low gears that make extended climbing easier but also slower. Finally, recumbents put you lower to the road. You're less visible to drivers, especially in traffic where you might be obscured by passing vehicles. It's smart to wear a bright helmet and jersey or even use a warning flag on a pole.

For an experienced cyclist on a lightweight recumbent, these negatives don't begin to offset the positives. Especially on a flat course, 'bent riders can rule the day. Frontal area is less than on a conventional bike, reducing air resistance as if you were drafting another rider. Add a transparent Zzipper windscreen fairing and you'll be quicker yet. Descending is the closest thing there is to street luge. You'll be miles per hour faster than on a regular bike.

There's no consensus in recumbent design. Only Trek among major bike manufacturers builds one, leaving the market to three dozen small, innovative companies. You'll find models with handlebars in front of your chest or under the seat, with the front wheel ahead of or behind your feet, and with all sorts of drivetrain configurations. Some models can be fitted with racks and panniers front and rear, making them a fine choice for touring. To learn more about these interesting bikes, there's no better source than Bob Bryant's *Recumbent Cyclist News,* a bimonthly magazine that includes an annual buyer's guide. The Web address is www.diskspace.com/rcn/.

Travel Bikes

Frequent travelers will do well to invest in a premium folding bike, such as one of the Bike Friday models from Green Gear Cycling. Each

Cover the bottom half of this photo and it looks like Ed Pavelka is riding a conventional bike. That's exactly Bike Friday's point!

of your authors has a Pocket Rocket, and this version or the Air Friday is owned by numerous serious riders we know. And we do mean serious. We've seen these bikes in long-distance events as rugged as Paris-Brest-Paris. The photo shows Ed Pavelka going through a water crossing at the 111-mile El Tour de Tucson. It was his first long ride on the bike, and a 22.6-miles-per-hour average speed provided all of the proof he needed of a Pocket Rocket's performance capability.

Each Bike Friday is built to the customer's specifications, with measurements taken from his or her best-fitting bike. The 20-inch wheels are light and fast, and allow the bike to fit into a hardshell Pullman-size suitcase (supplied) for safe travel. It also lets you avoid the exorbitant charge (as much as $100 round-trip) that some airlines levy for transporting a bike. When you check in with a Bike Friday, it's just another piece of luggage. If you fly frequently, the bike literally pays for itself.

A Bike Friday takes 15 minutes or less to assemble, and then it rides so much like your regular bike that you forget you're on something different. For touring, it can be fitted with racks and bags, and the suitcase can convert to a small-wheel trailer. The base Pocket Rocket costs about $1,800, equipped with Shimano 105 components. For information about the company's full line, including its tourworthy tandem (it packs into two suitcases) and a recumbent, check the Web site: www.bikefriday.com.

Another option for travelers is a bicycle of conventional design that's built with couplings from S&S Machine. These let you take the frame apart and put the entire bike in a case just big enough to accommodate the wheel diameter. Several companies and framebuilders give you this option for single bikes and for tandems, including Burley, Co-Motion,

Santana, and Longbikes. In addition, it's possible to saw apart (gulp!) your present bike and add couplings, if the frame is steel or titanium. This isn't a do-it-yourself job, of course. Check with a framebuilder.

Saddles

It wouldn't be right for us to recommend a particular seat. The fact that so many different styles are on the market is a testament to the fact that saddle choice is highly individual. There is wisdom, however, in using a saddle like two of our favorites, the Trico Split-Rail and the Specialized Body Geometry, which are designed to reduce the risk of nerve and blood vessel compression. This type goes a long way toward eliminating genital numbness and (in men) the possibility of erectile dysfunction. As a bonus, many riders find that such seats also reduce the frequency of saddle sores. When choosing a saddle, use the selection guidelines in chapter 11 to improve your chances of finding one that's comfortable and safe. Nothing takes the place of a test ride, so check at bike shops for samples you can try.

Helmets

You'll find various styles from the major companies, but virtually all have one thing in common—the ability to meet current standards for impact protection. This is indicated by an interior sticker from a testing agency, such as the Consumer Product Safety Commission (CPSC). Modern helmets also are light and well ventilated. The day is gone when these were critical factors in helmet selection. Now you can make your choice based on price, style, and extra features. We recommend a bright color for better visibility, and a head-cradling strap in back for a more secure fit—especially helpful on bumpy trails or roads. Some helmets come with a detachable visor that shields your eyes from things like rain, tree branches, and the glare of oncoming headlights. If your helmet doesn't have reflective material, add your own to improve safety at night. Your head is your highest point, so use this to your advantage. Helmet-mount lights will fit virtually any model.

Eyewear

Sunglasses have important functions (other than to help you look extra cool). We go into these vital safety benefits in chapter 13. Use that information to find models that give your eyes full protection, then make your selection based on price, style, fit, weight, and features such as interchangeable or prescriptive lenses. Close-fitting, wraparound sunglasses do the best job of keeping wind and airborne things out of your eyes. Light weight and a grippy rubber nose bridge will keep them from slipping down. Also available are eye shields that attach to the front of a helmet, providing room underneath for regular glasses.

Hydration Systems

A backpack-style hydration system is all but mandatory for long-distance cycling. The extra fluid capacity is an important advantage, of course, and studies show that the convenience of sipping through a hose results in more frequent drinking. Several companies make these systems, allowing you to carry anywhere from 70 to 100 ounces of fluid (the equivalent of about three to five standard water bottles). For mountain biking, choose a pack that lets you store your mini pump, tools, food, and spare clothes, thus keeping this weight off your bike— an advantage when carrying it over obstacles. For road riding, we like the CamelBak Razor and similar models that fit flatter for better aerodynamics. The Razor's pack has reflective Illuminite panels, another plus. It also has a removable foam liner that lets you put a reservoir full of ice in contact with your back, a proven way to lower your core temperature in hot weather. A reservoir with a wide-opening top saves time during an event by letting you add ice quickly rather than cube by cube.

Rear Suspension

A shock-absorbing seatpost can be installed on virtually any bike, adding rear suspension without a significant weight penalty. This obviously improves comfort on trails, but it can pay off on long road rides, too. A shock post adds efficiency and reduces fatigue, because it spares your body from hard impacts and vibrations. It lets you stay seated on rough surfaces so that you don't have to use muscles to support your weight.

When shock-post shopping, you'll find two designs. The simpler one looks much like a regular seatpost but with a bellows near the top. It contains elastomers or a spring and slides up and down in line with the bike's bottom bracket. Expect to pay $100 to $150 for this type. The other design is more complex, which makes it heavier and more costly, but it also tends to work a bit better. Atop this post is a paral-

SUSPENSION SEATPOST
A suspension seatpost with a parallelogram absorbs bumps by moving in an arc rather than up and down.

TELESCOPING SEATPOST
Telescoping seatposts are relatively simple and less expensive, but cause greater changes in saddle height.

lelogram, a four-bar linkage that absorbs bumps by moving horizontally more than vertically. It makes a sort of arc relative to the bottom bracket. This keeps the seat's height quite constant, though it does vary its distance to the handlebar. For most riders, the amount is too small to be bothersome.

Another option is a frame design that puts the saddle on a cantilevered beam. The beam moves to absorb shock. Softride does this with either a flexible carbon-fiber or hinged metal beam. Other examples are the resilient titanium beams used by Titan Flex and Green Gear Cycling's Air Friday folding bike. This type of suspension works—winning RAAM bikes have included a Softride (Danny Chew) and a Titan Flex (Gerry Tatrai)—but it does take some getting used to because the beams are always in motion, bobbing slightly in response to each pedal stroke as well as bumps. The resulting fluctuation in saddle height concerns some physiologists, especially if a cyclist has a biomechanical problem that might be magnified. Most beam riders report benefits rather than injuries, however.

It would be hard to find a new mountain bike that doesn't have front suspension, and now it's available on road bikes, too. For example, Softride makes a pivoting stem, Cannondale uses its HeadShok system housed in the head tube, and RockShox makes the Ruby SL fork that can be installed on most road frames. The HeadShok and Ruby have lock-out devices that let you stop their movement for more efficient out-of-saddle climbing. All of this said, front suspension is a dubious benefit on a road bike, in our view. Flexed elbows along with padded gloves and cork bar tape take care of bumps and vibration very well. If you're going to add the cost and weight of suspension, do it in the rear of the bike where the benefits are unquestionable.

Aero Bars

These have come a long way since Pete Penseyres made headlines by using a homemade version in winning the 1986 Race Across America. Now, they are all but mandatory for long-distance cycling for two reasons. First, the aerodynamic advantage can increase your speed by 1 mile per hour or more without additional effort. Second, the comfort of relaxing on your elbows reduces strain on your back, shoulders, arms, wrists, and hands. By keeping pressure off your palms, you avoid the risk of fingers becoming numb from nerve compression.

There are various styles of aero bars. We recommend a model such as the Profile Air Stryke ZB with elbow rests that flip up when you remove your arms, letting you have a bar-top grip. Some events, most notably Paris-Brest-Paris, prohibit aero bars to improve safety in big packs. Don't train with them if you can't use them.

Bar-Ends

These short forward extensions can easily be attached to the ends of most flat handlebars. They give you a more powerful position for climbing, and a lower, more aerodynamic posture for greater speed on flat terrain. Try a pair on your mountain bike or hybrid. You'll notice the improvement if you ride on the road, where you need to have different hand positions for comfort.

Multi Tools

Long rides will frequently take you to the middle of nowhere, far from help should a mechanical problem arise. To bail yourself out, pack an all-in-one multi tool that has the Allen wrenches, screwdrivers, and other items necessary for minor repairs and adjustments. Of course, a multi tool won't do you any good unless you know how to use it, so get familiar with repair procedures by using an illustrated book such as *Bicycling Magazine's Basic Maintenance and Repair*.

Chamois Lubricants

By reducing friction between your skin and the liner ("chamois") inside your cycling shorts, you can limit the chafing that causes tenderness and leads to saddle sores. Some cyclists prefer a medicated powder, which also helps absorb moisture. Noxzema skin cream has long been a favorite, though it doesn't have much staying power. If skin irritation does develop, experienced cyclists often turn to a product made for diaper rash, such as Desitin or A&D Ointment. Bag Balm, made to soothe the irritated teats of milk cows, can heal a cyclist's irritated skin, too. But for all-around prevention and treatment, it's hard to beat the cycling-specific lubricant called Chamois Butt'r. It protects well, and because it's nongreasy, it won't clog pores and washes easily from skin and shorts. An 8-ounce tube costs about $12 and will keep you and your chamois happy for months. It's smart to pack some for freshening up during long rides, too.

Rearview Mirrors

These improve safety in traffic, so it's a mystery why more roadies don't use one. A rearview mirror lets your eyes know before your ears when a vehicle is coming from behind. Just as important, it also lets you know when nothing is there so that you can relax and safely ride around debris, potholes, and broken pavement. As opposed to handlebar-mounted mirrors, a model that attaches to your helmet or glasses saves weight and clutter, and lets you scan behind by turning your head. If you object to the look of a mirror, get a miniature version that sticks to the inside corner of your sunglasses' left lens. Once it's positioned correctly and you get the hang of using it, it's very effective.

Fenders

Long rides can take you through a gamut of weather. To be ready for wet roads or muddy trails, install lightweight fenders (also known as mudguards). They're effective in reducing the amount of gritty water sprayed by the wheels onto your bike, bags, feet, and body. This is a blessing when you come to a wet section following a shower. If it's actually raining, you won't stay any drier, of course, but you will stay cleaner.

For a road bike, limit the aerodynamic penalty by choosing fenders that are only as wide as your tires and that fit close to their circumference. With some ingenuity, they can even be installed on close-clearance racing frames. In fact, we saw fenders on everything from Colnagos to Kestrels in the days when they were mandatory at Paris-Brest-Paris. Stay clamps can be used when dropout eyelets aren't present. To block water from spraying on your feet, fashion a mudflap for the front fender. (Cut it from a plastic milk jug or sheet of rubber gasket material.) Short mudguards that clip to the seatpost, seat tube, or down tube can be used to block muck on mountain bikes. This may be the only type that will work with some suspension systems.

Cleat Covers

In chapter 11, we discuss what to look for when selecting cycling shoes. If you don't have the walkable type with recessed cleats, you'll find $10 Kool Kovers handy. These rubber covers are made for Look or Time cleats. They prevent wear, slips, and that clip-clop sound that turns heads when you walk through stores. A pair fits easily into your seatpack or rear pocket.

Cue-Sheet Holder

In some parts of the country, a century ride may have a full page of turn-by-turn directions. We've ridden 600-kilometer brevets that have had four pages. It's a nuisance having to continually pull a cue sheet out of your pocket, so use one of two solutions that keep it right in front of you: a small handlebar bag with a clear plastic pocket on top, or a special cue-sheet holder. Our favorite is the $9 BYCUE, made by a small manufacturer that sells direct (800-522-2640). The BYCUE installs without tools and securely holds a folded sheet in front of the handlebar. Its simple wire frame is pliable, to help you position it around any other stuff you have on the bar.

Tires

Lightness is always important in wheels because they are rotating weight. A lighter, narrower tire rolls with less resistance and requires less energy to accelerate and decelerate. This efficiency is wasted, however, if you have to stop more often to fix flats. With this in mind, go light—but steer clear of gossamer racing tires. The best way to lessen weight without increasing the risk of punctures is with foldable tires that have Kevlar beads instead of conventional wire beads. (The bead forms a tire's inner circumference on either side.) A width of 23 millimeters to 25 millimeters in a 700C road tire is a good compromise between lightness and enough tread for long wear and puncture resistance. For loaded touring, go up to 26 millimeters or 28 millimeters, and consider tires with a puncture-resistant Kevlar belt under the tread. This material does add a few grams, but it's so effective against penetration that it's used in bulletproof vests.

For road riding, you can save money by using heavier, cheaper tires and wheels for the wear and tear of training, and then switching to lighter, higher-quality equipment for events. For mountain biking, however, it's best to use the same wheels and tires for all of your riding. That's the recommendation of Ned Overend, who explains that it's how you learn the nuances of handling and traction.

Wheels

Lightness counts, but too light could mean unreliability. Don't overlook the extra weight you may be adding to your bike for long, self-supported rides. The sparse spoking of lightweight aerodynamic wheels isn't intended for carrying loads. Consider the fix you'll be in if there's a problem with their unconventional hubs, rims, or spokes. Unless you have support with backup equipment, there are practical advantages to sticking with conventional 32- or 36-spoke wheels. Spare spokes are easy to carry, and in an emergency most bike shops will have the right size as well as replacement rims. On the other hand, the risk of being stranded by a wheel problem isn't a big issue in organized events, where assistance is available at rest stops or from other riders. Spoke problems disappear entirely when you use composite wheels such as those from Spinergy or Aerospoke. Be aware, however, that any wheel with a deep, V-shape rim or wide composite spokes may ride more harshly and be unstable in crosswinds, especially when used in front.

Crank Brothers Speed Lever

Compared with conventional tire levers, this handy, 31-gram gizmo makes removing or installing any tire easier and faster. One end hooks under the tire bead, while the other end snaps onto the hub axle. Then you rotate the lever to remove or install the tire without risk of pinching the tube. The Speed Lever folds to 6 inches so it's easy to carry, and it costs less than $10—a bargain the very first time it slips a stubborn tire onto the rim.

Pumps and CO_2 Cartridges

Mini pumps are light and little, both important advantages. Full-size frame-mount pumps are more durable and fill tubes with fewer strokes, but they can be impossible to install, depending on the frame design and what else you're carrying. One out-of-the-way place that may work is along the front of the left seatstay, wedged between the dropout and the seat cluster. Use a floor pump at home for routine inflation so that you avoid wear on your portable one. CO_2 cartridges are another option, reducing weight and filling tires instantly. The risk, as you can imagine, is having more flats than cartridges.

Seatpacks

You probably already have an underseat pack for carrying a spare tube and patches, tire levers, a multi tool, and emergency money. Not much room left, is there? For long-distance cycling, we recommend a larger pack that holds more to start with, and expands to give you room for such things as additional tubes, food, a vest, or a rain jacket. It's more comfortable when these things aren't weighting down your jersey pockets. Because a seatpack is hidden behind your legs, even a large one won't catch much air to slow you down. As with all bags, trunks, or panniers, increase your nighttime safety by choosing a pack that's made with Illuminite material or has reflective tape.

Rack Trunks

For long, self-supported rides, supplement or replace your seatpack with an expandable racktop trunk. The photo shows the carrying capacity that a good trunk provides, and because it's behind your body, it won't catch much air despite its size. To use one, you need a lightweight aluminum rack, which can be attached to frames without dropout eyelets by using seatstay clamps. When choosing a trunk, look for such features as waterproof material, large side pockets, cov-

SPEED
LIMIT
45

Using panniers and an expandable rack trunk, you can carry everything you need for a journey that lasts days—or weeks. This equipment can be adapted to most road sport and mountain bikes.

ered zippers, secure attachments (including a loop over the front of the rack), and shape-holding foam liner.

Panniers

For self-supported touring, you need the carrying capacity of panniers. These mount on either side of the rear wheel, and they can be fitted to a front rack, too. Used in combination with a rack trunk, you can carry what you need for a ride that lasts days or even weeks. For a camping tour, a sleeping bag and pad can be strapped atop the rack in place of a trunk. Panniers let you evenly distribute weight side to side and front to back, helping the bike feel more stable and not too top-heavy. To help, always pack heavier items in the bottom.

Well-designed panniers will be water-resistant and have storm flaps over the zippers (but it's still a good idea to put things in zip-shut plastic bags). External mesh pockets allow damp clothes to dry while you ride. You'll find lots of bells and whistles when shopping for panniers. Don't overspend for features that are unnecessary for your needs, but do spend enough to get good quality overall. You don't want leaking seams, sagging support, or an insecure attachment system to plague your tour.

Rear Racks

Lightweight but strong aluminum racks can support about 40 pounds when loaded with a trunk or panniers or both. Ideally, these bolt to frame fittings near the top of the seatstays and to threaded eyelets on the dropouts. Small clamps can be used for frames without these features. Or, you can use a cantilever-style rack that clamps to the seatpost and extends over the rear wheel. This also is the type you'll need for a mountain bike with rear suspension. Because this rack is not braced from below, it can't hold has much weight (about 20 pounds maximum), and it might spring slightly like a diving board. Performance makes a model that includes side brackets for attaching panniers (25 pounds maximum).

Travel Cases

When you need to fly to an event, make sure your bike arrives undamaged by packing it securely in a case that's made for abuse. Using a cardboard box from a bike shop's trash bin is just asking for trouble. In general, a plastic hardshell case offers the best protection, though well-padded soft-side models are effective, too. Most cases fit within UPS size limits, giving you the option of shipping your bike back and forth if you don't want to lug it through airports. Some cases are made for two bikes. They save money when you're traveling with another cyclist and the airline charges for bike transport. A good case is expensive (around $250 to $450), but chances of damage skyrocket without one.

Cyclecomputers

All models have the essential functions, so you're welcome to base your choice on price or extra features. The Cateye AT100, for example, tells your present altitude as well as how many vertical feet you've gained during the ride. It has a thermometer, too. Its backlit display is very helpful for checking distances between turns after dark. This model and several others on the market are wireless, receiving data from a front wheel sensor by radio wave (a good way to eliminate some clutter).

Be sure to calibrate your cyclecomputer precisely to prevent confusion or wrong turns when following a cue sheet. Most models come with instructions for measuring the circumference of your front wheel. When an exact size is entered during computer setup, accuracy to one-hundredth of a mile is possible.

Heart Rate Monitors

An HRM with the key feature you need for effective training—programmable target zones with alarm—will set you back less than $100. Or, you can spend around $500 for one that has half a dozen additional functions, plus hardware that lets you download ride data to a PC for analysis and storage. If this suits your approach to training, go for it. Otherwise, consider spending just enough for helpful extra functions such as time spent in the target zone, average heart rate, and heart rate at set intervals throughout the ride or at specific moments, such as the tops of climbs. These features can be fascinating and useful or merely overwhelming, so choose (and spend) wisely. All modern HRMs are wireless, transmitting from an EKG-like chest strap via a radio signal. The monitor itself is worn like a watch or strapped to the handlebar. For women who find a chest strap uncomfortable, Polar offers a sports bra with a built-in pocket for the transmitter.

PowerTap

This intriguing product from Tune, Inc., became available in 1999. It consists of a special rear hub, heart rate chest strap, and handlebar-mounted cyclecomputer/HRM. The PowerTap's key function is to measure the watts you are producing while riding your road or mountain bike. Previously, watts was a feature found mainly on indoor

TUNE POWERTAP
The Tune PowerTap brings something new and valuable to outdoor training—watts measurement. It's called the most accurate way to evaluate effort.

trainers. To be totally high-tech, you can get the PowerTap model that allows data to be downloaded to a PC, which can then generate graphs and charts for analysis.

According to well-known fitness authority Fred Matheny, "The main advantage of a PowerTap is that it's an objective measure of the power you're producing. You don't have to rely on other, less accurate ways like your speed, which varies with wind and terrain, or perceived exertion, which requires substantial experience." A major principle of training is overload—creating a level of stress greater than what you expect to experience in events. If a PowerTap tells you that you average 280 watts on long climbs during a century, for instance, you can ramp up your pace on training rides to wattages of 285, 290, 295 . . . gradually improving your ability to ride nearer to your lactate threshold and to climb faster in events. Or, if you know it requires 320 watts of power to stay with the better climbers in your area, and you can maintain only 300 watts while climbing at your lactate threshold, then you can design hill intervals that last 10 to 15 minutes at 320 to 350 watts without going too far above your threshold heart rate. This will improve your strength and power.

At this writing, the price of the basic PowerTap system is about $500 (plus the expense of having the hub built into a rear wheel). Not exactly pocket change, but it does compare favorably to the first such unit to reach the market, SRM, which costs several thousand dollars. Remember, too, that the PowerTap makes it unnecessary to buy a separate heart rate monitor. Full details are at www.power-tap.com.

Indoor Trainers

Most of us aren't in this sport to pedal in a closed room. But sometimes riding an indoor trainer (also called a resistance, wind, fluid, or mag trainer) is necessary to maintain a training program. Winter is the obvious time, but a trainer can be used to stay on track during any period of lousy weather or tight scheduling. At the minimum, you need a model that allows enough pedaling resistance for productive workouts. Fancier trainers with handlebar-monitor readouts for watts and other data include the Cateye CS-1000 Cyclosimulator, Tacx Grand Excel, and Performance Axiom PowerTrain. Trainers that use fans for pedalling resistance are cheaper but noisier than those that use fluid or magnets. Another noisemaker, for mountain bikers, is a knobby tire rumbling on a trainer's roller. You could install a slick rear tire, but a neater solution is a trainer that contacts the rim instead of the rubber.

This type is less apt to slip, too, when you're making hard accelerations during interval workouts.

Rollers are a different approach—the equivalent of a treadmill for cyclists. Unlike on a trainer, nothing holds you up. You have to balance the bike as its wheels spin on one front and two rear cylinders. This helps cultivate a smooth, round pedal stroke. Some rollers provide extra resistance to make workouts as tough as on a trainer. Rollers are a good investment for improving pedaling technique and adding diversity to a long winter of indoor training.

For the ultimate ride to nowhere, consider a CompuTrainer, a product that seems to be in the arsenal of nearly every serious long-distance cyclist. This high-tech resistance trainer simulates outdoor riding by automatically changing pedaling resistance to match the terrain of

COMPUTRAINER

CompuTrainer sets the pace for making indoor workouts both fun and effective. Options allow you and a partner to compete on video road courses with hills and descents that automatically alter pedaling resistance.

courses realistically displayed on your TV screen. You can get a very good workout by racing against the internal computer or your own previous best performance. Or you can use a CompuTrainer sans video for a structured workout based on power output in watts. Another feature, called Spin Scan, shows you how much pressure you're applying to the pedals all the way around each stroke. This helps you identify and correct poor technique or imbalances. A CompuTrainer costs about $1,000 or more, depending on features. This is a serious investment that makes indoor cycling about as interesting and effective as possible.

Battery Lights

Lights are another product category that gives you many choices. There seems to be no clear favorite, as you'll notice at any event that requires night riding. Some riders prefer lights such as the $20 Cateye Micro Halogen. It's small and uncomplicated and provides adequate light, but it runs only about 3 hours on four AA alkaline batteries— an ongoing expense. Other riders prefer rechargeable systems. These cost from $150 to $300 and have one or two compact headlights that put out enough light for safe riding at any speed. The downside is weight and wire clutter. These lights typically have large, heavy batteries shaped like bottles so that they can be carried in a frame-mounted cage. The battery may be lead acid, nickel cadmium (NiCad), or the latest development for bike lights, nickel metal hydride (NiMH). The last cuts the weight in half without lowering run time. With a rechargeable system, you'll need at least two batteries to ride through a summer night.

For trail riding, consider a helmet light. It lets you see wherever your head points, illuminating dark turns before a handlebar light can shine there. Roadies get the same advantage, which is handy for reading street signs at dark intersections. Helmet lights can be used alone or as a supplement to a bar-mounted system.

Generator Lights

Traditionally, generator lights have been too inefficient for serious night riding. That is, the convenience of being free of batteries wasn't overcome by the energy that the generator sucked from the bike. This has changed thanks to the German-made Schmidt Dynamo front hub and lightweight Busch & Muller Lumotec headlight and taillight. The hub weighs 1½ pounds, which is less than a standard hub and

GENERATOR LIGHT

The easy-rolling Schmidt/Lumotec front-hub generator eliminates the need for batteries. It unfailingly lit our way through several ultra rides in 1999.

rechargeable bottle battery combined. When the lights are off, drag is insignificant—the equivalent of climbing one vertical foot per mile. This increases to about 10 vertical feet per mile when the lights are burning, which is still not much considering the advantages. For example, you can burn the lights for safety on a rainy day without concern about having enough battery power for night. The hub spins quietly and has a service interval of 35,000 miles—enough for a lifetime of events that require lights.

The headlight can be mounted on the handlebar, or out of the way on a bracket that fits between a caliper brake and the fork crown, putting it in front of the head tube. The beam brightness is between that of a Cateye Micro Halogen and a rechargeable dual-beam system. Ed Pavelka was very pleased with the Dynamo/Lumotec's performance during Paris-Brest-Paris '99, where he noticed the system on dozens of Europeans' bikes. It looks like the coming thing. At this writing, the U.S. importer is Peter White Cycles in Acton, Massachusetts. Prices begin at $215 for the hub and lights. The shop also builds custom wheels using the hub. For additional information, check the Web site: www.peterwhitecycles.com.

Photon Micro-Light

This little light is about the size of a quarter. It shines when you squeeze it, or there's a tiny switch for constant illumination. Two LED beam colors are available, white or red (best for preserving night vision when checking your cue sheet or cyclecomputer). A Photon can easily be tethered to a cue-sheet holder so that it's always handy. It's more convenient than a flashlight around the bike, though it doesn't have the power to help you read road signs. And it's so small that you have to be careful not to lose it.

Undershirt

An undershirt made of a wicking fabric is a key to dressing in all but the warmest weather. On cold days it adds insulation, while in any temperature it helps keep your skin drier and more comfortable. And if you should crash, it may reduce abrasions because your jersey will slide against it instead of your skin. Should a cool start turn into a hot day, an undershirt can be removed and stowed during a rest stop. You can choose undershirts with long, short, or no sleeves, and in numerous brand-name synthetic fabrics, most being some offshoot of polyester. You've got the right stuff when the hang tag makes a big deal out of the material's ability to absorb and suspend perspiration.

Bib Shorts

This style has what amounts to built-in suspenders. The advantage, compared with standard shorts, is that they stay up better. When the chamois is snug in your crotch, there's less movement and friction that leads to chafing and saddle sores. The disadvantage (for guys) is the bit of contortion required to pull the front low enough to urinate, and (for everyone) the need to remove whatever you're wearing on top before you can pull the shorts down. As this is written, bib shorts with a hidden fly opening have just been introduced. Bib shorts cost a bit more, but they can't be beat for a secure, comfortable fit.

BIB SHORTS
The snug fit of bib shorts reduces chamois movement and chafing.

Gloves

For winter gloves, see the sidebar on page 88. For traditional half-finger cycling gloves, see chapter 11. We discuss them there in the context of avoiding all kinds of hand injuries. Gloves are just as important to your safety as they are to your comfort.

Vests

For lightweight torso protection in cool air, nothing beats a vest. Pearl Izumi makes two popular models, the Zephrr Classic and the Kodiak Barrier. The former has a wind- and water-resistant front, with a mesh back that helps prevent overheating. A drawstring waist holds it down and reduces flapping. When rolled up tightly, this vest is about the size of a fat banana, making it easy to stash in a jersey pocket or seatpack. The Kodiak Barrier is a bit bulkier and warmer because it has a solid back (which also includes a zippered pocket). For extra safety in the dark, Performance has similar vests made with Illuminite.

Rainwear

Cyclists in the Pacific Northwest don't tan, according to an old joke. They rust. Maybe all of that wet-weather riding experience is why Burley Design Cooperative in Eugene, Oregon, makes some of the most functional rainwear. We're speaking of its jacket in particular, which has features you should find no matter which brand you're checking. These include a waterproof material such as Gore-Tex that blocks water while allowing some heat to escape; a full-length, storm-flap-covered front zipper that opens from both the top and bottom; large, zippered underarm vents; an ample sleeve length with adjustable cuffs; a long tail to cover your butt and the seat; a mesh liner for comfort against your skin; a high collar; a drawstring waist to keep the jacket from billowing; and a bright color (yellow is best) plus reflective material to increase your visibility in inclement weather. Burley also makes thin, uninsulated, waterproof foot covers for summer conditions. In colder temps, your winter booties will help hold in body heat even if they eventually soak through. Rain pants aren't essential in summer as long as you have upper-body protection. In cooler air, tights or leg warmers can keep your working legs warm enough even though they're damp. When a ride starts in the rain or the entire day is expected to be wet, waterproof rain pants are in order. A waterproof, reflectorized helmet cover is the crowning touch.

ILLUMINITE FABRIC

When choosing clothes and packs for events that go into the night (or start before dawn), look for Illuminite fabric. The effectiveness of its microscopic mirrors is amazing.

For light rain or short showers, a rain jacket like the one just described is overkill. Have a simple, thin, inexpensive shell that you can roll up and carry in a bike bag or jersey pocket on a day that looks iffy. Useful features include elastic in the cuffs, a front closure with hook-and-loop material, and mesh panels along the sides and sleeves for ventilation. Choose yellow to make yourself more visible.

Illuminite Fabric

If you'll be riding in the dark for any reason, our advice is simple: Use clothing and bike bags that are made with reflective Illuminite fabric. The photo shows how effective this material is. The Illuminite process embeds the weave with millions of microscopic mirrors that shine light back to its source. You become a glowing human figure on the road, attracting maximum attention by drivers. The Illuminite process improves a garment's wind and water resistance, too. Its reflective properties aren't diminished by machine washing. Performance is the largest supplier of Illuminite products that we know of, carrying

Don't Get Cold Feet (or Hands)

Wet shoes in winter mean frozen feet. Use waterproof booties to keep them dry. For insulation, wear heavy wool or wool-blend socks that hold moisture away from your skin. If thick socks make your shoes too tight, the reduced circulation will chill your feet fast. Consider having a second, larger pair for winter cycling. Check into an insulated, high-top shoe designed specifically for winter.

When it's very cold (less than 20°F), switch to standard pedals with Powergrips. These straps let you enter and exit simply by rotating your feet. They're large enough to allow use of insulated, water-resistant "snow jogger" boots, which are sold by outdoor-apparel companies such as L. L. Bean. Get them big enough to accommodate your heavy socks (or even two pairs).

When selecting winter gloves, make sure they flex easily. A slightly loose fit may be warmer because it allows some air circulation. Avoid bulky gloves that make it difficult to work the brake and shift levers. Synthetic materials such as 3M's Thinsulate and DuPont's Thermolite allow manufacturers to produce gloves that are both trim and warm.

Wear mittens, not gloves, when the temperature is in the thirties or lower. Mittens are warmer for the simple reason that they trap hand heat in a single compartment. For extra insulation, wear a pair of thin glove liners inside them. These also work if you prefer the greater dexterity of "lobster"-style mittens, which have three compartments—one for the thumb and one each for the first two and last two fingers. These are warmer than gloves, but they help you operate a bike more easily than you can with full mittens.

For cold mountain biking, use insulated covers that fit over the handlebar and levers. They let you ride barehanded when you'd wear gloves, and wear light gloves when you'd need mittens. Your hands stay warm, and your ability to operate the bike, eat, drink, and adjust your clothes isn't hindered. These covers are known as Pogies from All Weather Sports and CliMitts from Sidetrak.

A lightweight balaclava protects sensitive ears and neck without causing overheating.

shorts, jerseys, tights, vests, and jackets, as well as packs and panniers.

Balaclava

These hoods fit close around your face, protecting your head, ears, and neck from cold air. We've found that a simple, lightweight polypropylene balaclava does the job in temperatures ranging from the forties down to the twenties. This type won't make you overheat, and it's thin enough that you won't have to change your helmet's sizing pads. For more brutal conditions, there are heavier fleece-lined balaclavas made of wind-resistant materials. Some are cut to give you the option of wearing them in any position from under your chin to over your mouth or nose.

Foot Covers

Full booties are essential to foot comfort when the temperature is in the forties or lower. Between needing them and needing nothing, you can keep the chill away with synthetic windproof socks worn inside shoes, lightweight "toe booties" that wrap around shoes from toe to heel, and uninsulated full booties that won't cause overheating. For cold conditions, choose fleece-lined booties made of a wind- and water-resistant material such as neoprene or Gore-Tex. These should have a beefy zipper than can work through muck, a sole opening just large enough for your cleats, a tall ankle for plenty of overlap with your tights, and reflective material for safety in low light.

6

Food for the Long Haul

When Ed Pavelka began riding bre-
vets to qualify for the centennial edition of Paris-Brest-Paris in 1991,
he learned a lot by firsthand experience. But one challenge of in-
creasingly long hours on the bike proved to be more difficult to solve
than any other. When people would ask him, "What's the hardest
thing about riding so far?", there was no hesitation in his reply:
"Eating."

This answer often drew a chuckle, but it was no laughing matter to
Ed. He had found that getting food down and digesting it well becomes more difficult as the miles pile up. Furthermore, any problems
with eating or drinking are bound to threaten every other aspect of a
long ride. Although years of improvements followed his first PBP, in-
ride nutrition was still Ed's chief concern as he was preparing for the
1999 event.

He's not alone when it comes to dietary dilemmas. When we sur-
veyed long-distance cyclists at a PAC Tour Endurance Training Camp,
questions about what, when, and how to eat topped the list. Few
riders, it seems, have discovered a fail-safe diet. Everyone wants to find
foods that are enjoyable to eat even after hours of riding, that digest
well, and that provide the energy and nutrients necessary for strong
performance. It's a tough order to fill.

One thing is certain: You can't be successful if you eat haphazardly.
At some point, almost all endurance cyclists run into problems that
better food and fluid choices might have prevented. Among these difficulties are gastrointestinal disturbances, heartburn, diarrhea, dehydration, impaired endurance, decreased strength, poor concentration,
and undue weight loss.

If you've already encountered such problems, you don't need to be
encouraged to read on. If you haven't, this chapter can spare you from
needless bad experiences.

Preride Nutrition

Lyn Gallagher, a newcomer to long-distance cycling, was looking forward to his first century. But he was having a problem. Even though he had trained well during the months leading to the event, he continued to bonk or "hit the wall" in the second half of long rides. This is a dilemma faced by many cyclists who are trying to build their endurance. Lyn's training program and muscle strength weren't failing him—his diet was.

No matter if you're a newcomer like Lyn or an endurance veteran, the principles behind eating and drinking for the long haul are the same. Never forget that nutrition is as crucial to top performance as training, so give it just as much attention.

FUEL SOURCES

Of the three fuels—carbohydrate, fat, and protein—that are available for muscular energy, only carbohydrate and fat are used to any great extent during exercise. And, if given an unlimited supply of all three, working muscles prefer carbohydrate because its energy is easily released and used by the body.

During moderately hard, prolonged exercise such as long-distance cycling, glycogen (stored carbohydrate) and fatty acids (the useful form of fat) are each used for energy. But when intensity increases, such as when riding in a fast paceline or going hard up a hill, glycogen becomes the muscles' primary fuel.

Here's the catch: The amount of glycogen stored in muscles is relatively small compared with what's necessary to fuel a long ride (let alone several consecutive days of long rides). In fact, testing on athletes at the Olympic Training Center in Colorado Springs has found that when carbohydrate is the primary fuel source, glycogen stored in the muscles and liver can be exhausted by just 60 to 90 minutes of hard exercise.

Because the body can run out of carbohydrate so quickly, energy must be derived from other sources. Here's where fat stores come into play. Even the thinnest cyclists have an abundant supply of fat—about 60,000 to 90,000 calories' worth stored in various parts of the body. That's enough fat energy to ride 800 to 900 miles. But here's another catch: Energy from fat stores cannot be supplied quickly to muscle cells, and fat requires more oxygen to metabolize. The result is that the glycogen content of muscles drains away if fat is relied on and carbohydrate is not replaced. And when the glycogen in working muscles becomes seriously depleted, fatigue hits hard.

As we'll see, protein can be a fuel source, too, during rides lasting more than 3 hours or in multiday events that allow minimal time off the bike. In such situations, protein may supply up to 15 percent of your energy. This is not a good situation, however, because it depletes your muscles' protein stores. To prevent it, you need to consume protein as well as carbohydrate during long rides.

GLYCOGEN LIMITS
The carbohydrate capacity of an active 150-pound male totals between 1,700 and 2,500 calories. Of these, 1,200 to 2,000 calories are stored in the muscles as glycogen, where they can be used directly as fuel. Another 400 or so glycogen calories are stored in the liver, where they can be released into the bloodstream in the form of the sugar called glucose. And about 80 to 100 calories are already in circulation as blood glucose. This, by the way, is the only fuel used by the brain.

The amount of glycogen that can be stored depends on diet and fitness. Trained muscles can hold more. While the above quantities may seem large, even a full supply of glycogen won't last long during high-intensity cycling. For example, if you maintain a brisk pace in a century, you'll burn between 600 and 800 calories per hour. Some fat and a little protein are also used as fuel, but if you don't replenish carbohydrate, your energy will be exhausted in less than 4 hours of moderate cycling (or in less than 3, if you're riding strenuously). For most of us, that's quite a while before a century is completed.

Interestingly, glycogen depletion also occurs during short, high-intensity efforts that are repeated several times. If a ride has hills and you climb them hard enough to switch on your anaerobic energy system, your glycogen will burn up much more rapidly. The same could occur if you get into a fast paceline. So, one key to extending your energy reserves on a long ride is never to exceed an aerobic pace. Another is to keep eating and drinking carbohydrate.

CARBOHYDRATE LOADING
How can you fill your glycogen tank before a long ride? Easy—consume a diet that's extra high in carbohydrate. This practice is known as glycogen supercompensation, but we'll call it by its more common name, carbohydrate loading.

To do it, you simply increase the proportion of carbohydrate from the usual 60 percent of daily calories to 70 percent. (One gram of carbohydrate equals four calories.) It wasn't always so easy, though. In the 1970s, the classical regimen of carbohydrate loading was developed.

This technique takes a week and begins with the very unpleasant depletion of glycogen through intense training for 3 days while on a diet low in carbohydrate but high in protein and fat. Fortunately, Michael Sherman, Ph.D., of Ohio State University in Columbus has shown that glycogen supercompensation can result from a much more palatable procedure that he terms the modified regimen. His method boosts glycogen stores to a high level while avoiding the scary and depressing lack of energy caused by a severe depletion phase.

Simply increasing your carbohydrate intake to 70 percent of daily calories, in combination with reduced training, will fill your glycogen stores. But the modified regimen's mild depletion phase causes a supercompensation effect that actually increases glycogen levels beyond normal. Depletion has another advantage, too. When lacking sufficient glycogen, your muscles are forced to become better at using fat for fuel. This adaptation spares glycogen during an event, helping your

Modified Regimen for Carbohydrate Loading

One carbohydrate loading method, created by Michael Sherman, Ph.D., of Ohio State University in Columbus, has been shown to boost glycogen stores to about the same high level as the more severe classical regimen, but with fewer side effects. It avoids the scary and depressing lack of energy felt during the depletion phase when very little carbohydrate is consumed.

DAY	EXERCISE TIME (min)	% OF CALORIES FROM CARBS*
1	90	50
2	40	50
3	40	50
4	20	70
5	20	70
6	rest	70
7	event	70

*50 percent equals 2 grams of carbohydrate per pound of body weight per day;
70 percent equals 4 to 5 grams of carbohydrate per pound of body weight per day.

reserves last longer. Also, your muscles become better at storing glycogen when they are periodically depleted and refilled.

You may feel bloated or that your legs are "heavy" after a week of eating extra carbohydrate while reducing training. This happens because the body stores 3 to 5 grams of water with every gram of carbohydrate. It's smart to try carbohydrate loading in training or before a minor event to see if you experience this feeling. It doesn't seem to affect everyone. But even if you are a victim, it's not necessarily a negative, particularly in hot weather. The extra fluid you retain can be used to produce more sweat to help keep you cool. Besides, at the moderate pace of a typical long-distance event, a heavy feeling won't harm performance and will soon fade away. The benefits of carbohydrate loading are well worth it.

WHEN TO LOAD
Carbohydrate loading isn't necessary for rides lasting less than about 3 hours. Your normal good daily diet of 60 percent carbohydrate (along with about 25 percent fat and 15 percent protein) supplies your system with enough glycogen to prevent bonking. For longer rides, boosting your carbohydrate intake to 70 percent for a couple of days beforehand will top off your glycogen tank. When a major long-distance event is a week away, go to the modified regimen to get the benefit of supercompensation.

The 70-Percent Solution
So far, so good. But you may find that it's not easy to eat a daily diet that's 70 percent carbohydrate. Remember that gram for gram, carbohydrate contains fewer than half the calories of fat (four versus nine). One way to increase your intake while avoiding extra plates of food is to use one of the high-carbohydrate drinks sold in sports or nutrition stores. These supply carbohydrate without bulk.

In addition, make complex carbohydrate a large portion of the 70 percent. Foods such as pasta, bread, cereal, grains, and beans provide vitamins, minerals, fiber, and protein, as well as carbohydrate. Limit your intake of simple carbohydrate in the form of sugars (sweets), because such foods are low in other important nutrients. The rest of your diet should contain good sources of protein and fat, including meats and dairy products. When carbohydrate intake is running at 70 percent, the remainder should be about 20 percent fat and 10 percent protein. Like carbohydrate, protein supplies four calories per gram.

Pre-Event Meal

Let's look at what to eat before an event, how much to eat, and when to eat it. Remember that a pre-event meal can't remedy inadequate training, an improper daily diet, or the failure to carbo-load. Your performance will depend on what you've eaten in the previous days and weeks, not what you cram down in the hours before the start.

It's particularly important to replenish liver glycogen before an early-morning event. The liver relies on frequent meals to stay tanked up. If you were not to eat for 6 or more hours prior to riding, you could experience a premature lowering of blood glucose once you begin. Research conducted by Edward Coyle, Ph.D., at the University of Texas found that a low-fat meal containing 75 to 150 grams (300 to 600 calories) of carbohydrate, eaten about 2 to 3 hours before an event, helps to ensure adequate levels of liver glycogen and blood glucose. This could be in the form of two or three slices of wheat toast with a banana, or a couple of cans of a nutritional "liquid meal" such as Ensure or Boost. As a rule, ingest no more than 1 gram of carbohydrate (four calories) per pound of body weight if you will finish eating just 1 hour before riding.

Experiment by eating before training rides that are similar to your events. First, eat about 3 hours before riding. If this presents no problem, move the meal closer. You want to begin long rides with your stomach empty enough to be comfortable, but you don't want to feel hungry on the starting line. Part of the timing depends on whether you get nervous about events. If your butterflies will be flapping, eat earlier (and perhaps less) so that digestion is more complete as the start time draws near. And remember, the morning of an event is not the time to try something unusual for breakfast.

During the ride, you want to maintain high blood glucose levels with a sustained release of food energy from your stomach. A combination of simple and complex carbohydrate will help this happen. On the other hand, avoid foods that are high in protein. They take longer to be digested and absorbed, and they increase urine output, which boosts the risk of dehydration. Keep protein to no more than 15 percent of total calories.

Likewise, avoid foods that are high in fat. Only 15 to 20 percent of your pre-event meal's calories should come from fat sources such as doughnuts, meat, cheese, cream cheese, and butter. Fat leaves the stomach slowly, which delays its conversion to energy and may make you feel stuffed. But when you have the correct percentages of fat and protein, they add to your long-term energy supply and help moderate the release of carbohydrate from your stomach. This in turn helps maintain blood glucose levels and wards off hunger pangs during rides lasting several hours.

If you don't want to be praying for a restroom in the middle of a long ride, stay away from foods that are high in fiber or the sugar fructose. High-fiber foods include whole-wheat products, bran cereals, fresh fruit with skins, and most raw vegetables. Fructose, in the form of fruit, juices, or some brands of sport drinks and energy bars, causes gastrointestinal (GI) distress and diarrhea in some people. If you're susceptible, check labels. Avoid products in which fructose is high on the contents list, meaning it's a major ingredient.

The final factor is fluid consumption. Whether you prefer water, juice, or a sports drink, swallow plenty on the morning of the ride—about 8 to 12 ounces every 30 minutes. This is extremely important. Don't rely on the fluid you consume during the event to prevent dehydration. Avoid coffee and other beverages that contain caffeine, which is a diuretic that promotes fluid loss.

On-Bike Nutrition

Your performance and even your health are jeopardized when inadequate amounts of food and fluid are consumed during a long ride. Add tough environmental conditions such as heat, humidity, altitude, or tough hills, and the need to eat and drink properly is magnified. Do it wrong, and dehydration, glycogen depletion, and low blood glucose levels are almost guaranteed. Then you can kiss your strength and endurance goodbye. The disturbing thing is that so many cyclists make key mistakes despite the wealth of knowledge that's available.

Heat and Dehydration

It's not uncommon to lose 1 to 2 quarts of fluid via sweating during an hour of riding in hot and humid weather. If this fluid is not replaced immediately, the resulting dehydration will limit your performance and increase the risk of heat injury.

Your body strives to maintain a relatively constant temperature. When excessive heat is produced during exercise, it must be dissipated to prevent your body temperature from rising to dangerous levels. In the high heat or humidity (or both) typical of summer rides, it becomes even harder for your body to cool itself.

Heat exchange between a cyclist and the environment occurs in four ways.

During hot weather, use a hydration system to help replenish fluid lost through heavy sweating. Most reservoirs hold between 70 and 100 ounces.

Convective cooling takes place as your body moves through the air, as long as the air temperature is lower than your body temperature. Or, heat can be lost by conduction, such as when it's pulled away by a cool rain wetting your skin. Or, it can be lost by radiation if your body temperature is greater than the air temperature. But the most important mechanism is the evaporation of perspiration. Should you fail to drink enough fluids during a long ride, the resulting dehydration reduces your ability to sweat. This leads to a progressive rise in body temperature, opening the door to premature fatigue and the risk of heat illness—dizziness, disorientation, nausea, and so forth.

The solution is simple: Keep your fluid intake on pace with your sweating. If you don't, a fluid loss of as little as 2 percent of body weight can begin decreasing your performance. That's just 3 pounds, for example, if you weigh 150 pounds. A quart of sweat, which can easily be produced in an hour on a hot and humid day, weighs a bit more than 2 pounds.

The problem worsens in sticky conditions, because the combination of heat and humidity makes it much more difficult for your body to regulate its temperature. Your ability to lose heat by radiation, convection, or evaporation is decreased. As a result, your body temperature can rapidly increase. Combine the effects of environmental heat stress, increased metabolism, and dehydration, and suddenly pedaling a bike becomes a real chore.

Shrinking Fuel Stores

A marathon runner "hits the wall." A long-distance cyclist "bonks." Both athletes are doing the same thing—encountering severe fatigue because they've drained their energy stores. As noted above, we all have enough fat in our bodies to fuel unbelievable feats of endurance. But it's our carbohydrate reserves that determine how long we can actually last.

Your muscles and brain need a continuous supply of carbohydrate energy. When you exercise for longer than 60 to 90 minutes, blood glucose levels dwindle. Just 3 hours of continuous riding at 65 to 80 percent of maximum effort may fully deplete muscle glycogen stores.

Quick Tips

- If you need to make a midride fuel stop at a convenience store, these are among the best high-carbohydrate, low-fat snacks: fat-free pretzels, fig bars, Milky Way and Three Musketeers bars (about two-thirds of their calories come from carbohydrate, much better than most candy bars), Twinkies (really), toaster pastries, low-fat yogurt, and fresh fruit. In addition, even small stores now stock sports drinks, and they may have energy bars. Always carry a few dollars in your seatpack so that you're able to get the nourishment you need.

- On long rides, conserve valuable muscle fuel (glycogen) by maintaining a steady spin. Accelerate smoothly, avoid blasting up hills, and don't try to stay with other riders who are faster than your best pace.

- Cut your bars and other food into bite-size pieces and store them in plastic sandwich bags. This makes it easier to eat while riding, particularly in cool weather when you're wearing long-finger gloves.

- The best place to keep food is in the rear pockets of your jersey, or in a handlebar bag if you're using one. Before reaching for the food, first grip the bar with one hand near the stem to reduce the risk of swerving. Nibble frequently while riding, then eat larger amounts when pausing at rest stops.

- The food or drink that tastes good and digests easily early in a long ride may not work nearly as well several hours later. Drinks, for

If you continue without food or sports drink, blood glucose levels reach a very low condition known as hypoglycemia. Because the brain can function only on blood glucose, you may lose your ability to concentrate and react quickly. When muscle glycogen levels also become exhausted, you've bonked.

Energy Replacement

To beat the bonk, researchers say, consume 30 to 40 grams of carbohydrate during each 30 minutes you ride. An 8-ounce serving of most

example, tend to taste sweeter as a ride wears on. Consider diluting the concentration in the bottles you'll be using in the second half. Learn these things in training, and never experiment with new foods or drinks on the day of the event.

- You must eat and drink early and often. Never wait till you actually feel the need. For a reminder, get a sports watch that has a countdown timer. Set it for 15 minutes. Each time it beeps, take a big swig from your bottle and nibble some food.

- During cold weather, keep energy bars inside your jacket close to your body so they won't become hard and tough to eat.

- Consider using a backpack-style hydration system. A study found that cyclists are more likely to sip frequently from a tube over their shoulder than if they have to use frame-mounted bottles. This is especially true when riding in a group or pedaling a mountain bike on singletrack. Hydration systems have the added advantages of holding as much as 100 ounces and keeping fluid cool if ice is added.

- Make food notes in your training diary after every long ride. How much did you eat and drink? What tasted good? What gave you indigestion? What became difficult to eat when the air got hot or you reached high altitude? The answers are your own personal instruction sheet for doing it right in important events.

sports drinks provides about 15 grams of carbohydrate. So, drinking 16 ounces each half hour should supply enough. (A standard water bottle holds about 22 ounces.) Alternatively, you can wash down an energy bar or packet of carbohydrate gel with water. Check the label to see how much carbohydrate your favorite product provides. By being conscientious about this feeding schedule, you'll supply your bloodstream, and eventually your muscles and brain, with plenty of their best fuel.

Well-trained endurance cyclists, such as two-time RAAM winner Gerry Tatrai, may consume up to 400 calories per hour while riding long distances. This is mostly carbohydrate, with some protein and fat. Gerry can do this because he's riding well below his anaerobic threshold, and because through many hours on the bike he has taught his stomach to process more calories per hour than recreational riders can.

Drinking plain water, which you could do for rides lasting an hour or so, is far better for your body than not drinking at all. However, research has shown that your body will absorb water more quickly from a sports drink that contains electrolytes such as sodium and potassium. So, you may want to use one even for short rides, especially if you sweat heavily.

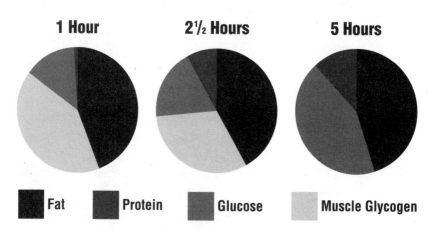

1 Hour　　　　**2½ Hours**　　　　**5 Hours**

Fat　　Protein　　Glucose　　Muscle Glycogen

These charts illustrate where energy comes from when you're riding at about 70 percent of your aerobic capacity (a typical long-distance pace). Note how muscle glycogen dwindles at 2 to 3 hours, then becomes exhausted. Blood glucose becomes a primary fuel source— but only if it's maintained though the steady intake of a high-carbohydrate sports drink or food.

The Best Sports Drink

The major goals of drinking during endurance events are to get water and carbohydrate into your system. Water is more important because, as we've noted, dehydration greater than 2 percent of body weight begins reducing performance. But carbohydrate supplementation is nearly as vital.

The carbohydrate in a sports drink is available for fuel within 15 to 20 minutes. It boosts your ability to make short, high-intensity efforts, and it allows you to sustain a higher overall intensity than when fat is the primary fuel. In addition, the sodium found in most sports drinks enhances the absorption of water, as well as carbohydrate, from the small intestine into the bloodstream.

Sodium (salt) is an essential electrolyte. It, along with others such as chloride, potassium, and magnesium, plays a key role in the maintenance of fluid levels, muscle contractions, and the transmission of nerve impulses. Sodium also is important for regulating blood volume. Inactive people lose little sodium, but a cyclist may lose as much as 1 gram per hour through sweat. After riding, the more rapidly we can replace the water, carbohydrate, and sodium we've lost, the more rapidly we can recover.

Simply put, where sodium goes, water quickly follows. This is why it's essential for sodium to be in a sports drink or to be taken in the form of salty foods or salt tablets. The other electrolytes play a relatively minor role—except in very long events such as a double century. On shorter rides, electrolyte losses other than sodium are minimal. But as hours of riding mount up, depletion may become significant—especially if you use only water instead of a sports drink.

Most sports drinks have between 6 and 10 percent carbohydrate (6 to 10 grams of carbohydrate per 100 milliliters of water). This is the concentration that most researchers say is best for maximizing fluid absorption and providing energy to fuel muscles and combat fatigue. This carbohydrate can be either simple or complex (also known as polysaccharides). The simple form is sugars such as glucose, fructose, or sucrose. The complex form is similar to starches found in bread and pasta in the form of glucose polymers or maltodextrin.

The better drinks contain both types of carbohydrate in a proportion that aids stomach-emptying. Their labels will indicate a higher concentration of complex carbohydrate by listing it as the next ingredient after water. Higher concentrations of maltodextrin tend to produce less gastrointestinal distress and fewer stomachaches when a large amount of sports drink is consumed. Research has found, however, that there is no difference between drinks containing simple or complex carbohydrate when it comes to the rate at which they're absorbed from the intestine into the bloodstream.

Stay away from drinks that have fructose right after water on the ingredient list. This sugar can slow gastric absorption and cause gastrointestinal problems in some people. However, if fructose is added as a second carbohydrate source for sweetness and energy, its concentration will probably be low enough to avoid causing problems.

If you're riding centuries or longer events, we recommend including some protein with your carbohydrate drink. Remember, during extended exercise your body begins to burn protein for fuel as your glycogen stores are depleted. A ratio of about 1 gram of protein to 4 grams of carbohydrate in a "long-distance beverage" will help fuel your muscles and protect them from breakdown. The best type of protein for this purpose is known as whey protein. You can buy it alone and mix it into a sports drink, or find it in products such as Endurox R4 and Champion Metabolol Endurance.

Finally, if you can get cool fluids during a ride, by all means do. These empty from your stomach faster than warm fluids. They also taste better, which helps you drink more. And by now you know that the more fluid you consume, the better you perform.

Postride Nutrition

With all due respect to Yogi Berra, it's still not over when it's over. At least not in long-distance cycling. What you do during the several hours following a 3-hour or longer ride is critical to your recovery and future performance.

In addition to restoring your body's fluid and electrolyte balance, you must replenish your depleted glycogen stores. And the sooner, the better. How fast you refill your muscles and liver determines how quickly you'll be ready to ride strongly again. Remember, even if you're a textbook-perfect example of eating and drinking during a long ride, you can't prevent glycogen depletion after about 2½ hours. All of the carbohydrate you take in is used as glucose to pedal the bike and keep your central nervous system operating. None of it is stored as glycogen.

When such a ride is finished, your muscles are empty. Now time becomes very important. Studies have shown that consuming carbohydrate during the first 30 minutes after exercise enables the body to rapidly restore glycogen levels. But for athletes who wait more than 2

Lunch during a long day on a PAC Tour means a roadside buffet of foods rich in carbohydrate and other essentials. A rider favorite: turkey sandwiches.

hours following exercise, glycogen replacement is about 20 percent less. The lesson is very clear: If you don't consume carbohydrate immediately after a long ride, you can't be your best the next day.

How Replenishment Works

Insulin, a hormone released by the pancreas in response to the intake of carbohydrate, is critical in regulating the creation of muscle glycogen. Ideally, the carbohydrate source should be glucose or other simple sugars after exercise, because they produce a quicker insulin response. Insulin assists the movement of glucose from the blood into the muscles, where it is changed into glycogen.

Insulin has a second important role, too. The creation of muscle glycogen from glucose requires an enzyme called glycogen synthetase. Insulin stimulates this enzyme, enabling the glycogen manufacturing process to proceed at a much faster rate.

Assuming that a sufficient amount of carbohydrate is available, the greater the insulin level after exercise, the faster the movement of glucose into the muscle cells, and the faster the rate of glycogen synthesis. The timing of this process is key. Muscle cells are most sensitive to in-

(continued on page 106)

Supplemental Advice

Sorry, there is no pill or powder that will magically turn you into an endurance champion (despite what you may read in magazine ads). Even so, most riders we know do take daily nutritional supplements. These range from general multivitamin/mineral tablets to doses of whatever specific product is currently the rage.

Remember, though, that extra vitamins and minerals can't make up for a poor diet. What they can do is correct imbalances and make sure you're getting the full RDA (recommended dietary allowance) in your daily diet, including the important antioxidants (see below). They help you cover your nutritional bases. At about a dime apiece, a daily supplement can be viewed as cheap insurance. When you're dedicating the time and effort it takes to ride long distances well, it's reassuring to know that your body isn't missing something important—even if you're eating as well as you can.

As for supplements that claim to enhance performance, they could fill a book by themselves. At least one—caffeine—has been proven to be effective for endurance athletes. In addition, ample quantities of antioxidants can be especially beneficial to long-distance cyclists.

Caffeine. Well into a long ride, you may want to take a pill or drink a beverage that contains caffeine. This naturally occurring chemical is a central nervous stimulant that perks you up and causes your body to release more fat into the bloodstream. Fat can then be used for fuel by muscles, prolonging your precious glycogen stores.

In his book, *Eat to Win,* Robert Haas states that "caffeine provides endurance athletes with an unquestionable, scientifically demonstrable advantage over opponents of roughly equal athletic ability." He's far from alone in this contention. Many athletes have used caffeine successfully.

If you decide to try caffeine for long rides, start with one or two cups of coffee (or 150 to 300 milligrams of caffeine from other sources) about 45 to 60 minutes before the start. It appears that about 5 milligrams of caffeine per kilogram (kg; 2.2 pounds) of body weight is a safe and effective preride maximum. You need to be careful, because if you ingest too much, you may experience headache, gastric turmoil, and espresso nerves, plus the time-wasting pit stops and dehydration caused by excessive urine production. Then, periodically take more as the ride continues. Some riders can tolerate up to 200 milligrams per hour. Remember, though, that caffeine affects everyone differently. Experiment in training (not in important events) to learn how it works best for you.

Antioxidants. After decades of promoting the benefits of physical fitness, scientists are now warning of a link between exercise and the formation of free radicals. Sounds like a group of terrorists, and, in your body, they are.

As cyclists, we ingest lots of free radicals—highly reactive, unstable, toxic molecules that are spawned by everything from the air we breathe to that pile of french fries to which we occasionally give in. Yes, it's even tougher to stop breathing than it is to ignore fries, but some of the chemical reactions triggered in the body by oxygen create just as much of a threat. Free radicals attack and damage the cell walls of the heart, muscles, and blood vessels. These cells' ability to function becomes impaired.

It gets worse. Cycling in smoggy conditions increases our intake of ozone and nitrogen oxide via deep and rapid breathing. When oxygen combines with these substances, even greater numbers of free radicals are produced.

Why is all of this important? Free radical damage has been linked to many bad things, including reduced endurance, muscle soreness, and several problems normally associated with aging—a weaker immune system, atherosclerosis, and Parkinson's disease.

Fortunately, our bodies are equipped to fight the ravages of free radicals with substances called antioxidants. They block or inactivate the dangerous molecular by-products and help repair cellular damage. But here's the catch: The more cellular activity there is, the more antioxidants you need.

What's the best strategy for fighting free radicals? First, eat lots of fresh fruits, vegetables, and whole grains. Citrus provides vitamin C. Two or more servings per day of dark-green vegetables help supply beta carotene. Fish and chicken are high in selenium. So are whole grains, which also provide zinc. Vitamin E is found in wheat germ, nuts, and sweet potatoes.

Of course, eating well is great in theory, but it may be difficult to consume enough of the foods that are high in antioxidants. Also, their content may be reduced by processing or overcooking. For these reasons, it's smart to take supplements containing the vitamins and minerals we've mentioned. And remember, the RDA for antioxidants probably isn't adequate for the hours of exertion and air quality that go hand-in-hand with endurance cycling.

sulin up to 2 hours after exercise. After 2 hours, cells actually become resistant to insulin, and this resistance continues for several hours. This underlines the importance of taking in carbohydrate immediately after you get off the bike.

Because insulin response is so vital in the muscle recovery process, researchers have investigated how insulin can be stimulated to an even greater extent. One way is to combine protein with the carbohydrate that's consumed. In fact, doing so almost doubles the insulin response, with the amino acid arginine playing a key role. (A study by John Ivy, Ph.D., of the University of Texas, found that arginine increases insulin response fivefold above that produced by carbohydrate alone.) But this is a case where more can mean less. Too much protein slows stomach emptying. That's not what you want when you're trying to replenish fluid and electrolytes after a ride. A similar delay can be caused by fat, so limit that in your postride meal, too.

The Magic Mix

The challenge is how to gain the insulin-boosting benefit of protein without its negative effect. Research has found that there is a critical proportion of carbohydrate to protein, which has been termed the "optimum recovery ratio." When the ratio is four to one—for example, 56 grams of carbohydrate to 14 grams of protein—protein does not seem to interfere with the movement of fluid and nutrients out of the stomach.

During some events you may be riding all day, which leaves little time to restore muscle glycogen before you're back on the bike. Recovery does not, however, require large quantities of carbohydrate. Above a certain amount (about 3 to 5 grams per pound of body weight per day), it won't improve the rate of glycogen synthesis. And remember, if you consume more carbohydrate, you need to decrease fat or protein calories, or both, or you'll gain weight. It's best to maintain the sensible balance of about 60 percent carbohydrate, 25 percent fat, and 15 percent protein.

Watch Your Weight

Immediately after a long or hard ride, your appetite may be suppressed. Eating solid food right away may not be appealing. But you probably will be thirsty. By using a sports drink or carbohydrate-protein beverage, you can rehydrate and refuel at the same time.

Your day-to-day energy level will let you know if you're doing it right. So will your body weight. By weighing yourself each morning, you can spot a trend toward chronic dehydration. A sure sign is the loss of several pounds from one day to the next. Such a drop is certainly due to fluid loss, not fat loss. You should always be within a pound of yesterday's weight. If not, you will begin today's ride dehydrated. This will reduce your performance and increase the chances of overheating and fatigue. Include sports drink, juice, skim milk, or water with each meal, and drink fluids throughout the day—not just before riding.

Even if eating solid food isn't a problem after riding, it's still a good idea to down a carbohydrate drink right away. A 150-pound rider, for example, should consume 16 to 30 ounces. Then, about 2 hours later, have a normal meal. At the 4-hour mark (maybe as an evening snack) have an apple or bagel with a glass of sports drink.

It takes about 24 hours to refill your glycogen stores after a long, hard ride, even if you consume the recommended 3 to 5 grams of carbohydrate per pound of body weight during this period. By the way, studies show that it doesn't matter whether you consume this carbohydrate in numerous small meals or in a couple of large ones. The rate of glycogen synthesis is about the same when the total carbohydrate intake is equivalent.

However, the type of carbohydrate you consume after riding does have an effect. Research has found that foods with a high glycemic index actually raise blood glucose levels and increase the rate of glycogen synthesis when compared with foods that have a low glycemic index. Bread and the sugar glucose are good high-glycemic foods. They help restore muscle glycogen twice as rapidly as, say, fructose or yogurt, which are low-glycemic foods.

7

The Mental Edge

Early in his long-distance career, Ed Pavelka was a classic mileage junkie. There was nothing more important, he believed, than miles, miles, and more miles in order to prepare for a transcontinental PAC Tour and the other endurance challenges he was eagerly seeking. This pushed him to an average of 405 miles per week during one year. To him, physical conditioning was paramount. Nothing else even entered his mind.

With this bit of background, you can probably imagine Ed's reaction the day he was reading an article about riding well in Paris-Brest-Paris and came across this statement: "It's 90 percent mental."

"Mental?" Ed thought. "Is this guy nuts? You don't pedal with your head. He's got it backwards—it's about 10 percent mental and 90 percent physical." After all, without plenty of long, hard miles in your legs, how could you expect to ride well in long, hard events? It's crazy to put mental ahead of physical.

Today, Ed knows better. He's still not certain of the exact percentage, but he understands why the mental aspect can be rated so high in long-distance cycling. As we'll see in this chapter, sports psychology is real and can definitely give you an edge. Training is essential, too, of course. In fact, it's responsible for one of the key mental components: confidence. That's when the light went on for Ed. He realized that all those miles were not just conditioning his body—they were also training his head. They were convincing him that he could succeed at distances even longer than he'd already tried.

Mind Over Muscle

Your potential in cycling is governed by three things: talent, training, and psychological readiness. In combination, they make a good cyclist better. But, no matter how strong or skilled you are, it's your psycho-

logical state—particularly motivation and determination—that determines whether you will achieve your goals.

Each of us has a certain amount of talent and potential. Part of it is
genetic—a gift from our parents. Another part is training. But, regardless of what we have inherited or developed, there is no guarantee
that we'll ever become the best cyclists we can be.

Why? Here's another perspective to consider. Eddie Borysewicz, the
former U.S. Olympic cycling coach, states that "75 to 80 percent of
your physical potential is inherited. The remainder comes from your
mind." He's saying that we should put great importance on the mental
value of training rides and events that test our physical limits. Long
hours of riding are an act of will as much as muscle. This is why motivated cyclists can outperform others who have more talent but are
less committed.

Develop Your Commitment

Commitment is the attribute that brings everything into focus. Commitment is what you do with your talent. It's the answer to questions
such as: How much training are you willing to do for your first century? How hard are you willing to work during the off-season? What
improvements are you willing to make in your diet? Commitment de-
fines how seriously you want to reach a goal.

Here are four ways to boost your commitment to cycling as well as
to overall health and fitness.

1. **Set goals.** What do you want to achieve during this cycling
   season and the next one? How are you going to get there?

2. **Be tough on yourself.** What are you willing to give up to
   become a better cyclist? Are you willing to do long rides in the
   rain? In the middle of winter?

3. **Know yourself.** Acknowledge strengths and weaknesses. If
   you're a poor climber, are you willing to spend time in the hills
   to work on your fitness and technique, or in the gym to
   improve your strength and power? What keeps you going
   when the going gets tough?

4. **Have a plan.** Use your strengths in cycling to carry you from
   one level to the next. Plan workouts and keep a training diary
   so you know how you arrived at today and where you're
   going tomorrow.

Two-time solo RAAM winner Pete Penseyres is a wonderful example of a cyclist with commitment. He had a normal amount of inherited talent, but an abnormal ability to set and fulfill goals once he
became determined to reach his potential in long-distance cycling.
Pete's greatest successes came while working full-time as a nuclear en-
gineer and raising a family. His legendary preparation for the 1986
RAAM—which included 400-mile weekend rides—paid off in what is
still the fastest average speed ever posted for a trans-America ride (including sleep breaks), 15.4 miles per hour. He was 43 at the time.
When you have the commitment of a Pete Penseyres, there's no telling
what level of performance you will eventually reach.

What are you waiting for? Start now, not tomorrow. Write down
goals that you feel passionate about achieving. List your resources and
support systems—family, local riders and coaches, equipment—and
think about how each one can help you improve your performance.
When you create a written plan, a quest becomes real and doable.
Circle key dates on your calendar, then backtrack to today, designing
your training with the advice from part 2 of this book. It may take a
few hours to piece it all together, but the result will give you a vital
sense of commitment for weeks and months to come.

Train Smart

Don't merely train hard. Anyone can go out and pound away. The
trick is to find the quickest, smartest, most efficient way to reach your
goals. Enjoy your successes, and embrace your failures. You can learn
so much from them and avoid messing up again, wasting your valuable time and energy. Remember, only you can determine how good
you can be in this sport. Talent is important, but so is the commitment
to doggedly work at it.

That said, it's also important to keep perspective. Many of us take
ourselves too seriously. We set high—perhaps unreachable—objectives, and then become overly disappointed when performances are
less than expected. This can do serious damage to motivation. When
you notice yourself becoming too self-critical or obsessed with your
placings in events, lighten up. Never forget the positive reasons you
got on a bike in the first place. Whether you finish first or 51st doesn't
matter as much as the fact that you are receiving cycling's many physical and mental benefits.

Be careful not to become too rigid. Your passion, and hence your
motivation, has its seasons. It's natural to experience occasional pe-

riods when interest wanes. Don't fight them. Take a few days off, cut back your distance or intensity, go hiking or swimming instead—anything that gives you a break from the routine that's weighing you down. Your desire for cycling will return as strong as ever. Pay attention to how your attitude toward riding fluctuates throughout the year. Plan changes in your routine for periods when motivation is low.

Go for the Goal

A cyclist once admitted, "I don't race much anymore because it interferes with my training." Well, there's nothing wrong with taking rides simply for fitness and enjoyment rather than event preparation. We'd be the last people to condemn that. But training, by definition, is not an end in itself. Having a concrete goal gives training a clear purpose. It's what motivates you to plan rides and then do them, rather than go out only when the sun is shining, the wind is calm, and you feel full of energy.

A goal can be anything that inspires you. Maybe you want to ride 100 miles for the first time. Maybe you're a veteran of several centuries and now want to beat your best time. Maybe you want to ride the brevet series and qualify for Boston-Montreal-Boston or Paris-Brest-Paris. You may want to complete an MS 150 ride in one weekend, or the Great Divide Ride along the spine of the Rockies in one summer. Maybe you want to lose 30 pounds and improve your cholesterol level. Each of these objectives is valid, valuable—and necessary. In the absence of a goal that's important to you, it's virtually impossible to persevere long enough to see a cycling program produce significant results. You'll soon ask yourself why you're on the bike so much. Without a good answer, you'll find reasons to ride less. A goal that you're committed to, on the other hand, gives you a way to measure what you're accomplishing. Progress produces more motivation.

To stay inspired, you can't become satisfied. You must keep setting new and higher goals. The only danger is in raising the bar too high (or too high too soon). We knew a cyclist who rode 11,000 miles in only his second season, and then announced his intention to enter the following year's Race Across America. By the time RAAM came around, he was out of the sport. You can't succeed if the objective is so difficult that it provides a ready reason to give up when things get tough. One person who knows this firsthand is Jerry Lynch, Ph.D., director of the Tao Sports Center for Human Performance in Santa Cruz, California. "In my work with elite athletes at the U.S. Olympic Training Center," says

Jerry, "the one major difference between those who reach their goals and those who fall short is their level of commitment. The stronger the commitment, the better the chances for obtaining objectives.

"This holds true for recreational cyclists as well. Many set unrealistic goals, then complain of the difficulties of reaching them. Or, they are not fully committed because there are other major responsibilities in their lives. If their profession or family is more important, then cycling will—and should—take a backseat. Realizing these situations exist will help you set more realistic goals and reach them successfully. Cycling must fit into the priorities of your lifetime goals."

Goal-Setting Strategy

The first step toward achieving a goal is to set one. Sounds easy? Many people don't do it right, and this puts them in line for frustration and failure. Use these six steps to establish a goal in a way that gives you the best chance for success.

Be specific. Specific goals direct you more effectively than vague or general goals. For example, if your goal is to "ride centuries better," you may always feel unfulfilled. Does finishing without bonking define a good performance, or not? What about finishing in less than 7 hours? What's needed is a clearly defined goal, such as: "Ride one century per month from June through September, and ride each one faster." Now the goal is precise and quantitative. It can be objectively measured so you know for sure if you're succeeding.

Create stepping-stones. Setting short-, mid-, and long-term goals aids performance more than setting only long-term ones. Use intermediate goals as steps on the way to your final objective. A good example is the sequence of brevets that qualifies cyclists to ride Paris-Brest-Paris. Each one is longer—200, 300, 400, 600 kilometers, plus an optional 1000 kilometers—leading to the 1200-kilometer event in France. This buildup gives riders at least four progressively tougher goals to achieve, making the huge challenge of PBP a lot more manageable.

Make goals hard, but not too hard. Up to a point, the more challenging or compelling the goal, the better. Past that point, however, a goal can seem so difficult that you stop taking it seriously. When a goal is both challenging and attainable, you'll have the highest motivation and get the most benefit from reaching it.

Record your progress. A goal works best if there is prompt feedback telling you how you're doing. Let's say you're going for your first or fastest century. Your main stepping-stones are progressively longer or faster weekend rides. By recording distance, elapsed time, and average speed, you have confirmation that you're closing in on your objective. Without these numbers, there's no positive reinforcement.

Have patience as well as persistence. Greg LeMond, after his hunting accident in 1987, set a long-term goal of winning the Tour de France again. While there were some setbacks along the way, he reached this goal in 1989. Ten years later, Lance Armstrong had several depressing low points during his comeback from cancer, but he stayed the course and eventually stunned everyone by racing better than ever. There will always be potholes and detours on the roads you ride. Some you can't control; others occur as a consequence of trying to improve but making mistakes. Use setbacks as lessons. Remember that it's almost never a straight line to success.

Become goal-oriented. Get in the habit of planning what you want to achieve in each long ride or event. This makes goal-setting an integral part of your approach to cycling. Goals can be as major as the overall time or distance, or simply something meaningful that you want to accomplish along the way. For example, plan to limit rest stops to 5 minutes. Do on-bike stretching every half hour. Pace yourself so that you ride the second half at least as fast as the first. Such objectives help to make each ride more beneficial. You improve, and you gain a sense of accomplishment.

As Kay Porter and Judy Foster state in *The Mental Athlete,* the effects of goal-setting are cumulative. As you achieve your first goals, you become more certain of what you want from yourself and how to accomplish it. Your goals become the framework that guides your training and competition. They are the motivation that pushes you through the rain and snow, the pain and injuries, and the times when you become stuck on a performance plateau.

Your goals should align with endeavors that satisfy you physically, mentally, and emotionally. Never lose sight of the fact that the journey toward any goal is just as important as the rewards.

Visualize Success

Many top athletes will tell you that finally winning a long-sought championship seemed almost anticlimactic. Why? Because in their imagination they had already captured that victory many times.

Visualization is the base from which your best cycling performances can be realized. It's a conscious process that takes place in a state of relaxation. In your mind's eye, you see pictures that directly influence how you ride. This works because the body's central nervous system doesn't distinguish between actual and imagined events; it responds to all images as if they were real. Visualizing yourself performing perfectly and achieving exactly what you want is a proven way to reach peak performance.

Think of visualization as a dress rehearsal that makes you more familiar with the actual task that lies ahead. When the time comes, says sports psychologist Jerry Lynch, you have the sense that you've "been there, done that." Visualization also rids the mind of images that block efforts to ride well, replacing them with images of success that relax the body and open the way to excellent performance. For example, if you imagine yourself climbing a tough hill with speed and power, your confidence will be higher and your performance will be better when you actually reach that climb. On the other hand, if you fear the hill and imagine a painful struggle, the tension and anxiety are guaranteed to make it hard.

Practice visualization several times each week. It may take a few tries before it comes readily to you, so don't get discouraged. The results are worth it. All you need is 10 minutes in a place that's free from noise and other distractions. Sit or lie in a relaxed position. Close your eyes. Take a few deep breaths through your nose, holding the air for about 5 seconds before slowly releasing it. You will begin to feel very calm. It's in this state that your central nervous system is most receptive to the images you focus on.

Imagine yourself on your bike. Feel it rolling over the terrain. Notice the wind separating around you and the power in your legs. Now put yourself on the ride that you're preparing for. Perform exactly as you want to, doing everything correctly. See yourself overcoming the tough sections and reaching the finish with speed and strength to spare. Feel the satisfaction that a perfect ride gives you. Tomorrow, do it all over again. Continue until the event takes place.

Many elite athletes use visualization, but you certainly don't have to be at their level to get the benefits. As you begin to train your mind, it will become stronger just like your body. Together, they'll power you to the kind of performances that once could only be imagined.

Psych Up

"Arousal" is a term defined by sports psychologists as "a state of eager readiness to play." Cyclists who are aroused before and during an event usually perform better than those with low levels of energy. But too much arousal can be just as harmful as too little. Your best performance depends on having the right level.

The graph below illustrates the three broad ranges of arousal: under-arousal, over-arousal, and a zone of optimal arousal. As arousal increases, performance improves up to a point, then it decreases. Each of us has a unique arousal-performance curve that depends on a variety of factors. These include stress, self-confidence, motivation, attention, experience, and thoughts.

Signs that you are under-aroused include low energy or lack of motivation. Signs of over-arousal are tension, headache, high heart rate, fast breathing, or the feeling that the pace is harder than it actually is. During a long ride, you may have to "cycle" through various levels of arousal to help produce your best energy output at key times.

To ensure an adequate state of arousal before or during an event, follow these guidelines.

1. Spend a few minutes each day visualizing how you want to perform. Don't wait until the morning of the event to do this.

2. Stick to your normal routine as much as possible.

3. Steer clear of conflicts and quarrels.

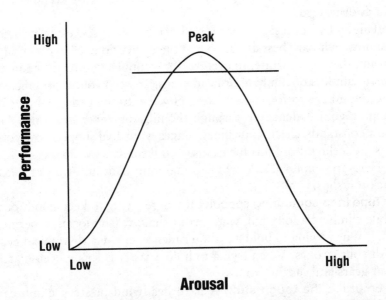

Optimum arousal or "readiness to play" will help you reach peak performance, but too much arousal can be as ineffective as too little.

4. Look forward to riding and reaching the goals you've set. All of the hard work of training is in the bank. Now the event should be fun.

5. Keep your level of arousal high as the event wears on. As you feel fatigue setting in, talk encouragingly to yourself. This will help get you through rough periods.

Keep Your Focus

Concentration is the most important mental factor during an event. You must stay tuned to what is taking place around you and to you. The environment and your body's reaction to it are always changing during long rides. You can't perform at your best without remaining aware.

Several years ago, sports psychologist Bill Morgan, Ph.D., of the University of Wisconsin did a study on marathon runners and what they thought about during a race. As he talked with these endurance athletes, who represented all levels from novice to elite, he noticed a consistent distinction. Almost without exception, the top runners put their attention on what they were doing and how they were feeling. In contrast, the less-accomplished runners tried to avoid discomfort and pain. They tended to think about other matters—school, work, family—ignoring distress signals as much as possible by keeping their minds distracted.

This and other research has found that the most successful athletes are those who are best at narrowing their attention. They don't daydream, they concentrate. In cycling, for example, you might be in an event with lots of climbing or headwinds. To keep your most efficient pace, you have to focus on putting power into the pedals while still keeping your cadence up through the hilly or windy sections. You must constantly check your inner gauges, your fuel supply, how your legs are feeling. Lose this focus, and you'll surely slow down.

Here are some specific ways to maintain concentration or get it back if it slips.

Tune in to something specific. If you're trying to keep good form while climbing a long hill, watch your shadow (sun location permitting). When trying to hold a certain cadence, create a rhythmical beat with your strokes. When trying to hold a faster rider's wheel, match your gears and cadence to his.

Embrace the tough stuff. A hard headwind or steep climb can make riders want to think about anything but. Those who ride well in these conditions see them as challenges, not agonizing difficulties. Put all of your attention into the task of getting through a tough section efficiently, believing that this attitude gives you an advantage over most other riders. It does.

Set a new goal. If you begin to doubt yourself or feel excessive fatigue during an event, focus on making it to the next rest stop. Setting this short-term goal will ease your fears. Pain and suffering are much more manageable when you're not dwelling on how long they'll last. You can always make it to the next break if you relax your upper body, breathe deeply, spin moderate gears, and keep eating and drinking.

Have faith in yourself. When the sun is blazing or the course gets vertical, don't let your confidence slip. Believe that these conditions will work to your advantage because you have trained well and survived them before.

Talk to yourself. When the going gets tough, rest assured that it's the same for everyone. The cycling gods aren't picking on you. Encourage yourself with positive thoughts, such as, "Everyone gets tired. If I hurt, they are hurting at least as much. If they can do it, then I can definitely do it." This is the approach used by Scott Dickson, the multi-time winner of Paris-Brest-Paris, as the hours pass and the huge pack dwindles to a small lead group. "It might sound perverse," Scott says, "but I look forward to the point where it starts to feel like a death struggle. I know I can handle it, but other guys begin to doubt that they can. By surging at the right time, I might make them give up and drop off the pace, even though I'm probably hurting as much as they are."

Mental Training Diary

Most cyclists are familiar with a training diary. It's used to keep a record of rides and other important information such as weight, diet, and equipment. But don't stop there. It's also a great place to chart the mental factors that play into your physical performance. Make notes about your arousal level—your eagerness to ride each day and your excitement about cycling in general. Write down motivational statements that are especially meaningful to you.

This is also the right place to record your short- and long-term goals. For example, a long-term goal may be to complete a cross-state ride in August, covering 75 miles per day for 6 days. To prepare, you set a short-term goal of averaging 75 miles per day over the 3-day Fourth of July weekend. Meanwhile, a daily training goal might be to ride a course with tough climbs as a way to work on the strength and technique you'll need for the hilly cross-state route.

You could set these goals in your head, but it's much more effective to write them down. This makes them a commitment, not just an idea. It gives you more motivation to schedule workouts and then complete them. This doesn't have to be elaborate. One sentence will do. For example, as you plan upcoming rides, you might dedicate one to working on climbing, one to increasing your cruising speed, and another to testing a new food or drink. After each ride, record your feelings about what you accomplished.

When writing about events, be more detailed. Search for insights that help you correlate your mental state with your physical performance. Ultimately, your diary should become the best book on cycling improvement that you'll ever own.

PART 2

The
Rides

8

Long Rides: Up to 100 Miles

"One hundred miles? On a bicycle? In one day? Golly, I hardly ever drive my car that far!"

Well, even Aunt Harriet, the dumbfounded speaker of these words, could probably ride a century if she had the desire and did the training. Don't get us wrong—100 miles make for a long and tough test of strength and endurance. But we've seen people of all ages, talents, and body types conquer the distance, achieving what for many is their ultimate goal in cycling—the century ride.

The challenge of riding triple digits made the century cycling's original long-distance adventure, dating to the era of the highwheeler. Now, it's cycling's most prolific recreational event. Each year in North America, more than a thousand centuries are held. Many are put on by local cycling clubs in September or October, giving riders a goal that culminates the season. These rides become annual traditions, with their dates circled on calendars throughout the land. In addition, century organizers often include fractional distances as a way to broaden their event's appeal to cyclists not yet at century ability. Common distances are the quarter-century (25 miles), half-metric (31 miles or 50 km), half-century (50 miles), metric (62 miles or 100 km), and three-quarter-century (75 miles). When there's a distance for everyone, the lure of achieving the next level brings cyclists back year after year.

In this chapter, we'll key on what it takes to build up to 50 miles and then a full 100 miles. If your goal stops at a shorter distance, you can scale down the training that we're recommending. Our approach here and in the next two chapters is to supplement the general endurance cycling advice that's found throughout this book with specific tips for success at greater and greater distances. Stop at the level you currently desire, but we'll bet that at some point the next longer challenge will start calling your name. That's the way it works in this sport. When it happens, you'll find the coaching you need in this section of the book.

Ready? Let's roll!

Training for 50 Miles

If you're a new cyclist, a half-century may seem monumental, and 100 miles all but unimaginable. But then you notice that many of the people who ride across the finish line of your club's annual century aren't Lance Armstrong clones. No, they're your fairly average citizens who spend their days working for a living, not cycling for a living. Hey, if these people can ride 100 miles, why can't you? Answer: You can! If you have the desire, all it takes is a sound training program.

Let's start with the first long-distance goal that many people strive for, the half-century. This distance has most people on the bike for 3½ or 4 hours. After following our training schedule for 6 weeks, you'll be ready. (We're assuming that you've been riding enough to have decent cycling fitness. If not, precede this training with about 6 weeks of steady rides in varied terrain, adding about 10 percent more time or distance each week. When you're up to about 75 miles or 5 hours per week, switch to this program.)

Note: The daily training intensities are defined by the heart rate zones described in chapter 1. Determine your zones so you can do these workouts correctly and make the best progress. Remember, all training rides start and end with short periods of easy spinning for warming up and cooling down.

Monday: Day off to rest and recover from weekend rides. Use this day for weight training if it's part of your program, but do upper body only—no leg exercises when you're on the bike almost every day.

Tuesday: 60 to 90 minutes with hills. Stay seated for most of the climbing, and work in the upper part of zone 2. Then, while seated or standing, do two or three efforts of 2 to 3 minutes apiece near zone 4.

Wednesday: Day off from riding, or up to 60 minutes at zone 1 pace. Weight-train as on Monday.

Thursday: 60 to 90 minutes in zone 2, except for one or two efforts of 8 to 10 minutes in zone 3.

Friday: Day off from riding, or up to 60 minutes at zone 1 pace. Weight-train as on Monday.

Saturday: 90 to 120 minutes with one 30-minute interval toward the high side of zone 2. Try to do this ride with a group of three to five cyclists for practice riding in a fast paceline. If necessary, stay on the front to maintain a steady heart rate during the interval. Use this ride to increase your training time or distance by up to 10 percent each week.

Sunday: 60 to 90 minutes in zone 2.

Training for 100 Miles

Next, here's a program you can use to graduate to rides of up to 100 miles. This training calls for additional hard efforts plus group rides. You need to become comfortable around other cyclists, because most events have large fields. You also need to experience riding in a paceline, a great way to conserve energy without losing speed (or even to gain some). If you follow this schedule for about 8 weeks, adding the magic 10 percent time/distance increase each week by extending the Saturday or Sunday ride, you should be able to complete a century with strength to spare.

Monday: Day off to rest and recover from weekend rides. Use this day for weight training if it's part of your program, but do upper body only—no leg exercises.

Tuesday: 75 to 120 minutes in zone 2, except for 30 to 45 minutes of sporadic high zone 3 efforts in the form of short time trials, hill jams, pushing into a headwind, and so on.

Wednesday: Day off from riding, or up to 60 minutes in zone 1. Weight-train as on Monday.

Thursday: 60 to 90 minutes in zone 2, except for one 30- to 45-minute interval in the low end of zone 3.

Friday: Day off from riding, or up to 60 minutes in zone 1. Weight-train as on Monday.

Saturday: 2 to 3 hours with a small group on flat terrain, using a fast paceline. Ideally, you will be at the higher limit of zone 3 much of the time.

Sunday: 2 hours in the hills, climbing in high zone 2 with short periods (2 to 3 minutes) in high zone 3. Between climbs, ride in the lower portion of zone 2.

Here are two additional programs that are more detailed. Each begins 10 weeks prior to the century. These were created by *Bicycling* magazine more than a dozen years ago. The reason they deserve to be repeated is that they work so well—they've helped countless cyclists achieve their first or best century ride. The one potential drawback, compared with the program just given, is their regimentation: There are very specific daily and weekly distances. This may or may not work for you, depending on the consistency with which you can train. But if you can stick to either program, success on century day is virtually guaranteed, according to the appreciative cyclists who have reported back to *Bicycling* over the years. Should you miss a day, simply forget it and do what's called for on the following day. Trying to make up missed miles will only upset the steady progression that this training relies on.

The first program is for riders who will be attempting their first century. It assumes a weekly foundation of about 45 to 50 miles. If you've been averaging more, increase the recommended distances slightly or jump to the more advanced second program. In both charts, "easy" (zone 1) means a leisurely ride for recovery, "pace" (zone 2) means matching the speed you want to maintain during the century, and "brisk" means riding faster than your century speed. For example, if you are scheduled to do 15 miles at brisk pace, ride the first 3 in zone 2, the next 8 to 10 in zone 3 with a couple of surges to zone 4, and the final 3 miles in zone 1 to cool down. If your century is on Saturday rather than Sunday, simply move the final week's training back one day.

PROGRAM 1: TO FINISH A CENTURY

WEEK	MON	TUES	WED	THURS	FRI	SAT	SUN	WEEKLY MILEAGE
	Easy	Pace	Brisk		Pace	Pace	Pace	
1	6	10	12	Off	10	30	9	77
2	7	11	13	Off	11	34	10	86
3	8	13	15	Off	13	38	11	98
4	8	14	17	Off	14	42	13	108
5	9	15	19	Off	15	47	14	119
6	11	15	21	Off	15	53	16	131
7	12	15	24	Off	15	59	18	143
8	13	15	25	Off	15	65	20	153
9	15	15	25	Off	15	65	20	155
10	15	15	25	Off	10	5 Easy	100	170

Use the next program if your average weekly training is more than 75 miles. This schedule will help you finish the century with strength to spare. It also can be used by century veterans to train for a personal record.

PROGRAM 2: TO RIDE A BETTER CENTURY

WEEK	MON	TUES	WED	THURS	FRI	SAT	SUN	WEEKLY MILEAGE
	Easy	Pace	Brisk		Pace	Pace	Pace	
1	10	12	14	Off	12	40	15	103
2	10	13	13	Off	13	44	17	110
3	10	15	17	Off	15	48	18	123
4	11	16	19	Off	16	53	20	135
5	12	18	20	Off	18	59	22	149
6	13	19	23	Off	19	64	24	162
7	14	20	25	Off	20	71	27	177
8	16	20	27	Off	20	75	29	187
9	17	20	30	Off	20	75	32	194
10	19	20	30	Off	10	5 Easy	100	184

Tapering

One rule of thumb for event week is to stay consistent. This isn't the time to make major changes in your diet, sleep pattern, or equipment. The one thing you must alter, however, is your training. This is called tapering. The objective is to create a reserve of physical and emotional energy.

Another rule of thumb is that it's better to be too rested for the event than not rested enough. Keep this in mind as you're tempted to do "just one more" long or strenuous ride when the century is only a few days away. It's very hard to resist, but you must. Eleventh-hour training is much more likely to produce a mediocre performance than a great one.

Begin tapering with at least 3 days to go. A full week is better if your training has put you on the brink of fatigue. Studies have found that the key is to substantially reduce mileage but keep intensity consistent with your normal training. A good example is found in the two training charts. Distance is reduced during the final training rides, but intensity stays the same. Don't stop riding entirely, which puts your body to sleep and makes you even more anxious about the training that you feel you're missing. Even on the day before the century, it's good to take a brief spin to loosen your legs and make sure your bike is working perfectly. Many riders like to include a couple of short sprints to raise their heart rate and open their lungs. Just don't do anything to make yourself even remotely tired.

How much performance increase can you expect from tapering? A review of more than 50 studies published in the *International Journal of Sports Medicine* found an average improvement of 3 percent. This translates to an 11-minute improvement during a 6-hour century, and more than 6 minutes during a 3½-hour half-century. Another benefit is psychological—the confidence that comes from feeling fresh legs and plenty of energy as you begin a long ride.

Nutritional Adjustments

To supplement the advice in chapters 1 and 6, we'll emphasize several points about eating and drinking specifically for distances of up to 100 miles. This includes training rides as well as events.

Distance: 15 to 60 miles

Intensity: zones 2 and 3

Time: 1 to 4 hours

Nutritionally, there are two dangers to avoid as rides get longer. The first is bonking—allowing your glycogen stores to become depleted. This usually can't happen unless the ride is more than 2 hours. The second is dehydration—a loss of body fluid sufficient enough to contribute to fatigue.

You can avoid both risks by using carbohydrate-rich sports drinks. However, plain water still has its place, especially on rides of 90 minutes or less. For this duration, sweat loss outweighs the need for energy replacement. Carry two bottles, one filled with a sports drink and the other with water. Alternately swig from one, then the other, every 10 to 20 minutes. Also, drink a tall glass of water about 20 minutes before every ride—especially in hot weather when you're sweating more.

Just to be safe, always ride with a high-carbo snack in your jersey pocket. This could be an energy bar or gel—something that will keep for the next ride if you don't use it. This is insurance if you start feeling hunger knock or something happens to make the ride longer than planned. (For the same reason, always keep a few dollars in your seatpack for emergency stops at convenience stores.) Generally, you won't need to eat anything during rides of 2 hours or less. For rides that extend to 3 hours, a combination of fluid and food that supplies 300 to 600 calories should be enough.

Distance: 60 to 100 miles
Intensity: zones 2 and 3
Time: 4 hours plus

A metric century or full century are tough to survive on bad nutrition. From what we've seen, inadequate eating or drinking during an event probably causes as many failures as inadequate training.

During the week of the event, modify your diet as you taper your training. This is the carbo-loading process. No radical changes are necessary—just make sure your meals are rich in high-carbohydrate foods (cereal, bread, pasta, rice, potatoes, vegetables, desserts). In other words, ample quantities of what every cyclist should be eating anyway. Besides pasta for your main course, you can have Oriental (stir-fried, not deep-fried), Eastern (including beans, rice, grains, and vegetables), or Mexican (choose nonfried dishes without too much meat or cheese)—but only if you know that such cuisine agrees with you.

During a century, you'll probably ride at a relatively steady pace compared with some of your training. This puts a premium on burning fat for energy. Nonetheless, carbohydrate stores are still the limiting factor. Your body will convert carbo-rich foods to glycogen, your muscles' preferred fuel. A full tank to start will give you enough energy for at least 2 hours of strong riding, but the objective is to protect this fuel till you really need it. You can do this by steadily consuming more carbohydrate during the ride, and avoiding efforts that drive your heart rate into zone 4, the range where glycogen is used rapidly.

On the morning of the century, eat a hearty breakfast a couple of hours before the start. This wouldn't be our recommendation for a more intense event, such as a road or cross-country race, when you must go hard from the gun. But for the typical long-distance recreational ride, you don't need (or want) a nearly empty stomach. A good breakfast could consist of fruit, oatmeal, and toast; pancakes with fruit; or an omelet, home fries, and toast. Some riders have been known to order all three, thank you. Ideally, eat the type and quantity of food that has proven to work well for you before long training rides.

Do protein and fat give you time-release energy that improves your endurance? Or will an omelet sit in your gut like a boat anchor? Know such things before you open the menu on century morning. Follow breakfast with at least one glass of water. Drink coffee only if it agrees with you and you're willing to sacrifice a few minutes to pit stops.

During the ride, start drinking before you're thirsty to ward off dehydration, a major contributor to fatigue. Your sensation of thirst lags behind your body's need, so get in the habit of taking a swig from your bottle or hydration system every few minutes. On a hot day, drink about 1 quart per hour (about a bottle and a half) while riding, and more at each rest stop. A sports drink is the best choice because it supplies calories along with fluid. Just make sure it's a brand that you've used successfully in training.

Similarly, don't wait till you feel hungry before eating something. Start nibbling in the first 30 minutes. Thanks to previous long rides, you will know the foods that are enjoyable, digest well, and keep you energized. Stick with them, even at rest stops. You might be tempted by a chunk of homemade nut roll, but if you've never ridden on something like that, steer clear till the postride banquet. On the bike, snack steadily to maintain a constant supply of food energy while not overloading your stomach. Strive for 250 to 300 calories per hour from food and drinks combined. Make it 400 if your system can handle it and there's a lot of climbing or you're pushing the pace.

At rest stops, go about your business briskly. Munch on something as you fill your bottles and your pockets, then do a few stretches to loosen and refresh your body (see chapter 17). Limit stops to 10 minutes or less so you don't cool down and begin getting stiff, thus making it tougher to resume your pace. The biggest mistake we see at stops is standing around for 15 to 20 minutes and eating the whole time. Muscles stiffen, and then there's a struggle for blood supply between your full stomach and legs as riding resumes. Your stomach loses, making it feel like you just ate a brick. Next comes indigestion, and there goes your chance for a successful ride.

Preride Preparation

Don't take anything for granted during the 24 hours before the event. If you don't think through everything, anything that can go wrong probably will. Ed Burke recalls going to his first mountain bike event, reaching into his gear bag, and pulling out two left shoes. Now he puts a greater effort into being less absentminded.

Let's look at a routine that makes sure all pre-event bases are covered. You'll feel more confident and sleep more soundly knowing that every detail has been tended to. And because they have been, all of the training you've done will have a better chance of resulting in a strong performance.

Day before. Final preparation begins with about 24 hours to go. By now, your bike should have been tuned up and test-ridden, and you should be well into the carbo-loading diet described in chapter 6. Eat a high-carbohydrate dinner at least 3 hours before bedtime to top off your glycogen stores. You should also have begun drinking plenty of water and other nonalcoholic, caffeine-free fluids. Stop hydrating at dinner to give your bladder a chance to empty before lights out. Otherwise, your sleep could be disrupted by bathroom visits.

Before you hit the hay, lay out your clothing, helmet, heart rate monitor, sunglasses, shoes, pocket food—everything you will need before, during, and after the ride (see sidebar). Don't risk restless sleep by waiting till the morning of the ride. Include a small first-aid kit and toilet paper, just in case. Think through everything, right down to details like filling and refrigerating your bottles, inflating your tires to full pressure, and packing some extra safety pins if numbers are to be worn. Don't forget your bottle of postride recovery drink. Is there a chance of rain? Include your wet-weather gear and zip-shut sandwich bags for the cue sheet and course map. Next, check everything twice.

After your gear is ready, relax and review your game plan. Consider the course features, and imagine how you'll do your best on the tough sections. Picture yourself relaxed and in control. See yourself finishing with energy to spare and feeling great about your performance.

Decide what time you need to get up, and then set your alarm for 30 minutes earlier than that. Then set a second alarm, just in case. Remove all anxiety about waking up on time or meeting a tight schedule. Settle down with a book, some music, or a TV program. Put the event out of your mind.

Turn off the light at your normal hour. If you have a hard time nodding off, just lie there comfortably and have faith that it's almost as restful as actually sleeping. Remember, it's the sleep in the last few nights before the event that's most important, not what you get (or don't get) the night before. Studies have proven this. If you've been getting your full quota up to now, you'll be fine.

Morning of. Get up in time for an unhurried breakfast. If you've been drinking enough, you'll first have to sprint to the bathroom. Plan this meal to yield about 70 percent of its calories from carbohydrate, and to end about 2 hours before the start.

Final hour. Unless you expect to ride with a fast group or you have your sights on a personal record (PR), a century doesn't require an on-bike warmup. Simply do about 5 minutes of stretching to loosen your lower back, shoulders, calves, hamstrings, and quadriceps. If the effects of adrenaline and your morning coffee are kicking in, you can stretch while in line for the Port-A-Potty.

If you do need to warm up, allot 15 to 20 minutes. Begin with easy spinning till your legs feel loose and you're breathing freely. Then do a couple of out-of-saddle windups to higher speed, followed by a few seconds of in-saddle pushing. You want to elevate your heart rate and break a light sweat, but avoid using any energy reserves. Time this to end about 5 minutes before your start. Stop briefly at your car for a few swallows of sports drink and final details, then begin the ride.

With experience, you can design an efficient pre-event routine

Make a List, Check It Twice

To reduce the possibility of forgetting something before an important ride, develop a pre-event checklist. Go through it the day before, with plenty of time to round up everything. Here are items commonly included. Your list might have more or less.

Arm warmers	License or	Sunglasses
Baby wipes	membership card	Sunscreen
Chamois lubricant	Lip balm	Sweatband
Chain lube	Pump	Tights/leg warmers
Emergency money	Puncture repair kit	Toilet paper
Energy bars, gels	Rainwear	Tools
Entry fee	Safety pins	Undershirt
First-aid kit	Shoe covers	Washcloth, towels
Food	Shoes	Water
Gloves	Shorts	Water bottles
Heart rate monitor	Socks	Windbreaker
Helmet	Spare tire	Zip-shut bags
Hydration system	Spare tubes	
Jersey	Sports drink	

that removes much of the anxiety that typically surrounds an important event. This will happen quicker if you think things through and leave nothing to the last minute—except extra time to deal with the unexpected.

Century Strategy

There are several right ways to ride a century. Several wrong ways, too. Use these tips to put together a strategy that comes as close as possible to producing your very best performance.

Start gently. You have a long day ahead. Roll into it like you would for a training ride, spinning an easy gear to warm up your muscles and cardiovascular system. Some rides start like those land rushes you see in old westerns, so don't get caught up unless your goal is a personal record (PR) and you're prepared to start fast.

Establish your pace. In just a few minutes, you'll find your groove. Settle in and keep a check with your cyclecomputer and heart rate monitor. It's common to be so excited, feel so strong after tapering, and be so distracted by the other riders that you don't realize you're riding several miles an hour faster than your intended pace. This can cost you dearly later, so pay attention.

Ride with a friend. If you have a regular training partner or know someone with the same time goal, a century can be more fun if you ride together. Trading pulls will help you both ride faster without more effort, and chatting makes the miles slip by quicker. Even when you haven't planned to buddy up, there will be opportunities from time to time as you encounter other riders going at your pace. Many new friendships have started this way.

Beware of fast pacelines. You're spinning along at your ideal pace. The ride is going great—feels like you're on cruise control. Suddenly, from behind you hear, "On your left!", and half a dozen guys in a smooth paceline come rolling by. It's so tempting to accelerate and slide in behind the last rider. We won't tell you not to, but be smart. By joining a paceline, you're obligated to take your turn at the front, and even one pull might cost you precious energy if the pace is too high. Much more time than you gain now could be lost later if your reserves become drained. Rule of thumb: Join pacelines that creep past; ignore those that make you accelerate to catch on.

Don't cross your threshold. Some of the best advice we ever heard for long rides was succinctly stated by Pete Penseyres: "Never go anaerobic." Pete knows from experience that playing near the lactate

Dwell at the postride feast, but keep rest stops to 10 minutes or less during the event. Otherwise, your legs will cool and stiffen. Fill your pockets, not your stomach, and eat on the roll.

threshold is dangerous business. Once you force your metabolism to switch—even briefly—from aerobic to anaerobic energy production, you may not recover for the rest of the ride. So beware of hard pulls, steep climbs, strong headwinds, and any other encounters that could boost your heart rate near the danger zone. Back off to remain aerobic and preserve precious glycogen.

Divide the ride. During the 1990s, Seana Hogan was unquestionably the world's best female endurance cyclist, winning the Race Across America five times and setting the women's transcontinental record of 9 days and 4 hours. But Seana still remembers the trepidation she felt when lining up for her very first century, thinking about the 100 miles that lay ahead. Now, she'll tell you that that's a major mistake. Instead of keying on the whole distance, she advises breaking the ride into doable segments, such as from one rest stop to the next. When your goal is a series of 20- or 25-mile rides, it's less intimidating. You know you can easily ride that distance. Just do it several times.

Eat and drink frequently. We've beaten this one to death, and we're not going to stop until you're automatically reaching for your bottle every 12 to 15 minutes and for your food every 20 minutes or so.

Keep stops brief. Remember, you'll actually feel better by resting less. Stops longer than 10 minutes will cool your body and make it necessary to warm up all over again.

Do a negative split. If you have trouble controlling your early pace, here's an effective tactic: Plan to ride the second 50 miles faster than the first 50. This is called a negative split and will make you ride at a conservative pace early on. Plus, it nearly guarantees that you'll have the energy left for a strong finish. It's a great feeling when you have the suds to make the final 20 miles your fastest of the day.

Stretch on the bike. Don't save stretching for rest stops. Use opportunities to do the on-bike stretches described in chapter 17 so your body doesn't stiffen in the first place. In a related technique, stand to pedal frequently to loosen your legs and back, plus reduce saddle discomfort and genital numbness. Just 30 seconds of standing every 15 to 20 minutes can make a big difference.

Talk to yourself. Michael Shermer is a psychologist as well as a pioneer in modern ultramarathon cycling. He'll tell you that positive affirmations are vital when the going gets tough—and it almost always will at some point in a century. Instead of dwelling on the hurt, pain, and agony, remind yourself that you've survived other long rides and have what it takes to finish this one, too. Remember that other riders are hurting as much or more. If they can make it, so can you. Keep setting small goals—reaching the next rest stop, the next town, the next silo you see in the distance—to keep the big goal manageable. Imagine the great meal you're going to have as a reward for your accomplishment. This is the tactic used by veteran endurance rider and coach John Hughes, who stays so busy mulling over every detail of dinner that the final miles melt away.

Go for broke. When you've done everything right and are feeling almost too good to be true in the final 15 miles or so, start using up what you have left. Don't ruin the ride by going over the edge, just pick up your pace so that you finish fast as well as happy. At this point, adrenaline may even be helping. Veteran long-distance riders swear that *something* kicks in near the end of certain rides, making the final miles the best of day. This mysterious force came into play for Ed Pavelka in Paris-Brest-Paris '99 when, after riding for 60 hours with one sleep break, he was able to average 23 mph during the final 3 hours. He can't explain it, but he'll never forget it.

Finish with a flourish. With the finish line finally in sight, perform this last important maneuver, as described by sage cycling writer Bill Strickland of *Bicycling* magazine: "Keep your left hand on the handlebar. Bend your right elbow and place your hand between your shoulder blades. Then give yourself a big pat on the back. You deserve it."

(continued on page 136)

Preparing for an Off-road Century

Check out the cyclists lining up for the Leadville 100, Cascade Cream Puff 100, or any other ultradistance off-road event, and you'll see quite a few sporting gray hair. People who ride in these events tend to be older than those who compete in traditional mountain bike races. It seems that the longer length has an appeal to riders not so intent on catching air and collecting scar tissue.

But 100 miles on dirt trails is tremendously risky in its own way. To be successful, you need more than just great endurance. You need to tolerate levels of discomfort and fatigue that are never seen in shorter off-road events and aren't approached in most road centuries, either.

The ultra off-roader must learn to be self-sufficient during the many hours it takes to ride 100 miles. There may be rest stops, but they probably won't be nearly as frequent as the hand-up areas on the relatively short laps of a mountain bike race. This makes it necessary to carry lots of food and fluids, as well as emergency tools and clothes. For some events, you may have to know how to use a compass and read a map. For every event, you should be able to repair a broken chain, true wheels, and perform other emergency bike repairs.

Want to make it even tougher? Then do the ride at high altitude. Ed Burke has ridden the Leadville 100 three times and can vouch for the added challenge of rare air. The start/finish in Leadville, Colorado, is at 10,150 feet above sea level, and the course tops out at 12,600 feet. During the ride, you're climbing and descending enough to accumulate about 15,000 vertical feet. Altitude sickness, delirium, heat, lightning, rain, snow, hail, and hypothermia are among the possible experiences along the way. Then there's the logistical challenge of arranging for a support crew and gear drops. You must anticipate what food and clothing you'll need at various times and distances. You have to drink gallons of fluid to stave off dehydration, so it's critical that you never run out.

If you blow it in these conditions, you're in serious trouble. But complete these 100 off-road miles with your head and body intact, and there are few greater achievements in cycling. You know you've done something that has been experienced by only a tiny fraction of cyclists. There may be some tangible rewards as well. For instance, if you can finish the Leadville 100 in less than 12 hours, you are presented with a silver belt buckle and a sweatshirt with your name and time emblazoned on it. If you can finish in less than 9 hours, you receive a belt buckle more than three times larger—big enough to draw envious stares from any hard-core cowboy.

In talking with fellow Leadville riders, Ed found about as many training techniques as brands of bikes. Some guys ride 300 or more miles per week, including one long ride of 6 to 8 hours on the weekends leading up to the event. Others ride progressively longer weeks, starting with about 50 miles and building up to 400 during 8 to 10 months of preparation. Some riders simply get into shape for relatively short and fast cross-country races, and then jump right up to century distance. This technique might best be described as mind over matter. They ride 100 miles in one day even though they may not total this amount during a whole week of training.

Ed's preparation consists of riding 10 to 15 hours per week on paved roads around his home in Colorado Springs, and on dirt roads and trails in the nearby Pike National Forest. The key as the event gets closer is the addition of several 7- to 8-hour off-road rides with long climbs and stretches of walking the bike up steep sections. Ed carries plenty of food and fluid in his CamelBak hydration system, simulating what he'll be toting in the event.

"Be more concerned with the time you spend in the saddle than the number of miles you cover," Ed advises. "My training is directed toward adapting to several conditions, including altitude, climbs and descents, rough surfaces, heat, cold, and the need for nourishment. I find that walking the bike for a few minutes every hour helps keep my cycling muscles loose and delays the inevitable fatigue of riding so far. It's more fun to walk short portions of the entire distance than to ride the first 85 miles till you're vine-ripened, then push your bike the rest of the way."

In addition, Ed has been known to go training no matter what the weather, and even to start out in the heat of the day—all to prevent surprises during the event. For the same reason, he tries different foods and drinks to find the ones that go down (and stay down) best during long and hard riding. He's found that taste and digestion change as fatigue sets in.

Somewhere past 75 miles, an off-road century becomes as much a mental ordeal as a physical one. This is why experienced cyclists stress the importance of training the mind as well as the body. "Keeping your pace under control, staying hydrated and fueled, and focusing your mind on the task are the keys to success," says John Stamstad, winner of many off-road endurance events. John and other top cyclists emphasize the need to manage both your body and your brain on event day.

Off-road champ John Stamstad contends that mental focus is as important as pace and nutrition.

After the Finish

Before joining in the postride festivities, stop at your car and clean up. Remove your jersey and use baby wipes or a wet washcloth on your face, neck, chest, and arms. Remove your shorts and do the same to your crotch. Then put on sweatpants if it's the least bit cool, or loose-fitting shorts in warm weather. Don't make the mistake of hanging around with clogged pores, damp clothes, and a germy chamois—the ideal breeding ground for a bumper crop of saddle sores. Keep your body warm to reduce muscle stiffness and avoid catching a chill. You've been through a lot, and your defenses are down.

Record your ride. As soon as possible, fill in your diary. Don't give your memory a chance to fade. Record the ride's weather conditions, what you ate and drank, how you felt at various points, what went right, and what went wrong. Think through everything, then give yourself advice to follow for the next century. This page can be the most important learning tool you'll ever have.

Take a rest. A century ride can become a problem if you're so fired up (or so disappointed) that you're out training again the next day. A short, easy, zone 1 recovery spin is okay, but don't do anything more. A walk and stretching session in lieu of riding is safer if you doubt your self-control. For a century ride to make you stronger, you must allow recovery. Letting your enthusiasm put you back into training right away is the fast path to overtraining. Have faith that some time off is the final essential step for successful century riding.

9

Longer Rides:
100 to 200 Miles

So, you've ridden several centuries,
100 miles is no longer the ultimate challenge it once was, and now
Peggy Lee is singing in your head, "Is that all there is?" Not hardly.
Perhaps you've already gotten a clue when hearing fellow century
riders use the word "ultra" in chatting about what lies beyond.
They're referring, of course, to ultradistance events, which mean an
ultra challenge and an even bigger dose of accomplishment.

In this book, we use "ultra" to designate 1-day distances of 100
miles off road or more than 100 miles on the road. It's a term recently
popularized in cycling and adopted by the principal organization for
endurance riders, the UltraMarathon Cycling Association. This outfit,
headed by renowned long-distance rider and coach John Hughes of
Boulder, Colorado, has nearly 2,000 members, from as far away as
Australia. The UMCA's annual calendar is the best source of ultra
rides in North America, and its bimonthly magazine, *Ultra Cycling,* is
a must-read for everyone interested in training, nutrition, tactics,
equipment, personalities, and event coverage. John serves it up with a
big helping of inspiration, keeping you excited to be involved in this
special part of the sport. Your authors are both longtime UMCA
members, and we encourage you to learn more at the Web site,
www.ultracycling.com.

In this chapter, we're going to key on how to train for and ride the
numerous ultra events that fall between 100 and 200 miles. Most of
these are road rides, including what could be termed "ultra centuries,"
such as the 111-mile El Tour de Tucson. Then there are the first two
(of five) brevet distances, 200 and 300 kilometers (124 and 186 miles),
plus the classic 200-mile double century. Lon Haldeman's transcontinental PAC Tours average between 110 and 140 miles per day, and

you will find numerous other organized events and tours in this range. In addition, 200 miles is the distance that many riders strive for in a 12-hour time trial.

Your Head Start

First, let's face facts. No matter how many centuries you ride, those last few miles are usually pretty tough. Rarely do you finish 100 miles and announce, "That was so much fun, I'd like to do another one—right now!" The prospect of pushing yourself even an extra 24 miles to complete a 200-kilometer brevet may seem daunting, and to ride the entire distance all over again to complete a double century may seem just plain impossible. Remember, however, that you probably felt the same way about riding a single century not long ago.

At this point in your cycling career, you have a big advantage as you contemplate riding beyond triple digits—the experience you've gained in century training and events. Look at how much you know now compared with when the long-distance bug first bit. You've learned how to alternate hard and easy training rides, sanely increase mileage, and avoid the pitfall of overtraining. You understand how to eat and drink to beat the bonk and extend your endurance. You have the self-restraint to pace yourself, knowing that if you begin a long ride like you would a 10-mile time trial, you'll pay dearly before the end. And you've learned a lot about how your mind works during 100 miles on the bike—and how to make it work for you instead of against you when the going gets tough.

In short, you know almost everything necessary to become a double-century cyclist. The experience of building up to a double will make future centuries seem easier and more enjoyable. Your fitness and confidence will be way above your former limits. No ride under 200 miles will seem too extreme again, and events beyond 200 miles may start whispering your name. Once you've doubled, the most astonishing events in ultra cycling are next in line.

Risky Business

It's a challenge to boost mileage without breaking down with injuries or falling victim to overtraining. But with planning and common sense, you can swing the odds in your favor.

As you read this, you have a current mileage limit. Every cyclist does. It's easy to see how your limit has risen over time, and there's no reason it can't be a lot higher still. One thing in your favor is that the difficulties that come with more miles don't increase in a straight line. For example, the tight lower back that develops at around 100 miles will not necessarily be twice as uncomfortable at 200. In most cases, you reach a physical plateau after several hours and dwell there for the remainder of the ride. This isn't to say that any problem can't blossom into a real difficulty, but it won't happen automatically. And sometimes just the opposite occurs, with nicks magically healing as the ride wears on.

The smart approach is to reduce the risk of injury in the first place. Don't even let one get a toehold. There are no guarantees, but these guidelines will make mileage increases as safe as possible.

Obey the 10 percent rule. During the span of several years, you can double or even triple your annual mileage. But increasing too quickly is almost certain to result in injury or chronic fatigue. While there is no scientific evidence telling us exactly how much we can safely increase in any given period, 10 percent seems to work very well.

Increase in steps. Don't add more miles every single week. This keeps stress ascending in a straight line. Instead, alternate longer and shorter weeks. Or increase for 3 weeks, then hold that level for 2 weeks before going up again. Another approach is to cut back mileage by 20 to 30 percent every fourth or fifth week to let your body recover. Use whichever technique (or variation) gives you the most effective combination of stress and recovery.

Don't let mileage become a goal in itself. There is no surer way to burn out and become chronically fatigued than to keep piling on the miles. In a way, it's the easiest (as in "most mindless") thing to do, and it provides a sense of accomplishment. But training that's focused on a goal other than more and more miles is more productive and less risky. If mileage is what drives you, you won't give yourself the breaks necessary for recovery and growth—until you're forced to by an injury, fatigue, or a bad attitude.

Be honest with yourself. High-mileage training isn't for everyone. Don't make cycling a chore by forcing yourself to ride more than you can stand. If you want to move up to a double century, there's no getting around the fact that you need a substantial mileage base. You must be enthusiastic about boosting your training. The trick is to do it in a way that doesn't gobble up every spare hour and overwhelm your life. This chapter will show you methods that work.

Advice from the Experts

In a survey of some of the country's most experienced double-century riders, *Bicycling* magazine asked: What advice would you give a recreational century rider who wants to try a double? Here are their insights.

Use your centuries as a guide. If you can ride 100 miles in 8 hours or less and not need cardiopulmonary resuscitation (CPR) at the finish, you have what it takes to advance to a double. In fact, many riders report that the increase from 25 to 75 miles as beginners is harder than from 100 to 200. When your body can handle a century, a double becomes more realistic than you might first imagine.

Do long weekends. A key to double training in most programs is consecutive long rides on several weekends. This is in addition to regular weekday training, of course. Before your first double, you need to do at least one ride of about 150 miles for experience and confidence.

Choose the right event. Pick a double that has a good reputation for its course and support, but don't fall prey to the hospitality. As with any long ride, keep stops short (10 minutes or less) to prevent cooling down. Also, you need to keep moving during a double if you want to avoid or at least limit the amount of riding after sundown.

Beware of hills. Two hundred miles is hard enough without the added difficulty of climbing, so choose a relatively flat first double. When you do find the road tilting up, keep your effort well below your lactate threshold to avoid switching from fat to glycogen as your primary fuel. Remember, if you go anaerobic even briefly, it could hurt you the rest of the day.

Ride with friends. It helps to have company on your first double. When you share the ride with another person or small group, it makes the hours pass more quickly and the ride more fun. The moral support is important, too. Conversely, don't extend the day needlessly by riding with people who are slower than your ideal pace. Easing up briefly to chat when you catch other riders is fine, but the ride will be more satisfying if you perform to your potential. And remember, faster riding equals quicker finishing. That's a formula everyone appreciates in the last few hours.

Eat early and often. It's been said that once a person achieves a certain level of endurance, it's possible to ride almost any distance as long as there's a fuel supply. In our experience, this is true. If you've read this book from the beginning, you now understand what to eat and drink for the best long-distance performance. During a double, the trick is to maintain a steady intake of those high-carbohydrate foods and fluids.

Training Programs

Training isn't a cookie-cutter process. Instead, there are numerous approaches that can prepare you to ride ultra events that go in distances up to 200 miles. Let's look at two. They have some similarities but also very important differences. Read through both approaches and the advice they contain, and then use the one that suits your approach to cycling and your lifestyle. Even if you can't follow it to the letter, it will provide the structure that's necessary to reach double-century fitness. In the end, it's not which program you pick, but how well you stick with it.

Bicycling's Sweet 16

Did you use one of *Bicycling* magazine's 10-week programs in chapter 8 to train for century rides? Did you like the precision of knowing the distance to ride and the effort to make every single day? Did your job, family, and other responsibilities allow you to stick with it? Yes? Good, because the same approach that helped you ride 100 miles can boost you to 200. But now, as the chart on page 142 shows, it takes a 16-week commitment.

You need a solid foundation before increasing your training to the level this requires. Take a look—you'll be riding more than 300 miles per week before double day. Everyone's different, but we don't recommend striving for this level until you have at least 3 full years of cycling behind you. If you're newer—and even though you may have knocked off a century or two without much problem—you still need to develop the physical conditioning that only several years of consistent training can produce. We mean everything from muscles to tendons to calluses in the right places. Ignore this, and your risk of injury becomes much higher.

In the chart, "easy" means a leisurely ride in heart rate zone 1 (see chapter 1). "Pace" means matching the speed you want to maintain during the double century, which is typically in the low to mid portion of zone 2. "Brisk" means riding faster than your double-century speed, including some efforts that push you at least into high zone 3. If you should miss a day of training, don't try to make up the lost miles. This will only upset the pattern of daily progressions. Simply do what's called for on the day you ride again.

Most double centuries are held on a Saturday, so the chart reflects this in the final week. If yours is on a Sunday, do about 30 "pace" miles on Friday and 10 "easy" on Saturday.

BICYCLING'S DOUBLE-CENTURY TRAINING PROGRAM

WEEK	MON	TUES	WED	THURS	FRI	SAT	SUN	WEEKLY MILEAGE
	Easy	Pace	Brisk		Pace	Pace	Pace	
1	10	12	14	Off	12	40	15	103
2	10	13	15	Off	13	44	17	112
3	10	15	17	Off	15	48	18	123
4	11	16	19	Off	16	53	20	135
5	12	18	20	Off	18	59	22	149
6	13	19	23	Off	19	64	24	162
7	14	20	25	Off	20	71	27	177
8	16	20	27	Off	20	75	29	187
9	17	20	30	Off	20	75	32	194
10	20	24	30	Off	24	83	32	213
11	23	26	33	Off	26	91	35	234
12	25	28	35	Off	28	103	38	257
13	28	31	38	Off	31	113	42	283
14	31	34	41	Off	34	124	47	311
15	34	38	45	Off	38	136	51	342
16	37	42	49	Off	42	150	56	376
Event Week	38	35	39	Off	10 Easy	Event	13 Easy	335

Doubling Up with John Hughes

John is one of ultra cycling's most astute coaches. Using physiological research and personal experience in events all the way up to the Race Across America, he provides personalized training programs to numerous ultra riders. We asked him to give you the same advice about riding double centuries that he gives to them. Although this lacks the customized, personal detail that he's able to provide in one-to-one coaching, it's a terrific overview of how to succeed in ultra rides.

Every four years, coach John Hughes rides the equivalent of nearly four consecutive double centuries in Paris-Brest-Paris, his favorite ultra event.

John's approach reflects the realities of modern life, in which time is limited, precise schedules can't always be kept, and cycling must fit within other important responsibilities. He begins with a list of keyword training principles that establish the foundation of any successful program.

Target. What are your key events for the year? Take time to identify these, and then plan your training so that you peak for them rather than arrive at the starting line under- or overtrained. You probably can't ride ultra events well on successive weekends, so decide which are most important.

Individual. We all have unique bodies, psyches, and cycling goals. Your training program should be as individual as you are. Take note of what other riders are doing, but do what you need to be doing.

Economy. The best training program is the one that enables you to achieve your goals with the minimum amount of time and effort. Do the miles that are necessary for success, but no more.

Intensity. Your leg muscles have slow-twitch fibers, which are good for endurance, and fast-twitch fibers, used for fast climbing and similar hard efforts. You can't train these different muscles and metabolic systems at one set cycling intensity. You need short, fast rides as well as long, steady ones.

Overload. When you do a hard ride, your body says, "Ouch—I'm not ready for this!" Then, somewhat reluctantly, it gets stronger. In order to improve, you have to increase the stress on your body even though this frequently causes discomfort.

Recovery. Your body doesn't get stronger when you overload it. It gets stronger when you rest it. Pay attention to the "ouch." Recovery is essential for rebuilding tissue and gaining strength.

Progression. What "ouched" you last month is kind of fun this month. Your body is stimulated, but no longer overloaded. So you must progressively do more to continue increasing the load and getting stronger.

Specificity. Cross-training is great during the winter, and you can do some in the early spring. But as the cycling season comes on, ride your bike.

Fun. Training may not always be a barrel of laughs, but the needle on your fun-o-meter should generally stay toward the positive side. Events, on the other hand, should be even more fun. Enjoy the challenge, exercise, movement, scenery, friendships, and, ultimately, your accomplishments.

Training Phases

In John's experience, your workouts and performance in events will be most effective when you section your training into four distinct phases, each with its own essential purpose.

1. **Build the base.** This takes 3 to 4 months, during which you develop the endurance for long rides. Gradually increase your weekly mileage by no more than 10 percent, and your weekly long ride by about the same. Ramping up faster risks injury. To ride a double century in May or June, you need to start building your base in February so that you have enough time to do it safely.

   Do two endurance workouts each week. These are rides of at least 2 hours at a moderate pace. Two workouts provide more overload and recovery than doing just one long ride on the weekend. Early in the season, you'll improve faster if you ride 50 to 70 miles on Saturday and 30 to 50 on Sunday, rather than grind out a century in 1 day.

   Later in this phase, you'll progress better if you ride 50 to 75 miles on Wednesday or Thursday, recover, then do 100 to 125 miles on Saturday. As a rule of thumb, total almost half of your weekly miles on the long weekend ride. On the other days, work on form and technique—a smooth spin, quiet upper body, comfortable aerodynamic position, and so on. Don't worry about pace or intensity during this phase. Your goal is to build endurance.

In addition, do crunches and weight training to strengthen the core muscles in your abdomen, back, and upper body. These are key to support and stability on the bike. Also, include exercises that develop leg muscles. See chapter 18 for recommendations.

If you've put on a few pounds during the off-season, now is the time to trim down to your riding weight. Do it gradually, by burning more calories each week than you consume. It's harder to control your appetite once you start intensity training.

2. **Increase intensity.** This takes 2 to 3 months, during which you work on speed to raise your long-distance cruising pace. During this phase, build mileage very slowly (no more than 10 percent per month) while progressively adding intensity. Significantly increasing both volume and intensity puts you at risk of overtraining. When you were building your base, you were putting miles in the bank. Intensity training starts to draw down your reserves a bit.

Twice a week (midweek and Saturday), do long rides to maintain your endurance. Increase the longest ride until you're at about 150 miles. Riding just centuries in training and then jumping up to a double is a sure way to a slow and eventually painful second hundred miles. During this phase, your training should become more event-specific. Ride in the types of terrain and conditions that you'll encounter in the double.

Once a week, do a pace ride. For 2 or more hours, maintain the heart-rate intensity that you'll strive for in the event. Each week, increase the length of this ride.

Once a week, do speedwork that drives your heart rate near the lactate threshold. After warming up thoroughly, climb hills fast or ride long intervals. Once each month, use this day for a long time trial on the same course so that you can gauge your progress.

On the other days, ride at a leisurely pace or stay off the bike altogether (especially if your self-control leaves something to be desired). These easy days are just as important as the others because they provide recovery.

3. **Create a peak.** This takes 4 to 6 weeks, during which your training becomes very event-specific, with long rides at or above your double-century pace. By the end of intensity training, you'll have the stamina to ride a double without much suffering, and you will have developed the aerobic power for short periods of greater effort. During the peaking phase, you maintain the endurance and extend the speed for longer distances.

This sharpens your form. Keep your weekly mileage the same, or even slightly less, than during the intensity phase. Every other weekend, do an endurance ride of 135 to 150 miles. Keep a steady pace, and minimize off-bike time. On the alternate weekends, ride fast centuries—faster than the pace you plan for the double. During the week, continue to do a lactate threshold ride, a pace ride of several hours, and a couple of recovery rides (or days off).

4. **Taper.** For at least 1 week, store energy for the big ride. You might as well, because it's too late to train effectively. The only thing long miles will do now is ensure that you go into the event tired.

"As event day approaches," Ed Burke warns, "your impulse is to continue training just when you should be cutting back. Yes, there's a paradox here. You need discipline and determination during the months it takes to get in shape for a double century, but then you need the same qualities in order to taper training. If you don't give yourself enough rest, you won't arrive at the starting line with a chance for your best performance."

Simply put, most cyclists don't rest enough. They realize they need to reduce mileage in order to reach a peak of strength and energy, but they wait too late, backing off with a couple of days to go. How much rest is enough? No set amount works best for everyone, but if your taper doesn't span at least 1 week following the demands of double-century training, it probably isn't sufficient.

So what do you do? Easy riding? No riding? As discussed in chapter 8, the key is to reduce distance considerably but retain some intensity. There should be a small amount of hard riding, a moderate amount of very easy riding, and a large amount of rest—all woven together by a tremendous amount of self-discipline. If you feel guilty about how little training you're doing, it's likely that you're doing enough. Here's an appropriate schedule beginning the weekend before the event.

Saturday: Last long ride. If you feel tired in the second half, cut it short. Do not let yourself become physically or mentally drained.

Sunday: Ride 30 to 50 miles, staying below 70 percent of your maximum heart rate. Keep your speed at least 2 miles per hour slower than your normal long ride pace.

Monday: Day off, or ride easy for 30 to 45 minutes.

Tuesday: Ride easy for 30 minutes to warm up, then do three or four efforts of 1 minute each to push your heart rate to about 95 percent of maximum. Ride easy for 15 minutes to cool down.

Wednesday: Ride easy for 30 minutes to warm up, then do a 10-minute effort at about 85 percent of maximum heart rate. Ride easy for 15 minutes to cool down.

Thursday: Day off. Use normal riding time to service your bike and make other preparations for the event.

Friday: Ride easy for 30 minutes. Throw in a couple of 30-second sprints to wake up your body and open your lungs. Then finish your preparations, eat a high-carbohydrate dinner, and relax with a book or movie. Stay off your feet as much as possible. Go to bed at your normal time.

Saturday: You're ready. Have a great ride!

Diet During a Double

The nutritional wisdom that applies to any long ride applies to double centuries, too. You just have to multiply it for the distance. However, this is one of those things that's easier said than done. It takes discipline to continue eating and drinking during a ride that lasts an entire day. There may come a point where you grow weary of the routine. You might actually lose your appetite despite burning so many calories. You could develop heartburn or indigestion. The thought of one more bite of that Putty Bar could make you gag. We've been there. That's why we say that eating can be the hardest thing to do right in ultra events.

Fortunately, in an organized double century you'll probably never be more than 35 miles from the next rest stop. The opportunity to get off the bike and pick from a variety of foods makes it easier to keep enough coal on your fire. Even if you find it difficult to eat much while on the bike in the second half of the event, rest stop repasts can save the day, providing enough fuel to get from stop to stop. Don't stuff yourself, of course, and keep using sports drinks to replenish fluids as well as calories.

If you get low on food—and especially fluid—but the next rest stop is still miles away, don't be reluctant to pull into a convenience store. Yes, this will cost you some time. But not as much as bonking and dragging through the rest of the day. Unless you really need a rest, quickly buy the items you want, fill your bottles, then eat while you're rolling again.

Because it's difficult to chew and digest enough food to keep pace with the 8,000 to 10,000 calories typically burned during a double century, competitive ultra cyclists have found that so-called liquid meals are the answer. These are the products such as Ensure, Boost, GatorPro, Suscatal, Met-Rx, and Endurox R4 that can be found in supermarkets or health or sports stores. A more specialized concoction used by some serious ultra riders goes by the name of Spizerinctum (Spiz, for short). These products are quick and easy to digest, and typically supply 300 to 400 calories per 8 ounces. They contain protein, fat, and various nutrients as well as carbohydrate. In addition, they usually taste good, like a chocolate, vanilla, or strawberry milkshake.

Perfect? Not quite. You need a way to get at least one serving per hour, and if the liquid isn't cold, you may find it distasteful. This means you'll need a support person who meets you at rest stops or other locations with chilled bottles of the product. This is doable, but it adds another critical element to the ride. Consider the fix you'll be in if the person fails to show up at your next scheduled spot for refueling.

Another problem can be lack of stomach satisfaction. After hours of nothing but fluids, you start craving something to eat. Your stomach feels uncomfortably hollow. You have to be careful, because eating at this point could create more problems than it solves. The trick is to eat just a little of something light. Rob Kish, the three-time RAAM winner, munches a few saltines or celery sticks to mollify a gnawing stomach. He's not eating them for nutrition, just satiety. In addition, Rob keeps popping sticks of gum to satisfy the urge to chew something.

Using a liquid meal doesn't cancel the need for water and a sports drink to supply energy and prevent dehydration. In general, the ratio should be about 24 ounces of sports drink for every 8 ounces of a liquid meal. Use sips of water to rinse your taste buds between swigs of the other two products.

Protein and Fat

Carbohydrate is the key fuel for energizing your muscles and nervous system, but protein and fat also are important energy sources. Protein can contribute as much as 10 percent of the energy consumed during an ultra ride. Interestingly, it also seems to have a role in reducing mental or "central" fatigue. This results from impaired function of the central nervous system. It doesn't affect your muscles directly, but it still reduces your capacity to perform during the later miles of a long ride.

Eric Newsholme, Ph.D., of Oxford University uncovered a correlation between the level of the amino acid tryptophan in the brain and the level of mental fatigue. When tryptophan enters the brain, it can depress the central nervous system, causing sleepiness. Usually, there are sufficient amounts of the branched-chain amino acids (leucine, isolucine, valine) in the blood to regulate tryptophan. But in one study, supplements of these protein-based substances improved performance in marathon runners. Research is ongoing, but for mental as well as physical energy, protein seems to be valuable.

Likewise, fat becomes important during long hours on the bike. It supplies energy at the rate of nine calories per gram, which is more than twice what you get from protein or carbohydrate. Plus, it provides a feeling of satiety, or, in plain language, it sticks to your ribs. Many ultra riders describe this as a "slow burn." As former *Bicycling* editor Geoff Drake puts it, fat feels like a log on the fire, while eating carbo is more like the dietary equivalent of tossing tissues into a furnace.

You can get fat and protein in commercial energy foods and drinks. All liquid meals have some, and you'll find various amounts in the different brands of bars. Those that have a 40-30-30 ratio of carbo-protein-fat seem to work well for endurance cycling, while bars that have a much higher percentage of carbo are more appropriate for shorter, faster events.

You also can get protein and fat in common fare such as sandwiches made with meat, peanut butter, or cream cheese. These can really hit the spot in certain circumstances.

Tips and Tactics

Ride a double century using the same smart techniques and strategies that help you succeed in shorter events. Here are a few additional tips that will help you conquer greater distances.

Know the course. By checking the profile ahead of time, you can

(continued on page 152)

Training for a Fast Double

How fast can you ride 200 miles?

In this chapter, coach John Hughes describes his training approach for a double century. Now let's look at his advice for riding a *fast* 200 miles, when your goal becomes not just to complete the distance but to get a personal record for it.

1. Maximize the time you spend riding at the threshold of anaerobic metabolism. This is dangerous territory, however. You must be careful not to cross the line, or you'll have to recover and that will slow you down. Going anaerobic also will consume glycogen at a rapid rate. On the other hand, don't drop into an easy, fat-burning aerobic pace. You need to dwell in a fairly narrow zone of higher intensity. And because this effort is primarily fueled by glycogen, you need to eat lots of carbohydrate during the event.

2. Maximize the power you can sustain without going anaerobic. How? With training that's based on your lactate threshold (LT)—the point at which your body switches from primarily aerobic metabolism to primarily anaerobic metabolism, which produces lactic acid. It's no mystery when the switch occurs, especially to your heaving lungs and burning legs. The way to get a good estimate of your threshold heart rate is to ride a 30-minute time trial while wearing your HRM. Go as hard as you can, and note your average heart rate (or the highest heart rate you were able to sustain if your HRM doesn't average it for you). That's your heart rate at LT.

Note: If you do this in a competitive time trial with your juices really flowing, rather than in a training time trial, your average heart rate will be about five percent above your LT.

When you know your LT heart rate, you can pay attention to which of these energy systems you're using during training rides:

- *Fat-burning*—heart rate less than 75 percent of your LT. You'll be at this level during recovery rides and the easy portions of longer rides.

- *Aerobic*—heart rate between 75 and 90 percent of your LT. To ride a fast double century or other all-day event, you should keep your pulse in this zone. To do your best time, keep it in the upper part of this zone.

- **Anaerobic**—heart rate more than 95 percent of your LT. This training helps you raise your threshold. At a slightly lower 91 to 94 percent, however, you are in kind of a no-man's-land. You're starting to switch from aerobic to anaerobic metabolism, but not riding hard enough to get the benefits of anaerobic training. Slow down or speed up, depending on your goal for the ride.

Even though you will ride the double century primarily in the aerobic zone, you need to train in all three zones. Riding in your fat-burning zone increases mitochondria—where enzymes metabolize fat—and the blood supply to your muscles. Riding anaerobically raises your LT so you can go faster before going anaerobic.

Progressive Speed Workouts

Let's look at three distinct workouts that develop sustainable power and speed for an all-day ride. All are stressful. The majority of your training time each week will still be in the fat-burning and lower aerobic zones. Mix in any two of the following workouts on 2 days per week. Do this training in terrain that's similar to what you'll find in the event.

Warning: Don't try any of these workouts until you have at least 3 months of solid training for the season. Cyclists who have been riding for less than 3 years should add just one of these workouts per week.

- Threshold workouts at 85 to 90 percent of your LT heart rate. This training increases your muscle endurance, and your ability to sustain a strong pace for hours. Early in the season, start with two or three intervals of 10 to 20 minutes apiece in this zone, with full recovery between each one. Gradually increase the number and duration of the intervals. Later in the season, go for rides of 2 to 3 hours in this zone, building up to a century or more.

- Subanaerobic workouts at 95 to 100 percent of your LT heart rate. These workouts will raise your LT so that you can ride faster before going anaerobic. For example, if you currently can sustain 150 beats per minute for 30 minutes, after several months of this training, your LT could increase to 155 or 160 bpm. Don't begin this harder work until

(continued)

Training for a Fast Double (cont.)

you've done threshold training for at least 1 month. Begin with two intervals of 8 to 10 minutes, with full recovery between them. Gradually increase the number and duration of the intervals. Time trials are excellent for subanaerobic training.

- Superanaerobic workouts at more than 100 percent of your LT heart rate. After several months of subanaerobic training, you'll stop improving. The way to create more overload and jump-start your progress is with intervals that push you as high as 105 percent of your LT. These intervals are typically just 3 to 5 minutes long. They're done in sets of three or more *without* full recovery. Generally, the rest interval is half of the work interval—for example, 4 minutes hard with 2 minutes recovery.

These three workouts help you prepare for a fast double in two ways. The threshold training increases your specific muscle endurance—the power that you can sustain for hours. The sub- and superanaerobic training increase your lactate threshold so that you can produce more power without going anaerobic.

Your training should culminate with event-pace workouts. If your goal is to ride a 12-hour double century, then practice by riding at the required pace (about 17 miles per hour) throughout your long training rides. Learn to sustain the speed you need without ever going much slower or faster.

On double day, have self-control. If your excitement causes you to blow past your lactate threshold on the first big climb, you'll pay for it during the rest of the ride. Strive to stay below 90 percent of your LT heart rate as much as possible—but not much below. When you follow this specialized training with a steady, strong, smart effort in the event, you'll get your personal record.

avoid the struggles that result from insufficient gearing. The best way to make sure all bases are covered is to have a triple crankset.

Start early. Most events allow you to depart at any time after the official start. Don't wait to get going. The earlier you begin, the less time (if any) will be spent riding in the dark.

Have a good light. It may still be dark when you set out, or you may not finish till after sundown. Make sure your headlight is bright, reliable, and powered by fresh batteries. It's a drag to ride more slowly than your capability simply because you can't see the road very well. Don't forget your taillight, required by law and common sense.

Start cautiously. If it's a predawn start, be careful around other riders. Some may not be accustomed to riding in the dark. Their perception of speed and distance might be off. Settle into your best pace and let the rabbits go. You'll catch most of them later. A good way to ensure a safe and sane start is to stay off the large chainring for the first half hour, no matter what.

Pace yourself. Make it a goal never to ride so hard that you couldn't carry on a conversation. This goes for climbing, too. Join only those pacelines that let you remain at 70 percent or less of your maximum heart rate. A good one can help pull you through difficult times—and you're bound to have some, especially in the last few hours.

Upsize your seatpack. A larger or expandable underseat pack gives you room to store extra energy bars, gels, and even a supply of powder for mixing your favorite drink. Be sure to tuck in some money. It's wise to pack a lightweight rain jacket, too. Lots can happen to the weather during an all-day ride, particularly during the summer thunderstorm season.

Keep moving. We keep emphasizing this because we see so many riders mess up. By limiting stops to 10 minutes or less, your legs won't turn to concrete. So fill your bottles, fill your pockets, visit the facilities, stretch a bit, and roll off. Eat while riding instead of standing around. By going through rest stops quickly, you could save 30 minutes or more—enough to get to the finish before sundown.

10

Longest Rides:
200 Miles . . . and Beyond

Ten years ago, when Ed Pavelka was getting hooked on endurance cycling and riding events longer than he'd ever tried, each new distance was a mix of delicious anticipation and nervous trepidation. His goal was to ride the centennial edition of Paris-Brest-Paris, the classic 1200-kilometer (744-mile) randonnée that attracts cyclists from around the world. To earn the right, he had to complete the standard series of four brevets, plus a special 1000-kilometer (620-mile) brevet to meet the 1-year qualification rules that were in effect at that time. This for a guy whose longest ride was 127 miles—an accidental personal record when he missed a turn during a century.

The first brevet, 200 kilometers or 124 miles, was barely within Ed's confidence zone. Then began a long journey through uncharted territory. The 300-kilometer (186-mile) brevet kept him on the bike nearly 4 hours longer than he'd ever ridden. The experience taught him a lot, but even more significant was learning one of the truisms of endurance cycling from a fellow rider—a PBP veteran with whom Ed rode a few of those miles. As the 300-kilometer was finally nearing an end and Ed was feeling all of the effects of 12 hours on the bike, his thoughts turned to 3 weeks hence and the 400-kilometer (248-mile) brevet. Gulp! Ride this far, and then do 62 more miles? "How is it possible?" Ed asked the brevet vet.

"Don't worry," the rider replied. "After 200 miles, nothing changes."

You Have What It Takes

Well, that's a slight exaggeration, but it's essentially true. After around 10 to 12 hours of riding, you seem to be in equilibrium. Then, if you keep eating, drinking, stretching, and using all the other tips we've given to maintain energy and comfort, very little does change as the miles go on and on. Otherwise, how would it be possible to ride events that take you far beyond a double century? If fatigue were to ascend in a straight line, and energy were to decline at a similar rate, you'd reach the point where you couldn't take another pedal stroke. Do things right, however, and you can ride practically forever. A great example is Scott Dickson, who has finished PBP six times by riding the entire 1200 kilometers straight through. No sleep, and no more than 5 minutes off the bike at any stop during 44 hours.

No sleep? Ah, yes—here's the key difference in events that take you beyond 18 hours or so. It's what does change. Depending on your pace, riding while you're sleepy is something you may need to deal with in a 400-kilometer brevet, and it certainly comes into play in the 600-kilometer one (372 miles) if you try to ride it straight through. Then there are the 24-hour events that are growing in popularity both on road and off. For most riders, anything beyond triple-century distance introduces sleep deprivation. This is also the case in multiday events such as PBP and Boston-Montreal-Boston, where sleep breaks are usually short and insufficient because of the need to reach the next checkpoint on time. For this reason, we're dedicating this chapter to coping with sleep deprivation and riding at night.

As for most of the other advice you need to ride beyond double-century distance, you already know the essentials from chapter 9. The same training, nutrition, and techniques that help you cover 200 miles in a day are exactly what you need to go beyond. Sure, there are certain tips, tricks, and training adjustments that will help you specialize in ultramarathon events from 24-hour races all the way to the Race Across America. If you decide to move up to this elite level, it's essential to join the UltraMarathon Cycling Association and, especially if PBP or BMB is a goal, Randonneurs USA (www.rusa.org). The UMCA is the best how-to source for the wide range of ultra events.

Be assured that once you are training for and riding double centuries, you have what it takes to go beyond—even *far* beyond. The main limiting factor will be riding with insufficient sleep, so let's look into that now.

Sleep Deprivation

When riding centuries and double centuries, you'll probably never pass the point where you should be sleeping. Now, consider riding a 24-hour race or being competitive in longer events, such as the Furnace Creek 508, Bicycle Across Missouri, Firecracker 500, Quadzilla, or RAAM qualifiers. These keep riders on their bikes for more than 30 consecutive hours. In addition, sleep deprivation becomes a key issue (if not *the* key issue) for riders in the ultimate randonnées, PBP and BMB.

And then there is RAAM itself. To be competitive, you need to ride 3000 miles in less than 9 days on 3 or fewer hours of sleep in each 24. This is why the event has been called a contest of sleep deprivation by some critics who, it must be admitted, have a point. Seana Hogan, the five-time women's winner, confesses, "I'm most likely to hit the doldrums in RAAM between 2:00 and 4:00 A.M., when my body's fighting sleep. I allow myself about 2½ hours a night. This seems to be enough to prevent the serious hallucination problems some other riders have."

Writing in *Ultra Cycling,* John Hughes and Warren McNaughton discussed sleep deprivation from personal experience and from what they've learned by talking with fellow ultra-endurance riders. Here are their key findings.

- Lack of sleep isn't going to stop you in relatively short events. A cyclist can still perform quite well for 2 days despite little or no sleep. It seems impossible to start an event at 5:00 A.M., ride all day and through the night, and then keep going to an afternoon finish. But 600-kilometer brevet riders do it every season, on training that never exposes them to sleep loss.

- Don't start an event with a sleep debt. During the week, go to bed earlier than usual to become well rested. You want as much sleep as possible on the eve of an event, but even sound sleep often will be cut very short by an early start time. Many long brevets, for example, begin at 4:00 or 5:00 A.M. If you fall asleep by 11:00, you're still not going to get more than half of your normal amount. This won't matter as much if you've banked some Zzzs earlier in the week.

- Improve your ability to sleep the night before the event. It's not unusual to have a hard time nodding off on the eve of a big ride. If this happens, you've just added another sleepless night to the one you'll be riding through. Calm down by making your final preparations as early in the day as you can. Remove anxiety by planning well, so the morning of the ride will be simple and efficient. After you climb into bed, think about the excellent training you've done to reach this point. Feel confident, relax, and let sleep come.

- Take your pillow and plugs. If you're staying in a motel or other unfamiliar place, having your favorite pillow will help the bed seem more like your own. Because there may be unaccustomed sounds, earplugs can keep you from being disturbed. The danger is that you won't hear your alarm, so request a wake-up call, too, and ask another rider to knock on your door after he's up, just in case. A less deafening alternative to plugs is one of those devices that emits the soothing sound of rain, surf, a gurgling brook, or the hum of white noise.

- Take your medicine. Some riders use melatonin for its ability to induce sleep. Although this isn't a knockout drug like traditional sleeping aids, it may still leave you feeling a bit groggy after a short night. Don't risk it for an event until you're sure of its effect on you. Other natural relaxers include kava, chamomile, peppermint, and vitamin B complex. Also effective is a couple of aspirin, ibuprofen, or acetaminophen. These help relax you by alleviating niggling aches and pains. You may nod off sooner and sleep more soundly.

- Don't let minimal sleep worry you. It's the same for everyone, so accept it and turn your attention to the ride.

Night-Riding Strategies

Here are seven effective tactics to use during an overnight ride.

Make time for sleep by making time on the bike. In the long brevets, it's possible to get several hours of sleep and not miss the time limit at checkpoints. To do this, you need to ride at a relatively fast pace to put time in the bank. Improve your speed through interval training. Also, get good at navigating with maps and cue sheets so that you don't waste time being lost. Always move through checkpoints quickly.

Know how insufficient sleep affects your performance. There's no substitute for experience when it comes to understanding how your mind and body cope with sleep deprivation. Your fatigue will increase and your mental sharpness will decrease. How much, and how this affects your pace, bike control, and outlook, is different for everyone.

At Paris-Brest-Paris '99, Ed Pavelka learned something about sleep deprivation by being awake (sort of) for 88 out of 94 hours.

Once you understand your personal reaction, the changes should have a less traumatic impact.

Make sleep breaks a multiple of your sleep cycle. The normal human sleep cycle is about 90 minutes. Therefore, plan sleep breaks to last for 1½, 3, or 4½ hours. Studies have found that people feel more rested if they wake at the end of a sleep cycle rather than in the midst of one.

Here's a specific example. During his record-setting RAAM, Pete Penseyres took his first sleep break 744 miles into the race, at 4:00 A.M. His second through sixth sleep breaks were also taken just before dawn, with the general plan being to sleep for 90 minutes. But this was modified if Pete was in REM sleep. His crew wouldn't wake him if they could see rapid eye movements behind his closed lids, because REM sleep is the most restful. So, Pete's actual off-bike time ranged from 1:38 to 2:14. He went quickly from the end of sleep cycles to rolling down the highway, a remarkable feat of self-discipline.

Wake up at dawn. Like Pete did, plan sleep breaks so you are up and riding again at the crack of dawn. As opposed to starting out in the dark, this can trick you into thinking that you've had a regular night's sleep. It's a psychological lift to ride in daylight, too.

Sleep only in the dark. Keep moving during daylight, then take your sleep break when it will reduce the amount of night riding.

Ride farther into the lane. Take advantage of the minimal late-night traffic and the fact that headlights give you plenty of warning when a vehicle is coming up from behind. By riding farther from the road's edge, you'll miss more potholes, cracks, and debris. A moment of sleepy inattention will be less likely to drop your wheels off the edge.

Keep moving. Your pace will always be slower at night, so don't lose even more time by stopping more often than absolutely necessary.

Techniques for Staying Awake

When all is said and done, most ultra cyclists enjoy night riding. There's a sense of calm and quiet that pervades the midnight hours. Traffic fades into long gaps between passing cars. Towns and villages are like ghost towns as you silently glide through. The farm dogs are asleep. You stop for a moment to check your cue sheet or water a bush and are struck by the unique sounds of night. An owl hoots, a fox scampers. Overhead, a sky full of stars glimmers in a way you rarely notice.

Paris-Brest-Paris is scheduled to occur under the full moon of every fourth August. After riding PBP twice, it's the night visions that make the event most memorable to Ed Pavelka. In fact, the enjoyment of riding through the veil of white satin is what prompted him to forgo sleep on the second night in 1999 and continue on to Paris. Instead of blackness all around, there were views of farm fields and distant hills silhouetted by the moon's glow. Riders were switching off headlights on open stretches to save their batteries for times when artificial illumination was actually needed. They chatted to waylay drowsiness so that they could keep riding in the ideal conditions.

To enjoy nights like this and make the most of others that may not be so perfect for cycling, use these stay-awake tips we've gathered from personal experience and endurance coaches such as John Hughes.

Set your watch's countdown timer to beep every 15 minutes as a reminder to eat and drink. This activity keeps you awake, and the calories help your blood sugar stay stable. This is thought to be the key to preventing or at least minimizing hallucinations. The beep also might catch you just as you nod off, preventing an excursion into a roadside ditch.

Stay warm enough so that your core temperature doesn't drop. Remember what happens to people who freeze to death. First, they lie down because they're feeling so sleepy. Pack your arm and leg warmers even in midsummer to ward off the chill of the wee hours.

Stand frequently. Stimulate yourself by pedaling out of the saddle for a few seconds even if the terrain doesn't require it.

Keep your head up. Use the bar tops so you can sit higher, which helps avoid nodding droops. Be wary of using aero bars when you're sleepy. The position is too comfortable, and your hands are too far

(continued on page 162)

Off-Road Ultras

Historically, endurance cycling has meant road cycling. That's why this book has so many references and examples from the traditional long-distance road events. But during the 1990s, a new form of ultra cycling began swelling in popularity—24-hour races held on the tough trails of scenic places such as Moab, Utah, and Donner Pass, California, plus the place that launched the phenomenon: Canaan, West Virginia. Here, Ed Burke describes the attractions and distractions he found in one of these wild events.

"The 24 Hours of Moab isn't about winning, at least for us mere mortals. It's about adaptation, riding hard, and survival.

"At high noon, you run to your bike in a Le Mans–style start. It took me 7 minutes to churn through the cloud of choking red dust kicked up by hundreds of feet. Then I began the first 16-mile-long loop. I was competing with two dozen cyclists in the solo division, while there were about 1,500 other cyclists making up the 350 teams in the relay division.

"Team riders switched off every lap and made me feel really slow as they sprinted by. In addition to the nerve-wracking experience of negotiating tricky drop-offs and grinding, technical climbs, it was a little scary riding with cyclists from teams with names such as One Short of a Six Pack and Poor White Crash.

"At the end of the first lap, I returned to the valley floor and the Woodstocklike camp city. A massive sound system belted out appropriate music, including the Ramones ('Twenty-twenty-twenty hours to go, I wanna be sedated'). Me, too. I'd crashed, and got up with my shoulder and hip looking like someone had plastered them with ground-up raspberries. After a quick bite to eat and a check with my wife, Kathleen, to make sure our health insurance was paid, I rode several more laps under a cloudless sky until nightfall.

"Somewhere between darkness and dawn, the whole game changes. I arrived at the rational decision to ride only one lap after sundown when I discovered that practicing in a dark city park doesn't quite make you ready for Moab's slickrock at midnight. So I retreated to camp until day 2 dawned and I returned to the battlefield for one more lap.

"In the minutes before the finish at noon on Sunday, a few team riders raced into the control tent, trying to beat the deadline for one last exchange. I suspected that these were the same cyclists who had sprinted by me on the first few laps—type A personalities who still didn't realize that Moab is about survival, not about who covers the most laps. Then I noticed a group of riders like myself. One was being admonished by his teammates to make sure the race clock hit noon, thus saving

Twenty-four-hour off-road events are attracting thousands of team relay riders as well as a few brave solo cyclists.

them from doing another lap in the hot desert sun. Now that's real teamwork!

"After shaking the red sand from my shoes and the ordeal from my system, I began to reflect happily on the 24 Hours of Moab. I overlooked the knotted muscles in my shoulder and the raspberry on my hip. I quit thinking about carrying my bike down Nose Dive Hill and up the matching ascent, known as Up-Chuck. Visions of homely sagebrush retreated, as did the sinking feeling of my rear wheel spinning out yet again on the sandy rock of a steep climb, making me get off and push my bike as if it were an overloaded shopping cart. I forgot about walking the rutted and rocky downhill at the 10-mile mark, where several riders crashed every lap and looked eerily like roadkill.

"Instead, I remembered the uncountable stars that illuminated the perfect night sky, and the shouts of encouragement from support people each time we rode through the camping area. I recalled the salmon-colored sunset and the fun of riding a roller-coaster section of banked turns through slickrock formations. To me, there is something very special, even mystical, about being part of an off-road endurance event like Moab. I savored the sheer joy of reaching the finish, feeling that I had experienced one of the best 24-hour periods of my life."

from the brake levers. This creates a dangerous situation when combined with your slower reaction time.

Watch your surroundings. Make a game out of how much you can see around you at night instead of focusing entirely on your lighted patch in front. Using your eyes and brain like this helps prevent a hypnotic stare.

Chew gum. It's a simple trick that works for driving, and it can help when cycling, too—as long as it doesn't keep you from eating frequently enough. It's theorized that by using the jaw muscles, chewing encourages bloodflow to the head, which perks up the brain.

Ride with someone. The conversation will help each of you stay more alert. Ride side by side instead of drafting late at night, when a moment of sleepy inattention can cause wheel contact and a crash. If riding two abreast isn't possible, keep several yards between the bikes.

Beware of descents. A long climb may make you wide awake, but as soon as the exertion stops and coasting starts, you can nod off in a hurry. It helps to stay busy by turning the pedals and alternately applying the front and rear brakes in short bursts. Keep your speed down, to compensate for your slower reaction time. Keep your weight back, for better control when hitting unexpected bumps. Never outrun your headlight.

Understand your pattern. You can go from alert to sleepy to alert again very quickly. Don't automatically give up and stop for a snooze when the sandman won't leave you alone. If your goal is to ride through the night, use the techniques we've just described to get through the inevitable sleepy patches.

Consider using caffeine. This natural stimulant can help you perform better in rides when sleep deprivation is an issue. Or it can make you perform much worse, with jitters, an upset stomach, or dehydration (because caffeine is a diuretic). Many ultra riders do use caffeine successfully and benefit from its two main attributes: central nervous system stimulation that produces alertness and the sensation of energy, and the release of free fatty acids into the bloodstream, where they can be used for endurance fuel. The only way to know if you'll get more benefits than drawbacks is to give caffeine a try. You can take it in beverages (coffee, tea, or caffeinated soft drinks) or in pill form (Vivarin and similar over-the-counter products). Remember, caffeine's effects are reduced if you're a regular daily user, which is why some cyclists abstain for several weeks before a big event. For more information, see chapter 6.

Don't let your confidence sink
with the sun. Night riding is
safe and fun once your
nocturnal knowledge
is up to speed.

Equipment and Safety

Night riding is risky for obvious reasons. Even though there is much less traffic as the hour grows later, the drivers who are on the road won't be expecting a slow-moving cyclist. Attract their attention by becoming a two-wheeled Christmas tree. You simply can't have too many lights, reflectors, and pieces of reflective tape on your body and bike. Go way beyond state law and good taste. You want drivers to see you far in the distance, become alert as they wonder what the heck that dazzling thing is, then slow down in amazement and pass with a wide margin. The crowning touch is shorts, tights, vests, jackets, and bike bags made with Illuminite fabric. It looks normal until hit by headlights. Then it glows like it's plugged in.

In addition, here are six light-related tips.

Use a separate, independently powered taillight so your headlight battery lasts longer. A taillight is required by law in all states. Many events insist on a steady beam because a flashing light can be an aggravating distraction to riders behind.

Aim your headlight to match your speed. By keeping your handlebar-mounted headlight just loose enough, you can rotate it forward or back to concentrate the beam at the ideal distance.

Especially for off-road events, use a helmet-mounted headlight

as well as one on the handlebar. The helmet light lets you see where you turn your head to look, a big benefit on curvy trails.

Don't forget your high beam is on. With a dual-beam headlight, battery life is dramatically shortened when using the high beam. Save it for special occasions, such as descents, when you need more light for safety—and then remember to switch it off as soon as your speed decreases.

Carry spare batteries and bulbs. Some events require you to display these before you can start. Depending on the bulb-changing procedure for your system, it may be better to pack a small emergency headlight that fastens quickly to the handlebar.

Pack a flashlight for reading the cue sheet, looking in bags, or making repairs. If it's small enough, you can hold it between your teeth so you can use both hands.

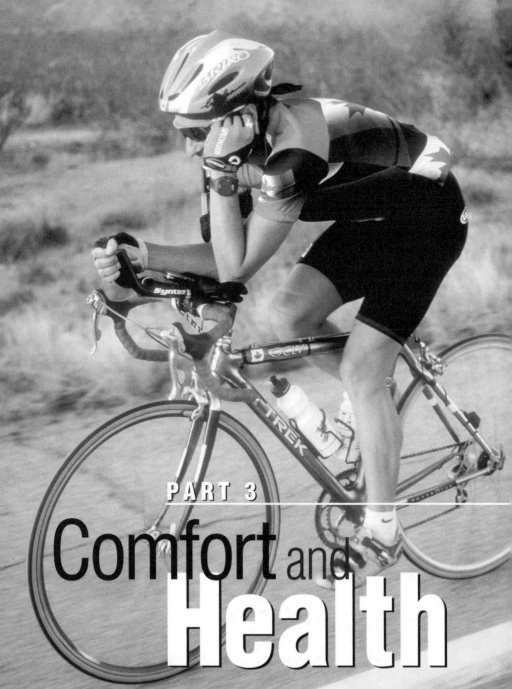

PART 3

Comfort and Health

⑪

Danger Zones

When making a list of things that can go wrong at the places a cyclist touches the bicycle—hands, feet, and seat—there's no better source than the Race Across America. When you ride for 20 hours per day for 8 to 10 days in a row, these points of contact become points of hurt, pain, and agony. The riders who solve these problems (or at least reduce them) are the ones who have the best chance to reach the finish.

The toll can be devastating. In the very first transcontinental race, Olympic cyclist John Howard suffered hand numbness that not only made holding the handlebar difficult, but also left his fingers weak and tingling for months. Feet can swell and ache so badly that riders are forced to cut away the toes of their shoes in order to get relief. Invariably, the first thing RAAM riders do at the finish is take those blasted things off their feet.

But it's the seat that plagues more cyclists than anything. RAAM riders have tried just about every type of design and padding imaginable to endure their long hours of saddle time. One of the greatest sufferers has been Muffy Ritz, the two-time women's runner-up. In one race, the pain got so bad that she had to lash a bed pillow to her seat in order to continue. Here was a superbly fit cyclist reduced to a crawl because of what's descriptively known as "the trauma of the saddle."

You don't have to be a RAAM rider, however, to experience a debilitating point-of-contact problem. Whether your event lasts for 8 days or 8 hours, burning feet or a tender crotch can put a real damper on your performance—or even your ability to reach the finish. It's probably safe to say that no long ride is ever completed without some point-of-contact discomfort. The trick is to minimize it through a combination of clothing, equipment, riding position, and technique. When you succeed, more than your comfort will increase. You'll see improvements in your speed and endurance, too.

Hands

Hands that aren't covered or cushioned, or that must bear too much weight, can fall victim to tingling, numbness, raw skin, or blisters. Cushioning is provided by gloves and handlebar tape or grips, while proper weight distribution results from having a good riding position. Refer to chapter 3 to make sure your setup is correct. Although riders have been known to tilt the nose of the seat up from its ideal horizontal position in order to force themselves to sit back and take weight off the bar, this is likely to turn hand discomfort into crotch discomfort.

Start by using a firm but relaxed grip. You don't want white knuckles, but you also don't want your hands to bounce off the bar when you hit an unexpected bump. Your wrists, elbows, and shoulders should be loose enough to absorb shock and avoid fatigue caused by tense muscles. Just as important, change your hand position frequently. This relieves grip pressure, and makes sure your upper body doesn't stay locked in one posture. A road bike's drop bar provides several hand positions. Here's how to use the three main ones.

DROP BAR POSITIONS

Hands on tops. To sit upright, place your hands on the flat portion of the bar (known as the tops) that passes through the stem. This is a good position for casual riding on the flats or for seated climbing. Remember to keep your elbows bent and loose. Move one hand next to the stem when taking the other one off the bar for any reason. This lessens the risk of inadvertent swerving. Also, you'll be safer if you wrap your thumbs under the bar rather than rest them on top. Otherwise, your hands could slip off on a bump.

Hands on levers. This position helps you move more weight from the seat to the bar. It puts your hands farther apart for better steering leverage, and gives you immediate access to the brakes. Because you're also fairly upright, this is a good position for pack riding (it helps you see ahead) and descending (if you want your chest to catch air to temper your speed). It's ideal for climbing, too, because it opens your chest for easy breathing. Standing is a simple matter of pivoting forward. As you do so, wrap your fingers around the levers so you can pull against your pedal strokes. As the right leg pushes down, the right hand relaxes. Same for the left. This establishes a swaying rhythm that helps you use body weight to power the pedals.

Hands in hooks. Leverage and aerodynamics are best when you have your hands in the curved portion of the bar. Keep your wrists

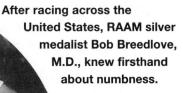

**After racing across the
United States, RAAM silver
medalist Bob Breedlove,
M.D., knew firsthand
about numbness.**

straight, which
produces a deep
bend in the elbows
and maximum pull on
the bar. This position
lowers your upper body and
helps you drive the pedals—exactly what you want for sprinting, time
trialing, or boring through a headwind. In general, there's not much
advantage in moving your hands farther back onto the drops. It
just means that you'll have to move them forward again to brake or
shift. However, this can be a relaxing position on a long, flat stretch of
open road.

Drop handlebars come in various sizes from end to end (width).
You'll also find variations in the distance between the tops to the
drops (depth) and from the tops to the hooks (length). When
choosing a bar, first make sure its width matches the width of your
shoulders, measured from their bony ends. Bar widths commonly
range from 38 to 44 centimeters. If in doubt, go to the next larger
size. Next, consider the depth, which determines how well your
hands fit into the hooks. You'll find a variety of anatomic shapes that
improve hand support and put your wrists in a relaxed, neutral position. Finally, think about how the length affects your reach to the
levers. If your stem is a bit too short, for example, a bar with more
distance from the tops to the front of the hooks can effectively
lengthen your reach. Some touring cyclists prefer a randonneur bar,
which has tops that slope slightly upward from the stem. This makes
their riding position a bit higher. Fans of this bar also say that it puts
their wrists at a more comfortable angle.

MOUNTAIN BIKE BARS

These, too, come in a range of widths, usually from 21 to 24 inches. A wider bar is better for slow-speed control. A narrower one makes you a bit more aerodynamic, quickens steering response, and helps you squeeze between trees when riding tight singletrack. A wide bar can easily be narrowed with a hacksaw or pipe cutter, but don't overdo it. Before performing this surgery, move the levers inward and take a test ride to check how the bike responds. You can always cut off more bar, but you can't add any if you cut off too much.

Another variable is a bar's upward bend. For years, all mountain bike bars were flat, but now riser bars are stock equipment on many new bikes, and they can be added to any older model. These bars bend upward a couple of inches or so. This lets you ride a slightly smaller frame or have a lower stem. Or, it raises your handlebar for less lower-back stress without the need to switch to a taller stem. Compared with flat bars, wide risers may also flex more, which helps absorb shock and reduce vibration, improving hand and upper-body comfort.

To double the handholds on a mountain bike, install bar-ends and use them frequently. (Check with a shop first, because they shouldn't be used with some ultralight or nonmetal bars.) These forward extensions give you a longer, lower position that helps aerodynamics and, even more important, improves comfort during a long ride. While you're at it, check the position of your brake levers. They should be positioned to give you a straight wrist when you grasp them from the attack position, with your weight back and your butt just off the seat. This is the posture you're in when descending and using the brakes a lot.

AERO BARS

For safety reasons, aero bars were banned from Paris-Brest-Paris beginning in 1995. Too many riders were using them in the big packs, a no-no because they don't allow quick braking or steering. But what was good for the overall safety of the peloton was bad for the comfort of the individual cyclists. On a long ride, aero bars let you relax your upper body and keep numbing pressure off your hands. They also raise your average speed, even at a subsonic randonnée pace. You don't need to be going 25 miles per hour in a time trial to get a benefit.

In most events, aero bars are still permitted. Consider adding them, too, for tours and long training rides. You'll find several models when you go shopping. They may come in set lengths and widths, or allow a range of adjustment. For a comfortable, stable, long-distance position,

RAAM champion Gerry Tatrai shows fine form in an aero position usually seen only among short-distance time trialists.

the forearm rests should be about 8 inches apart (measured from the center of one cup to the center of the other). Of course, narrower is faster, because it reduces your frontal area. If your main goal is rapid centuries, you may want to move the rests closer by as much as 4 inches.

The length should be such that you can grip the end of the aero bar when the rests are 2 or 3 inches in front of your elbows. Make this happen with the aero bar adjustment, not by moving your saddle fore or aft and disrupting your proper riding position. You have it right when your upper arms are approximately vertical. If they're angled too far forward (a common mistake), there will be more stress on your shoulders than necessary. Another variable is the aero bar's angle to the horizontal. Wind tunnel tests show that a 30-degree upward slant produces the most speed, but some riders may never find this comfortable for long distances. Fifteen degrees is a good compromise, and may still be faster than horizontal.

For regular cycling, don't change your stem height. You want your bar tops and drops to be in their normal, comfortable position for all non-aero riding. But for special events when you want more speed, lower is better. Drop the stem a quarter-inch at a time, interspersed with test rides to check control, comfort, and power output. Keep lowering it until your back is horizontal. Not every rider can achieve this position, so don't force it. On the other hand, if you can adapt to a very low position, as double RAAM winner Gerry Tatrai has, the aero benefits are significant. Gerry has managed to find coast-to-coast comfort (and lots of speed) in a horizontal posture usually seen only among 4000-meter pursuiters on the velodrome.

GLOVES

Ed Pavelka recalls writing an article about cycling equipment for a general-interest magazine. The editor, who didn't know a spoke from a seatpost, removed the section on traditional half-finger gloves, dismissing them as a silly, unnecessary affectation. Ed managed to convince him otherwise by explaining these benefits.

- Protection from hand numbness caused by pressure, vibration, and shock

- Protection against blisters and raw skin

- Protection from abrasions in a crash

- Protection when you use a hand to brush debris off a spinning tire

- A better grip when hands are moist from rain or sweat

- A way to wipe sweat from your face and eyes (assuming the gloves have absorbent terry cloth on the thumb and back, as most do)

A good fit is important if you want to maximize these benefits. For typical half-finger gloves, the palm padding should flex easily when you grasp the handlebar, without any bulky bunches. The fit should be snug when new (but not tight) because gloves tend to stretch with use. To prevent tearing the stitching when you remove them, don't tug at the fingers. Instead, peel them off inside out.

Padded gloves help you avoid a cycling injury commonly called handlebar palsy. This condition is caused by shock, vibration, and pressure on the ulnar and median nerves that run through the wrist into the heel of the hand. It's marked by tingling and weakness in the fingers, particularly the ring finger and pinkie. Usually this is a temporary nuisance that occurs now and then. But once you experience it, additional episodes are more likely. Sometimes cycling must be curtailed because it's difficult to control a bike with fingers that lack feeling or can't grip strongly. If the condition persists, surgery may be necessary, just as it is for sufferers of carpal tunnel syndrome.

Avoiding handlebar palsy isn't difficult. You need only to wear padded gloves, use cushy bar tape, change your hand position every few minutes, keep your elbows bent to dissipate shock, and make sure your riding position doesn't cause you to put too much weight on the bar.

What kind of glove padding is best? The two main choices are foam or gel, the common term for viscoelastic polymer. Gel actually adds a layer of lifelike synthetic tissue between your own tissue and the bar. This absorbs and evenly disperses pressure. In addition, gel doesn't compact over time (as foam can) and lose its shock-absorbing ability. However, gel is relatively heavy, and in lesser-quality gloves it might squeeze out of position. Foam is light, tends to stay in place, and protects well if it is properly positioned. Several glovemakers, including Specialized and Shock-Tek, place their padding strategically around the nerves.

If you're experiencing hand problems that aren't relieved by these measures, you should stop riding until improvement occurs or switch to a recumbent. Consult your doctor if time off the bike doesn't help. Once you start cycling again, use good gloves and technique.

GRIPS

In addition to padded gloves, mountain bikers should use a pair of moderately soft grips. The key word is moderately. If they're too thick and cushy, you'll tend to use excessive grip strength, which causes hand fatigue. If they're too firm, they won't absorb shock. Nerve injury could result.

Besides handlebar palsy, mountain bikers can develop tenderness at the base of the thumb from using finger-operated shift levers such as the Shimano Rapidfire type. Pushing the thumb shifter all day on a long ride can place lots of stress on this area. If you run into this problem and repositioning the levers doesn't help, consider switching to twist-grip shifting. This type lets you shift with your whole hand and wrist, taking your thumb out of the action.

Feet

When Pete Penseyres was winning 3000-mile races across America, he learned that he couldn't take foot comfort for granted. To keep his pups from blowing up faster than a drill sergeant's temper, he wore a low-tech-but-comfortable pair of touring shoes with slightly flexible soles. Because his feet could bend a bit, he found that they retained circulation better than if they were pressing on the unyielding soles of racing shoes for 20 hours a day. Following Pete's lead, ultra riders have come up with various innovative ways to enhance the comfort of those delicate appendages that Leonardo da Vinci once called "a masterpiece of engineering and a work of art."

SHOE SELECTION

It seems that each year another athletic shoe company enters the cycling market. It typically does so with claims of new research that proves its materials and designs are superior. Well, perhaps they are. But this doesn't mean that the latest, greatest shoes will fit *your* feet. Marketing claims, or the fact that your favorite Tour de France racer wears a particular model, don't count for a thing if your rides end in the agony of de feet.

Sorry, couldn't resist. But the point is that it's critically important to find shoes that fit right, stay comfortable for hours of riding, and help you pedal efficiently. Two main considerations are stiffness and ventilation, but these don't come into play until you're certain that the fit (length, width, toebox, and heel counter) is ideal. Here's how to tell.

Soles. Most riders will find advantages in stiff soles, even though there are exceptions, such as Pete. Stiff soles disperse pressure from the pedals and protect your feet from feeling uncomfortable edges. By inserting a thin, resilient insole, you can add cushioning for more comfort.

Stiff soles also maximize power transmission into the pedals. Softer soles, especially those that don't have a rigid shank through the cleat area, waste some energy as they flex and compress. As your feet eventually feel this pressure, you'll tend to reduce pedaling force to ease the discomfort. Guess what happens to your speed then? This is why shoes made for running or tennis aren't suitable for serious cycling. As biomechanist Peter Francis, Ph.D., notes, "Cycling maintains a fairly constant tension on the plantar fascia [the major ligament in the arch of the foot]. The last thing you need is the middle of the shoe sole flexing and putting additional stress on this ligament."

Generally, roadies doing centuries should go for light and stiff racing shoes. Tourists and randonneurs should look into so-called "walkable" shoes with two features that make them better off the bike. First, like Pete's shoes just described, they have a bit of forefoot flex that allows a more natural walking gait. Second, the soles have recessed pockets for the cleats, keeping them out of contact with the ground during strolls at convenience stores or rest stops. This makes walking safer and quieter on hard surfaces, and it spares cleats from wear or damage. If this shoe style is your choice, make sure your pedals can work with recessed cleats, or switch to a shoe/pedal "system" for guaranteed compatibility. This is also the right type of shoe for mountain bikers. The soles should have lugs for traction in addition to cleat recesses and a midsole stiffener.

Sizing. When shoe shopping, wear the type of socks you ride in. Take your insoles or orthotics, too, if you use them. It's smart to shop late in the afternoon because feet swell during the day and become about the size they'll be after an hour or more of cycling. Be prepared to try on several brands and models. You want the sole to be curved in the shape of your foot, producing full and uniform contact. Some brands will fit better depending on whether you have flat feet (less curvature) or a high arch (more curvature, with a taller heel).

Don't be too concerned with sizes—sizing varies slightly among manufacturers, and the number doesn't matter at all as long as the fit is right. For each pair, stand and press your feet firmly against the sole. If they feel roomy, about like your everyday shoes, they're a bit too big. Try a half size smaller. You need some space between your toes and the front of the shoes, of course, but your feet shouldn't be able to slide inside. As you're deciding your ideal size, remember that leather uppers will stretch over time and conform to the shape of your feet. They should be slightly tight when new. Synthetic uppers don't stretch. The fit in the store will be the same that you'll feel on your first ride or your one-hundredth one.

Women typically have narrow heels, which can make it difficult to get a good fit. Too often they've had only small sizes of men's shoes to choose from, but more manufacturers are including models designed for the female foot. If you're a woman and men's shoes don't feel right, find a store that carries women's models. Instead of settling for an okay fit, get a perfect one.

Heel counter. This counter is the portion of the upper that wraps around the rear to cup your heel. It should be firm to prevent the heel from rolling inward during the downward power phase of the pedal stroke. In addition, a firm heel counter stops shoes from breaking down quickly. Cyclists who use orthotics will get better performance from shoes with a stiff sole and heel counter.

Material. If you ride much in wet weather, synthetic uppers will last longer than those made of leather, which soon stretches and loses its form-fitting shape.

Shoes should be replaced if the uppers or heel counter become flimsy and no longer give proper support. You're asking for biomechanical trouble by trying to milk more miles out of shot shoes.

Closures. Because feet tend to swell during long rides, it's an advantage to have hook-and-loop straps rather than laces. You can reach down and adjust straps while riding to make tightness just right. Shoes that have both straps and laces are overkill—they complicate the quest for comfort rather than help it. If the shoes that fit you best have both, simply remove the laces and use the straps.

Other features. Most uppers have mesh sections or holes to improve air flow and let out water. Any reflective material on the shoe is a plus for night riding. On racing-style road shoes, look for a rubbery section at each end of the sole. These reduce damage and slipping when walking.

CLIPLESS SYSTEMS

So-called "clipless" pedal systems—clipless because they hold feet to the pedals without using toe clips and straps—have been a savior for many cyclists with foot, ankle, or knee problems. Most models allow feet to rotate laterally on the pedals—some as much as 25 degrees—before the cleats snap free. This rotation, also called "float," lets your feet find their natural angle, reducing stresses that could result from being locked in a fixed position. No longer is precise cleat alignment necessary.

In our view, every long-distance cyclist should be using a clipless system. The advantages multiply with the miles. The various systems offer distinct features, so shop around to find those that are useful to you. One thing to consider is the size of the pedals, especially if you have large feet. Some minimalist designs may not disperse pressure as well as pedals with a larger platform. You'll find a full range of brands

ROAD SHOES
Road shoes have a rigid sole and externally mounted cleats. They're great for power transmission, but not for walking.

MOUNTAIN BIKE SHOES
Mountain bike shoes have a semirigid sole and a recessed cleat pocket. Walking is about as easy as in street shoes.

in racing-style road systems, while the off-road market with recessed cleats is dominated by the Shimano SPD system. Several other brands use the same sole slots for cleat attachment, giving you a choice.

When they aren't recessed in the soles, cleats wear down quite quickly from normal use and from walking. Excessive wear causes difficult releases. When you notice this happening, or any time that cleats get damaged, replace them to restore smooth, reliable operation. Before you do that, though, be sure to outline the old cleats on the soles so that you can put the new ones in the positions you've become used to.

FOOT MALADIES

Hot feet. This may be the most common problem cyclists encounter on long rides. Or, it's a close second to saddle discomfort. Although the sensation is one of heat, and riders sometimes try to douse the burning with squirts from their water bottles, the condition is rarely temperature-related (unless you happen to be riding the Hotter'n Hell Hundred or Furnace Creek 508). What feels like heat is actually the result of nerve compression, reduced circulation, and numbness at the ball of the foot.

If you experience this painful problem, there are several remedies to try. First, make sure the forefoot of your shoes is wide enough. Remember, feet swell. Shoes that fit fine early might become too tight and restrict circulation. You may have to go up half a size. Second, install a thin, resilient insole to alleviate some vibration and pressure. (This could make things worse, however, if your shoes are borderline tight.) Third, get in the habit of occasionally pulling up against the top of your shoes instead of always pushing down. Doing this for just a few pedal strokes removes the pressure that restricts blood flow and compresses nerves. It works surprisingly well.

However, if these measures don't help, Lon Haldeman's solution is likely to do the trick. For years, he has ended hot feet for riders on his 140-mile-per-day transcontinental PAC Tours by moving their cleats rearward by 1 to 2 centimeters. Traditionally, cyclists are advised to place their cleats so that the balls of their feet are directly over the pedal axle. This position, however, causes maximum pressure right where hot foot occurs. By moving cleats rearward, the afflicted area is in front of the axle and pressure is relieved. When Ed Pavelka tried this, it quickly ended foot pain that had been bad enough to drive him to a sports podiatrist for cortisone injections. The new cleat position takes only a few rides to get used to, and we have yet to hear of it causing a problem. The one snag may be the need to drill new holes in your shoes to get the cleats far enough rearward for this fix to work.

Discomfort on top of the foot is likely caused by shoe closures that are too tight. This can cut off circulation or cause a bruise. Laces can't be adjusted while riding, which is why we recommend hook-and-loop straps. Usually the top one is the key to comfort because it's near where the ankle flexes. Keep it just snug enough to prevent your foot from moving inside the shoe. There's no need to pull it tighter unless you'll be tugging hard on steep climbs or accelerating during interval training. As a ride wears on, be aware of increasing tightness from swelling feet, and adjust straps before there's actual discomfort. Once a spot becomes tender, it's harder to find the comfort zone.

If your shoes fit great but late-ride swelling often causes a pressure point (say, where your big or little toe presses into the upper), don't be reluctant to perform a little minor surgery. On the shoes, we mean. Plenty of experienced endurance riders have used a razor blade to slit or even remove a toebox to alleviate hot spots. In fact, we've seen the better portion of some shoes missing. And then there's Gerry Tatrai, who has suffered extreme problems with swelling and pressure points because of his misshapen feet—the result of car and motorcycle accidents. His solution was to get custom shoes that are actually more like sandals, with only straps for uppers. The rigid composite foot beds work like an orthotic on the top and a sole on the bottom. They look cool, and they are.

Blisters. If you do a great job with shoe selection, blisters shouldn't be a problem. But they could still arise if conditions allow friction between your foot and the shoe. Socks are the usual culprit, so always wear a clean pair to start a ride. Socks that are the wrong size or are damp, wrinkled, or stiff with sweat can literally rub you raw. Synthetic fabrics seem to work best because, unlike natural fibers (cotton in particular), they don't sop up moisture.

To reduce friction on areas you find susceptible to blisters, apply foot powder or a lubricant such as petroleum jelly. If your feet sweat heavily, rub them with underarm antiperspirant. In addition, cover a blister-prone area as soon as you sense trouble—or even before beginning the ride. Bandages, moleskin, or a synthetic skin covering should be part of every long-distance cyclist's supply kit.

If a blister forms, some doctors advise draining the fluid. Others recommend leaving it alone unless it's in a weight-bearing area. If draining is your choice, clean the area first with alcohol, then use a sterilized pin or needle to puncture the blister along the side. Always leave the roof of the blister intact. It acts as a barrier against infection while protecting the tender tissue underneath.

Corns and calluses. Like blisters, these result from the body's attempt to protect skin from irritation. Calluses form over wide areas like the ball of the foot, while corns occur on smaller spots, such as on or between toes. The main causes are shoes that don't fit correctly or improper foot mechanics that cause pressure and rubbing. In the first case, change to better shoes. In the second, consult a sports podiatrist for evaluation. Orthotics or other corrective devices may be necessary. Meanwhile, you can self-treat corns and calluses with pads that contain a medication called salicylic acid, available without prescription at drugstores. Or you can use a pumice stone or emery board to reduce the thickened skin.

Ingrown toenails. Cycling doesn't cause this problem, but that's little consolation when an ingrown nail makes pedaling painful. Generally, the cause is a nail that's been incorrectly clipped, leaving the skin around it vulnerable to inflammation. Don't trim your toenails too short, and cut them straight across the top, not curved like fingernails. Use a file to smooth sharp edges. If you have more than one pair of shoes, wear those with the widest toebox while an ingrown nail is healing.

Orthotics

Many cyclists can benefit from orthotics, which are rigid inserts that fit like insoles between your feet and shoes. Orthotics actually change the way forces are transmitted to and from the feet. They correct improper angles and movement, improving your pedaling power.

Over-the-counter orthotics are widely available, but most brands are made for walking and running. They focus on heel strike and do little to stabilize the forefoot, which is where pressure is applied to the pedal. It's much more effective to be custom-fitted by a sports podiatrist who is savvy about cycling. To find one near you, contact the American Academy of Podiatric Sports Medicine, Box 31331, San Francisco, CA 94131 (800-438-3355; www.aapsm.org).

Seat

Saddle woes are certainly nothing new. In fact, Jerome K. Jerome waxed philosophical about this potentially painful part of cycling way back in 1900 when he wrote a book called *Three Men on Wheels* and penned these classic words: "It has always been an idea of mine that the right saddle is to be found. I said, 'You give up that idea. This is an imperfect world, a world of joy and sorrow mingled. There may be a Better Land where bicycle saddles are made out of rainbow, stuffed with cloud. In this world, the simplest thing is to get used to something hard.'"

There are two basic types of saddle pain, and it sounds as if Mr. Jerome knew them well. The first is the result of pressure on the tender tissue that covers the ends of the pelvic bones, known as the ischial tuberosities or, more simply, the "sit bones." This problem is usually most severe during the early part of the season, when you are getting back on the bike following minimal winter riding. Without saddle contact, the skin softens. Once you begin cycling regularly again, the discomfort peaks and then gradually diminishes (assuming the saddle fits you correctly).

Posterior pain also can be caused by a bad saddle position. If your seat is too high, your hips will rock with each pedal stroke, sawing your crotch and chafing your skin. If it's too low, you will tend to slide forward onto the narrow nose, taking weight off your sit bones and putting it on the tender tissue between them. The same will happen if the saddle is tilted down, while an upward tilt presses the nose into your crotch when you lean forward to the handlebar. Horizontal is the way to go.

The saddle that you're positioning must fit your body and riding style. In general, narrow seats are intended for competitive cyclists, who bend low and sit forward much of the time with their weight on the narrow part of their crotch. Long-distance cyclists, on the other hand, tend to sit more upright. They need support farther back, where the sit bones bear their weight. A slightly broader saddle usually works better.

If we sound like we're hedging a bit, we are. Posteriors come in all shapes and sizes, so blanket recommendations are irresponsible. Go to any long-distance event and you'll see the gamut of saddle brands and models. Most riders arrive at their current choice after considerable trial and error. The seat that one person loves may be despised by the next guy. There are some guidelines, though, that can help you to narrow the field to a manageable number of choices.

Width. The rear must be broad enough to support your sit bones on top, and not let them press on the edges. Beware of seats that have a domed top (when viewed at eye level from the back). These put your sit bones lower than the center of the seat, increasing pressure on the nerves and blood vessels in the crotch.

The quest for crotch comfort sometimes leads to extraordinary measures. Note, however, that this rider is not sitting down.

Profile. When viewed from the side, a seat should have a minimal
dip between the nose and tail. Lay a ruler along the length to judge this.
Excessive curvature leads to positioning and comfort problems. When
the nose is horizontal, the rear will be angled up and unpleasant to sit
on. Level the rear and the nose will point up, increasing crotch pressure.

Padding. A thin-to-moderate layer of gel or dense foam will
cushion the sit bones and absorb some vibration. Many riders assume
that if some padding is good, more must be better. For short cul-de-
sac cruises, maybe. But for long rides, thick padding can result in uncomfortable numbness. This happens because the sit bones sink deep
into the plush stuff, causing the center of the saddle to press into the
crotch. Instead of more comfort, you get less during a ride of any
length. If you can't solve sit-bone discomfort, try a seat cushioned by
the new polymer gel. This material distributes your weight over a
larger area and does a good job of absorbing vibration.

Anatomical designs. In response to concerns about genital numbness and even erectile dysfunction caused by bike seats, manufacturers have introduced numerous designs to reduce crotch contact and the resulting pressure on nerves and blood vessels. Riders who will be spending long hours on the bike may want such a saddle. Again, it's impossible for us to say which model you'll find effective and comfortable. In fact, we've tried nearly every "safe saddle" on the market, and each of us has a different favorite. See chapter 5 for more information.

How Suspension Helps

Ed Burke finds it useful to simply "think light" when riding in long mountain bike events. This reminds him to keep his upper body relaxed, his elbows loose, and his hands gripping firmly but not tightly. Strive to feel at home on the bike, he advises—as comfortable as if you are sitting in your favorite chair.

A bigger help, though, is a well-tuned suspension system. It absorbs small bumps so you don't even feel them, and it takes the bone-rattling jolts out of hitting holes and rocks. This increases arm and leg comfort, especially when you're seated and your built-in "springs" are not in action. Suspension allows you to relax, conserve energy, and ride farther with less fatigue.

Pedaling across a series of obstacles involves both reactive and anticipatory muscular effort. In other words, you stand and pull on the handlebar to get over a rock, which uses some energy, and you also brace yourself, which uses more. By studying the relationship of shock absorption to total energy expenditure, it's possible to put numbers on the physiological benefits of suspension.

Research conducted at the German Sports University, Cologne, in cooperation with suspension maker RockShox, looked into the impact of jolts and vibrations on cyclists. Tests were run on bikes with front suspension only (suspension fork), bikes with front suspension and a suspension seatpost, and dual-suspension bikes with a fork and integrated rear-frame suspension. A specially designed apparatus simulated the range of shocks that might be experienced on a trail. Monitoring pads (accelerometers) were attached to various parts of the riders' bodies. When results were compiled, the average overall reduction in impacts and vibration thanks to suspension was more than 20 percent. The dual-suspension bike had the biggest benefit on the lower back—a 33-percent reduction. The suspension seatpost was surprisingly efficient in this area, showing a 25-percent reduction.

Cycling Shorts

Once your saddle and position are right, cycling shorts are the key to comfort. And the keys to great shorts are the crotch liner ("chamois") and its padding. Most companies offer their own special type of soft and absorbent liner material, designed to cushion your crotch and hold moisture away from your skin. Some liners even have an antibacterial treatment to reduce the risk of infection if skin becomes

The head of this study summed it up by saying, "Back problems occurring during or after a ride are not simply a result of tired muscles. They are more the outcome of stress fatigue caused by shocks and vibrations that hammer straight into this weak spot of the human body. If someone wants to put suspension on his bike, he should start at the rear. That is where the spine needs it most."

Ed Burke participated in research that found additional performance benefits from suspension. Working with John Seifert, Ph.D., of St. Cloud State University in Minnesota, Ed had 12 experienced mountain bikers ride a front-suspension bike, a dual-suspension bike, and a bike with no suspension for 1 hour on singletrack at a steady 10 miles per hour. Mean heart rates were 146 beats per minute during each ride on both suspension bikes, compared with 154 beats per minute on the rigid bike. Like heart rate, perceived exertion also was higher without suspension.

Another part of the study measured a special hormone (creatine kinase) that's found primarily within muscles but increases in the blood when muscle damage occurs during exercise or other trauma. Can you guess the result? Right! Significantly less of this hormone was in the cyclists' blood after they rode the suspension bikes than after their rigid-bike ride. This means you'll suffer less muscle damage when using suspension, and that the advantage is multiplied in an event which lasts for hours.

The results of these studies confirm what Ed and other cycling physiologists have suspected for years: Bicycle suspension doesn't just increase comfort and control, it also reduces fatigue and muscle damage. There's no reason to doubt that these benefits apply to road riding, too—though they'll be less pronounced because the surfaces aren't nearly as rough.

broken. Compared with the traditional leather chamois in wool shorts, the modern synthetics are eons ahead in performance, durability, and ease of care. Some companies also offer shorts designed especially for a woman's anatomy, with liners that avoid stitching in potentially uncomfortable places.

We recommend that you buy the best shorts you can afford, and always have at least two pairs so one is clean for the next ride. Top-line shorts are constructed from eight distinct sections ("panels"), which make them more form-fitting than six- or four-panel models. It's up to you whether to choose a drawstring or elastic waist, or a built-in bib top that works like a pair of suspenders. Some riders prefer the latter because the shorts won't sag in the rain. Off-road endurance champion John Stamstad says a bib top even reduces the risk of saddle sores because it holds the chamois more firmly to the crotch, reducing movement that causes chafing. On the other hand, the additional material covering the lower torso can make you feel hotter on summer rides. And, of course, you can't lower bib shorts without first removing your jersey.

Despite the many advances in chamois design and materials, chafing and pimplelike saddle sores are still a threat to long-distance cyclists. In the next chapter, we'll tell you how to limit the risk, plus how to treat sores if they develop.

End Saddle Sores

At the Villaines la Juhel checkpoint
620 miles into Paris-Brest-Paris '99, a middle-age French rider was lying facedown on a table in the emergency medical room. His jersey was still on, but his shorts were off. The lower portion of his butt, right where a saddle fits, was beet-red. It looked like he'd sat on the business side of a steam iron. He glanced up with a tired shrug, as if to say that he'd gone as far as he could before asking for help. Maybe too far. A doctor was beginning to apply large bandages. Whether this rider completed the remaining 150 miles to Paris isn't known. If he did, the agony of those last few hours was probably exceeded only by the pain of the bandages being peeled off.

Although this is an extreme example, it's safe to say that it's the rare cyclist who makes it through PBP or any other long ride without some amount of saddle trauma. In France, finishers are on their bikes anywhere from 44 to 80-plus hours. That's a lot of concentrated pressure and friction on the part of the anatomy where everything in cycling hinges. To reduce the risk of suffering like the Frenchman, you must keep chafing to a minimum. In addition, cleanliness is essential for preventing the infection of broken skin that results in sores or boils.

The type of lesion often called a "saddle sore" typically begins with irritation to hair follicles, which leads to a small, pimplelike bump. The predominant bacterial infection, staphylococcus, is forced into the skin by saddle pressure or additional friction, and a sore is born. In most cases, its life span is just a few days. During this time, though, it may become hard, inflamed, and quite painful. In some cases, the infection spreads to adjacent tissue and creates a boil or cyst that necessitates surgery. Some pro racers have been forced to have an operation in midseason when they were unable to continue because of the pain. When you consider the excellent medical care that pros are given, you can appreciate how hard it is for the rest of us to avoid saddle sores.

The problem is that you can't dodge the main causes. Friction occurs with each pedal stroke, as leg action moves the crotch on the saddle. The risk of chafing rises when sweat or rain softens the skin. Bacteria multiply in the warm, moist environment, ready to invade at any opportunity. Then there's body weight, pressing the supporting bones of the pelvis against tender tissue. You need to fight back. Here's how.

Saddle fit. The keys to correct fit are width, curvature, and padding. Revisit the design guidelines in chapter 11. No seat can eliminate saddle sores, but one that fits your anatomy correctly will minimize the risk. Also check our advice on riding techniques in chapter 4. Move on the saddle to relieve pressure points, and stand frequently.

Saddle position. Besides being the correct height, be sure the seat is horizontal or tilted down in front a maximum of one or two degrees. A level saddle lets you move fore or aft to change weight distribution and pressure points. A slight downward tilt can ease crotch pressure when you ride in a low position or use aero bars. See chapter 3 for setup instructions.

Hygiene. Because oily, salty sweat is a major contributor to saddle sores, cleanliness is very important. Own enough pairs of shorts so you always have a clean pair to wear. Riding in dirty shorts is a shortcut to disaster. Ideally, you should also wash your crotch with an antibacterial soap before each ride. Then, apply powder or a greaseless skin lubricant such as Chamois Butt'r or Noxzema to your skin and the chamois to reduce friction. Many experienced riders develop their own system. For example, endurance veteran Jim Smith, who has ridden coast-to-coast PAC Tours half-a-dozen times, says that he controls chafing by applying an over-the-counter product called SBR-lipocream before riding, followed after showering by an abrasion-healing prescription product called DesOwen lotion. In general, avoid heavy products such as petroleum jelly that can clog pores and are difficult to wash out of shorts. (Save it for rainy rides, when you need a lubricant with staying power.) Always shower as soon as possible after riding. At an event, get out of your shorts and clean your crotch with soap or rubbing alcohol. Have fresh clothes to put on so you won't be socializing in a damp, germy chamois.

At home, wash your crotch regularly with an antibacterial soap. Products such as Hibiclens and Betadine Surgical Scrub work well and are available at any drugstore. Regular use will reduce the chance of skin infection. Plain soap isn't as effective because it doesn't contain germ-killing agents. To control crotch dampness or excessive sweating,

Keys to Comfort

The way you ride can do a lot to reduce saddle trauma. Here are three effective techniques. Make them habits, and begin using them early rather than when you're already in distress.

Stand frequently. Make use of opportunities to get out of the saddle, even if only for a few seconds. Hills are a prime time, so climb at least part of each one standing. When Lon Haldeman rode Paris-Brest-Paris '99 on a one-speed bike, he was probably the only finisher feeling no crotch discomfort. Why? Because he was off the saddle so much, standing on every climb. (His quads weren't so pain-free, though.) When you're coasting on descents, crouch with your butt just above the seat. Stand whenever you're pedaling up to speed from a turn or stop. If you're on long stretches of flat roads that don't naturally create position changes, shift to a higher gear two or three times every hour and stand for a minute or so.

Ride like a jockey. Mountain bikers call it the "attack" or "ready" position, and roadies can use it, too. Level the pedals, keep your elbows and knees bent, and let your butt hover just over the seat. In this position, the bike can chatter across washboard ruts, railroad tracks, broken pavement, or any other rough stuff without the seat hammering you.

Change your location. Instead of sitting in the same area of the saddle all of the time, sit on all of the saddle some of the time. Scoot to the back, move to the middle, slide toward the nose. Each position alters the contact area and pressure points. Moving in this way also relieves muscle tension in your upper body and legs, reducing stiffness and keeping you feeling fresher.

If you should experience genital numbness, don't simply write it off as an unavoidable side effect of cycling. It's not. Men who let bouts of numbness continue could be in line for more serious problems. The link between bike seats and sexual dysfunction isn't certain—after all, many 20,000-miles-per-year pro racers are happy fathers—but we do know that some unfortunate cyclists have lost sensitivity or the ability to get a suitable erection. At the first hint of a problem, visit a urologist for a full exam. Numerous health and lifestyle factors can contribute to sexual dysfunction, so you need to pinpoint the causes and pursue the solutions.

apply talcum powder, baby powder, or Zeesorb after washing and drying. Consider sleeping without your pajama bottoms so your crotch will stay air-dry all night. This is helpful, too, if you're using any topical medications.

Shorts. Always wear clean shorts with a large, smooth, padded, absorbent liner. Some chamois, like in Giordana RT 800 and Performance Elite shorts, are treated to minimize bacterial growth. Almost all liners are made of synthetics nowadays (rather than hard-to-care-for leather), with names such as Suedemark II (Hind), Microsuede (Cannondale), and Biosuede (Pearl Izumi). Combined with high-tech fabrics such as CoolMax or other synthetics, they give you high performance, durability, and ease of care.

Treatment Techniques

Okay, despite trying to do everything right, there it is—a growing, painful, pimplelike sore that's making you grimace and ride sidesaddle. Don't be too discouraged. It happens to all of us sooner or later. The trick now is to help that thing heal quickly so that your downtime is limited.

First rule: Don't treat the sore like a typical boo-boo and cover it with a salve or ointment. These applications may actually keep bacteria alive. Instead, wash with one of the above-mentioned antibacterial cleansers three times each day and leave the sore unbandaged. Ed Pavelka and Fred Matheny are two riders who've found applications of Erythromycin Topical Gel very effective at the first sign of a sore. Unlike a salve, this prescription product dries in seconds. Put on clean underwear after each washing.

If the sore is looking more like a boil, help it come to a head and drain by taking three hot baths a day lasting 15 to 20 minutes each. The warmth will also increase bloodflow to the area, allowing your body's bloodborne infection fighters to flood in and reduce inflammation.

A stubborn sore can be helped by what's known generically as a "drawing salve," made to bring a boil to maturity so that it will drain. Check with your doctor or pharmacist for availability. It's applied to the sore, then covered with an adhesive bandage. You should see results in a couple of days. Drawing salve can be combined with an over-the-counter product called Boil Ease, which contains a topical painkiller that may reduce discomfort enough to let you continue riding. In fact, saddle pressure combined with the effect of a drawing salve can help a sore discharge. You'll pull off your shorts and the bandage to find a bit of a mess, but the pressure will be gone and the sore will start healing.

Another effective product is Bag Balm, particularly for raw areas caused by chafing. Available at pharmacies and veterinary stores, Bag Balm was developed "to soothe a milk cow's irritated teats." We're not kidding. It works for irritated bike riders, too. In fact, dermatologist Bernard Burton, M.D., says, "When it's applied after your shower, it will usually clear up the problem overnight." Be careful, though, until you learn how your body responds to this product. Some riders who have tried using Bag Balm as a daily crotch lubricant report an adverse skin reaction.

A serious sore will make you cut back your mileage or modify the way you ride. For example, when masters racing champion and cycling author Arnie Baker, M.D., developed a bumper crop of saddle sores, he changed how he trained in order to stay fit while keeping pain to a minimum. How? By alternating days of hill sprints, long climbs, or uphill intervals—all done out of the saddle. He stayed strong until the next time he could sit down comfortably.

Arnie's technique won't work, though, if the sore strikes while you're in the midst of a multiday event or tour. If this is the predicament, you can reduce pressure on the sore by cutting a donut from a piece of moleskin (available in drugstores). Position the donut so the sore is in the hole. The moleskin will stay put and prevent direct pressure. You could even fill the hole with drawing salve and Boil Ease, then seal it with a bandage.

Other emergency solutions include moving your saddle fore or aft to alter your sitting position. Or you could wear two pairs of cycling shorts to get extra padding (lower your saddle a bit to account for the extra thickness). And then there's the age-old solution of slipping a piece of raw meat between your skin and the chamois. This may make you laugh or make you queasy, but it really can save a ride. One cyclist we met at PBP '99 made it to Paris on a slice of ham.

If self-treatment doesn't produce a quick cure, you should consult your butcher . . . er, doctor or dermatologist for professional treatment and stronger medications. You may be ordered to use a broad-base oral antibiotic such as erythromycin, dicloxacillin, or keflex, or topical antibiotics or cortisone creams. Some cyclists have experimented successfully with Accutane (another prescription product), which is a synthetic form of vitamin A. Accutane must not be used by pregnant women, however.

13

Body Shop

Although skin problems may not
be as dramatic as head injuries, or as painful as cranky knees, they
rank high on cycling's annoyance list.

Think about it: Skin is your body's most vulnerable organ, susceptible to sun, wind, heat, cold, moisture, pollution, abrasions, and infections. Skin is composed of two layers: the epidermis (outer) and
dermis (inner). The epidermis, which contains the pigment responsible
for skin color, is continually being sloughed off as new cells are
formed. The underlying dermis is often called the true skin. It contains
sweat glands, nerve endings, small blood vessels, and hair follicles.

Skin is vital for conserving fluids, preventing dehydration, and regulating body temperature. When you're riding in the heat, blood is
shunted to the skin, where sweat glands produce perspiration that
cools you as it evaporates. Thanks to the numerous small vessels in the
dermis, blood is cooled, too. This is extremely important in preventing
overheating during long rides—particularly in hot, humid conditions.

Of all a cyclist's organs, the skin takes the most daily abuse. Fortunately, the problems that this can cause are avoidable. Understanding the potential dangers and knowing how to prevent them will
keep serious discomfort to a minimum during all of the hours you're
on your bike.

Sun Protection

While the sun may feel good on your skin, it is far from good for it.
Recently, a panel of medical experts who spoke at a National Insti-
tutes of Health conference stated that athletes should avoid summer
outdoor exercise between the hours of 10:00 A.M. and 3:00 P.M. This
is when the sun's ultraviolet rays are at peak intensity, exposing the
skin to radiation that can cause cancer. But they conceded that giving

Ultra cyclists such as RAAM champion Danny Chew get toasted in more ways than one. Sun protection is paramount when your skin is exposed for long hours during summer rides.

this advice is easier than making people heed it. We all know that not riding at these times is impossible during long-distance events. The solution is protection.

Begin by using the proper sunscreen, one with an SPF (sun protection factor) of 15 or higher. This number indicates the amount of time you can stay in the sun before you burn, compared with using no sunscreen at all. The higher the product's SPF rating, the greater the protection. Use lots, and frequently add more. Creams, which bond well to the skin, last longer than alcohol-based lotions or oils. Put on your base coat about 30 minutes before a ride, and then apply more every 2 to 3 hours.

If you're fair-skinned or are riding at high altitude or near the equator, use a sunscreen with an SPF of 30 to 50. In addition, use only sunscreens labeled "broad spectrum," which means they block all harmful rays. On a cloudy day, don't change a thing. Up to 80 percent of the sun's cancer- and wrinkle-producing rays bore right through the cloud cover.

Sometimes you'll see cyclists, like lifeguards at the beach, with their noses covered by opaque creams or pastes of zinc oxide. If you are overly susceptible to burning, applying this stuff to danger areas is 100 percent effective because it prevents sunlight from reaching the skin. Another way to block burning rays is with a long-sleeve jersey made of a lightweight, light-colored fabric. This method was used by numerous RAAM riders in years when the course crossed the Mojave

Desert from a Southern California start. In fact, two-time winner Gerry Tatrai's sun-defeating outfit included women's white stockings as well as removable white sleeves. Despite temperatures of 110°F or higher, he avoided sunburn and actually felt cooler without the intense rays on his skin. Some riders put a bandanna under their helmet to shield their face, ears, and neck.

Lips can get badly sunburned, too, so use lip balm that has a high SPF factor. It also will prevent drying and cracking. Failure to protect lips can result in so much discomfort that it's hard to keep eating and drinking. In a pinch you can apply sunscreen, being careful to limit the amount that gets into your mouth.

Okay, now what happens if you blow it and wind up with a sunburn during a tour or other multiday ride? Your skin is hot, red, and tender, yet you still have more hours of riding and sun exposure. Take aspirin or ibuprofen. These drugs ease the pain and alleviate swelling. Continue with two tablets every 4 hours throughout the ride. Use a high-SPF sunscreen to avoid further burning, or cover the scorched skin as best you can.

Mouth Matters

In 1999, endurance cycling legend John Stamstad rode the 2465-mile Great Divide Mountain Bike Trail in 18 days. He was unsupported, carrying all of his gear and stopping for food at the occasional grocery store or gas station. Reflecting on the physical ordeal of this accomplishment—the fastest anyone had ridden this rugged route along the Continental Divide between Mexico and Canada—John commented, "The sorest thing was my mouth."

During the same summer, former RAAM champion Lon Haldeman was back in the saddle, riding the 14th Paris-Brest-Paris randonnée. A lot can go wrong when you compact 765 miles into 3 days or so, which may be why Lon was so quick to cite one thing that went right. "I didn't have any mouth problems at all," he said, adding that this was something he usually couldn't say after an ultramarathon ride.

What's going on here? How can your mouth become such a problem during a long ride? For some people, it's because of the dryness caused by deep breathing for so many hours (sip more frequently to alleviate this). Or because their lips had become sunburned, swollen, or cracked (use a lip balm that contains sunscreen). Usually, though, when riders complain of mouth maladies, they're talking about tenderness of the mouth lining, gums, and even the tongue. This is painful discomfort that makes it tough to keep eating.

John Stamstad lays the blame on acidic foods, noting that sources of these can seem innocuous—fruit-filled pies or pastries, for example—but they take a toll over time. The sugar that's in these and most other snacks and energy foods is a problem, too. The bacteria that are found in plaque (the film that accumulates on teeth) can convert carbohydrate into tooth-dissolving and gum-tenderizing acids. In other words, those energy bars, gels, and sports drinks that are fueling your long rides also are providing loads of raw material for mouth problems. The danger is increased if you already have a sore in your mouth or gums. Americans at PBP are warned to be careful when eating French baguettes because the hard crust can cut their mouths. This seemingly minor nuisance can develop into a major problem as the ride wears on.

To minimize acid buildup, eat some foods that contain fat and protein, not just sugary carbohydrate. This will stimulate the secretion of saliva, which helps neutralize plaque acids and washes away or dissolves food particles and sugar. In fact, chewing of any kind stimulates saliva flow up to 10 times normal levels. By chewing sugarless gum and taking an occasional swig of plain water, you will keep your mouth cleaner.

John has two more tips. First, he finds that dairy products, such as yogurt, help neutralize mouth acid and can even relieve soreness. Second, he's found that an occasional rinse with mouthwash can thwart the development of sores. When in need, he'll buy a small bottle at a convenience store.

Analgesics

Visit the staging area of any bike race on a chilly, damp day and you're bound to smell menthol in the air. The source will be Musculor, Cramergesic, Ben-Gay, Icy Hot, or a similar product. Technically known as analgesics or counterirritants, these products come as an ointment, cream, or liniment. Racers use them to warm up muscles or relieve soreness.

These products produce a skin reaction that creates a sensation of heat. This can range from mild to intense. The perceived strength depends on the skin's sensitivity. For example, a mild analgesic such as Ben-Gay will probably feel different to you than it does to the next cyclist. In addition, it will feel different depending on where it's applied. Your thighs and your neck, for instance, have different sensitivities.

The most popular ingredient in analgesics is methyl salicylate. It's found in wintergreen oil or made synthetically. When applied, it causes skin to turn red and feel warm. Methyl salicylate is safe when used no more than three times per day. But be careful if you're sensitive to aspirin, because they're chemically related.

Menthol is the second most widely used ingredient. It can be produced synthetically or extracted from peppermint oil. Menthol stimulates the nerves that perceive cold and depresses those that feel pain. The immediate sensation is coolness, followed by warmth.

When menthol and methyl salicylate are combined, a mixed message of cold and heat is sent to the brain. This diminishes the perception of pain, which is why these products are used after a hard ride that produces muscle soreness. Interestingly, the presence of a fragrance such as menthol may also serve as a distraction to take your mind off discomfort. (No, don't put some on your nose!)

Can these products also help you warm up for a ride? A study conducted at the University of California at San Diego measured the effect of using an analgesic (Ben-Gay) before strenuous exercise. One group of runners applied it to their legs, and then warmed up. Another group warmed up without it. Everyone then took a long treadmill run. After analyzing their level of discomfort at various times during the run, it was apparent that those who had used the analgesic ran with significantly greater comfort for a longer period. In terms of endurance cycling, a product like Ben-Gay can be helpful when warming up isn't practical, such as before an event that has a predawn start. It can make the early miles feel smoother and easier.

In cool, damp weather, a product with an oily or gel-like base will coat your skin to block water and wind. It's smart to have someone apply the stuff for you so it's not on your hands later when you touch your eyes, nose, or lips. Don't forget to roll up your shorts to get the upper thighs, and to roll down your socks to get the Achilles tendons. It's also helpful to rub some on your lower back, as well as on your arms if they'll be uncovered. After the ride, use rubbing alcohol and a towel to wipe your skin clean.

Never apply analgesics to bruised or broken skin. The methyl salicylate or capsicum found in some creams will interact rapidly with exposed pain receptors and make you wish you had a crank bolt to bite on. If a rash develops, stop using the product and try a different one after your skin heals. Of course, keep these products well away from sensitive areas, including your face and crotch.

Eyewear

For cyclists, sunglasses are much more than fashion. They are an essential piece of equipment—as important as anything else for your safety. Without eye protection, the combination of bright sun, wind, and glare can cause a malady known as astheopia, which can lead to headaches and general fatigue. By wearing good sunglasses, you can dramatically reduce the stress on your eyes and avoid these symptoms. In addition, your overall vision, including acuity on cloudy days or in fading afternoon light, will be sharper.

Before you run out to buy a new pair of shades, let's go over a few points that will help you make the best selection. This is important, considering the stiff price of eyewear as well as the value of your eyesight.

It's the unseen wavelengths, both longer and shorter than visible light, that can damage your eyes. On long rides, particularly at high elevations where the thinner air blocks less light, you should be wearing sunglasses that remove 100 percent of the ultraviolet (UV, short-wavelength) radiation. Without such protection, exposure to UV radiation causes eye irritation and inflammation. Worse, it can lead to brown cataracts—the gradual accumulation of pigment in the eye's lens—and loss of vision. To prevent such problems, ultraviolet inhibitors are put into lenses made of glass, plastic, or polycarbonate.

Infrared (IR, long-wavelength) radiation is less damaging. Yet after your eyes have been exposed to the sun for an extended period, you may develop a raw, burning sensation that leaves you feeling tired and irritable. To prevent this, wear glasses that filter most infrared rays as well as ultraviolet ones.

How can you be sure? In 1989, the Food and Drug Administration announced a voluntary labeling standard for eyewear. It was developed by a consensus of eye-care professionals and educators, plus federal and industry agencies. Look for this label when you purchase your next pair of sunglasses. You'll find some models that block 100 percent of both infrared and ultraviolet radiation.

Lens density or darkness is important, too. Visible light may be less

EYEWEAR

Sunglasses with a large, curved, close-fitting lens are essential for protecting eyes from wind and debris.

damaging than the light you can't see, but it's fatiguing if you have to squint through a long ride on a bright day. On the other hand, lenses that are too dark for the conditions can be dangerous. If the ground goes black in shaded sections, there's no telling what you might ride into. And wearing darkly tinted glasses that don't block ultraviolet light can be worse than wearing no eye protection at all. Your pupils will widen to let more light enter, which also lets more radiation enter.

Just What the (Eye) Doctor Ordered

If you can't wear contacts while riding but need vision correction, most major sunglasses companies offer models that can incorporate your prescription. This is a boon to riders who long for the advantages of the protective, wraparound-style eyewear that works best for cycling. Until recently, they couldn't use these large lenses because the size and curvature didn't accommodate prescriptions.

Now, popular brands such as Bolle, Briko, Smith, and Rudy Project have models with corrective-lens inserts. These let you put your prescription lenses behind the sunglass lenses, which also makes it easy to change tints for different light conditions. A wide range of prescriptions, from +3.00 to −6.00 diopter, can be accommodated. To use this type of sunglasses, you must first obtain the prescription lenses from your optometrist or optician.

The prescription-lens insert is integrated with the frame's nosepiece, and can easily be snapped in or out. Because it's behind the tinted lens, the sunglasses have a normal look and feel. Also supplied is a standard nosepiece, should you want to use the glasses without the insert. If you sometimes wear contacts, this gives you two pairs of sunglasses for the price of one.

Oakley takes a different approach by integrating "Rx Implants" into the lenses of its sunglasses. Thus, the prescriptive lens is a single unit, which eliminates the insert. This streamlines the design and saves a bit of weight, but doesn't allow tint changes.

There are two main reasons to wear sunglasses—to protect your eyes and to look cool. Thanks to these systems, cyclists who need vision correction have a solution that's both functional and fashionable.

As for lens tint, many opticians recommend gray because it softens all colors but eliminates none. Amber/brown and persimmon also work well for cycling. Yellow sharpens vision on a cloudy or rainy day, and it actually helps brighten the gloom—a nice psychological plus. Clear lenses are best for night riding, of course. In sparkling sunlight, a reflective mirror coating reduces the total amount of light reaching your eyes, while standard dark lenses actually absorb light. This is another reason they must block ultraviolet rays.

High-quality sunglasses are expensive, so durability is important. Even the most resilient frames can be broken in a crash, but you certainly don't want lenses to shatter when hit by an object. This means that polycarbonate or plastic lenses are the way to go. They're nearly indestructible, although they do scratch fairly easily unless a special coating is used.

For cycling, a close-fitting wraparound design works best. This reduces air penetration, shielding your eyes from dust, bugs, debris, and pollutants. Less drying wind means more comfort on long rides, especially in low-moisture environments. This is a big help if you wear contact lenses.

14

Aches and Pains

The more you ride, the greater your chance of developing an injury. By now, you know that the best way to minimize the risk as well as the severity of an injury is to have the best possible riding position that you can develop. But even when you do, the repetitive nature of pedaling, combined with hours on the bike at a time, can result in nagging aches and pains. Think of it as Murphy's Law for long-distance cyclists: If something can hurt, sooner or later it probably will hurt.

So, what we need to do as endurance riders is to expect problems to crop up, and then be smart about correcting them. Most discomforts are minor and easily remedied with position tweaks, better conditioning, or even smarter nutrition. With this in mind, let's look into several common ailments you might encounter, and the remedies that will get you healthy again in a hurry.

Knees

A long day of riding will cause a number of minor discomforts, all soon forgotten in the afterglow of accomplishment. But knees are different. When your hinges hurt, the pain can ruin a ride and continue to plague you for days, both on and off the bike. Although knee problems may be less common in cycling than in sports that involve running, they're still high on the list of complaints.

The term "cyclist's knee" is an umbrella for several repetitive or overuse conditions. These are often linked to anatomical problems in the foot or lower leg, improper foot position on the pedal, or pushing inappropriately big gears. Most people, even those with chronic knee problems, can ride comfortably once the reason for the pain is understood and corrected.

Often described as a hinge joint, the knee's chief role in cycling is to flex and extend the leg. The knee slides and glides around a moving center of rotation at the end of the thighbone. To permit this movement, the knee is a poetic combination of bones, muscles, ligaments, tendons, cartilage, bursa, and joint capsule. The cartilage (meniscus) acts as a shock absorber and stabilizer, while bursa and synovial fluid lubricate between moving parts.

What happens when this mechanism goes haywire? At the first International Olympic Committee Medical Conference in Colorado Springs, James Holmes, M.D., and Andrew Pruitt, Ed.D., disclosed what they've learned from treating some of the world's top cyclists. Anterior or frontal knee problems, specifically chondromalacia (inflammation to the back of the kneecap) and patella tendinitis (inflammation of the tendon that connects the kneecap to the lower leg), were the most common knee injuries—found in 63 percent of the 134 cy-

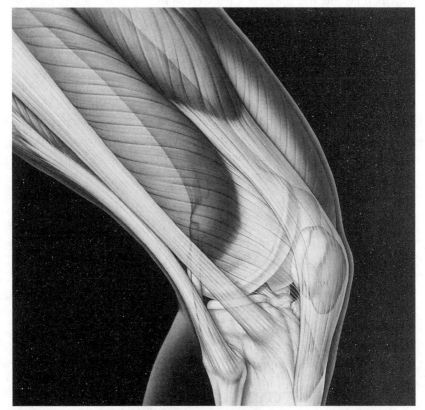

The knee is complicated, so treat minor aches and pains before they become injuries that curtail your riding.

clists who visited their clinic for help. Medial knee injuries (inner side) were diagnosed in 21 percent of the cyclists and accounted for the second largest category of overuse injuries.

The significant bend in the knee that occurs at the top of the pedal stroke can cause a thickening of the medial retinaculum, according to Holmes and Pruitt. The retinaculum is a spiderweb of connective tissue that stabilizes the kneecap. In some cyclists, especially those who push big gears, the medial condyle—it's like one of those two rounded bumps at the end of a chicken bone—can contact the retinaculum and cause it to harden and become chronically inflamed. You'll know it by a strange sort of pain along the medial side of the kneecap during or after riding. Because this injury is relatively unknown in other sports, most doctors will not recognize it, even with the aid of an arthroscope. If untreated, the thickening or hardening may continue until the victim can no longer ride comfortably. Dr. Holmes has perfected a procedure in which he cuts out the thickened section of the retinaculum, thus relieving the pain-causing friction.

Another potential problem is known as iliotibial-band (ITB) syndrome. This is the injury that forced Davis Phinney, the winningest road racer in U.S. history, out of action for a few months during the height of his career. Common sufferers include bowlegged people; their curved thighbones tighten the ITB, which extends from the hip to the lateral (outer side) of the knee. It's also a problem seen in quite a few women, who, because of their relatively wider pelvises, have a more radical angle between their hip and knee bones.

In most cases, rest will quiet an inflamed ITB. In the rare case when surgery is called for, a special procedure, again developed by Dr. Holmes, removes a small piece of the band at the point where it rubs on the knee. Most surgeons slit the band to lengthen it, but this may not alleviate the painful rubbing for cyclists, who subject their knees to such a consistent range of motion.

Holmes and Pruitt reported that training modifications, exercises, rest, ice, and changes in riding position improved the symptoms in 75 percent of the knee cases they treated. No surgery or other drastic action was required. Most knee injuries, they noted, occur in the preseason and summer, when mileage is high, big gears are being pushed, and clothing may not be warm enough for some weather conditions.

SEAT HEIGHT AND FOOT POSITION

Riding position is discussed in detail in chapter 3. But in terms of knee problems, two points are worth emphasizing here. First, a saddle that's too low creates excessive knee bend at the top of the pedal stroke. This can result in strain or damage to the patella tendon. Second, a saddle that's too high creates excessive leg extension, which can put undue stress on the tendons and ligaments behind the knee. Hence, Andy Pruitt's simple maxim: If your knee hurts in front, raise the saddle. If it hurts in back, lower the saddle. In addition, work to develop a smooth pedaling style. Ragged leg action increases the strain on tendons.

If you're a relatively new cyclist and suffering knee problems, you're probably making two mistakes, according to orthopedic surgeon Thomas Dickson, M.D., the former medical director of Pennsylvania's Lehigh Valley Velodrome. "First, new riders tend to set the saddle too low and, second, they use gears that are too high. By cranking along slowly in a big gear, a rider is increasing the force across the knee joint. Conversely, the rider who uses high revolutions per minute and low resistance subjects the joint to much less wear and tear, and substantially increases his aerobic efficiency as well."

Other key factors include how your knee aligns with the pedal as force is applied on the downstroke, and how your foot is positioned on the pedal. Each foot may want to angle inward or outward or point straight ahead, and your right foot may differ from your left. If your cleat position doesn't permit this natural alignment, knee ligaments and tendons will be stressed and pain will probably result. This is why we recommend pedal systems that allow your feet several degrees of unrestricted pivoting ("float") before the cleats disengage. This makes a precise cleat position much less critical, though they still must be in the correct fore/aft location.

After a crash, check your cleats, pedals, and crankarms. Cleats can be twisted out of position, and other parts can be bent. If you ride for long with these problems, knee pain may soon follow. Outline your cleats with an indelible marker so that you can tell when they've moved. And, if you can't tell whether the crankarms or pedals were damaged by a crash, have them checked by a mechanic to make sure the parts are still straight and strong.

Proper clothing during cool weather goes a long way toward preventing knee problems. Wear leg warmers when the temperature dips below 70°F. On warmer days when the mercury might drop, carry them rolled up in a jersey pocket or bike bag. In colder weather, say, under 45°F, wear tights that have windproof material on the front of the legs (or at least over the knees). When it comes to knee protection, it's always better to have too much than too little.

KNEE THERAPY

Here's how to treat cycling's most common knee injuries. Be aggressive about these remedies, or you could develop a chronic condition that disrupts your riding for weeks or months.

Frontal knee pain. Apply ice for 15 to 20 minutes right after riding. Take a pain-reducing anti-inflammatory, such as aspirin or ibuprofen, every 4 hours with food (but not for longer than a week at this rate). On the bike, reduce resistance by using lower gears that you can spin without strain at about 90 revolutions per minute. Raise your saddle a few millimeters. Wear leg warmers if the air is the least bit cool.

Iliotibial band. Use ice and anti-inflammatory drugs, as above. Widen your stance by moving your cleats as far toward the inner edge of the shoe sole as possible. Get even wider by putting washers between the pedals and crankarms (but don't overdo it; make sure plenty of pedal threads engage the crankarms). Use a pedal system that allows more float. Check your saddle height. A low seat combined with lots of hard miles is what usually triggers ITB problems. A stretching routine that works on the outside of the leg should help. If these fixes don't lead to fast improvement, stop riding! Once an ITB injury gets established, it's hard to correct.

Patella tendinitis. Again, use ice and anti-inflammatories. Raise your saddle 2 or 3 millimeters. Do not ride hills or use big gears. Keep your knees warm. Tendinitis usually requires prolonged conservative treatment, including easy spinning or complete rest.

Medial knee pain. Ice, plus aspirin or ibuprofen, plus easy spinning should produce improvement. Stay away from hills or big gears until all pain is gone. If you try to ignore the discomfort and continue riding as usual, ligament injury could result. Then surgery may be the only solution.

Now, what happens if a knee flares up during a long ride, tour, or other multiday event? You can't stop riding, at least until reaching the day's destination. Stop at a store where you can get aspirin or ibuprofen, plus some ice in a plastic bag. Take two or three tablets while you eat, rest, rehydrate, and hold the bag on your knee for 10 to 15 min-

SHOE INSERT
Orthotics for cyclists must extend to the forefoot, because that's where the foot contacts the pedal.

utes. Stay in low gears when you start riding again, and baby the hills. Yes, your speed will drop, but that's nothing to be concerned about now. After finishing, ice again and take more anti-inflams when it's time. Continue downing the medication every 4 hours.

If you have to ride the next day, raise the saddle a bit if the pain is at the front of the knee; lower it if the pain is behind the knee. Keep taking medication, icing when you can, and minimizing resistance by staying in low gears. As soon as the ride is completed, get off the bike for several days while continuing treatment. If you don't have rapid improvement, visit a sports medicine physician.

Leg-Length Discrepancy

Many people are born with a slight variation in their leg lengths. And for most of them, this discrepancy is never a problem. It can be different for cyclists, though, because of the repetitive nature of pedaling. Even a small discrepancy tends to be magnified over time, eventually resulting in foot, ankle, knee, hip, or back injuries. These can be cured, or avoided altogether, with corrections to cycling shoes and off-bike footwear.

If you experience chronic stiffness, soreness, or pain in the body parts just mentioned, especially during or after riding, get checked for a leg-length discrepancy. There are various methods. The most accurate is a scanogram x-ray, which is made with a ruler beside your legs so differences in bone length can be precisely measured. A difference of just a quarter-inch (about 1 centimeter) can put undue stress on your musculoskeletal system. In most cases, saddle height is unknowingly set for the longer leg, which makes it too high for the other one.

In time, chronic overuse injuries can develop on either side of the body because of this improper position. The longer leg may experience greater loads from cycling and other activities, with the result that the foot's arch collapses toward the inside (pronated position) in an attempt to compensate. Conversely, the foot of the shorter leg may roll to the outside (supinated position). These responses help level the pelvis, but stress on the ligaments and tendons of both feet can lead to persistent injuries.

Compensation also may occur at the knee, leading to ligament and tendon soreness there, too. In chronic conditions, the longer leg may bow in or out. It may become hyperextended (pushed backward). If these conditions are allowed to persist, tendinitis or knee instability can develop, and surgery may be the only remedy.

And it doesn't end there. Because the leg bone is connected to the hip bone (as the old song goes), the forces produced by the unequal legs can put undue stress on the hip joint, too. This, in turn, can affect the alignment of the pelvis, leading to abnormal loading of the spine and pain or injury in the lower back.

Do we have your attention? Again, this scary chain reaction can begin with an unremedied leg-length discrepancy as small as a quarter-inch. When problems arise from a skeletal difference, the condition is termed structural. Or it can be functional, which means that actual leg lengths are the same, but they seem to be unequal because of muscle imbalances, problems with riding position or pedaling technique, or faulty foot function. To make it even more complicated, most people with leg-length discrepancies have a combination of structural and functional differences.

If you're experiencing mysterious pain somewhere between your feet and back, do your own leg-length test to see if it makes sense to have a professional evaluation. There are a couple of quick checks. First, strip down and stand barefooted with your feet together on a hard surface in front of a full-length mirror. Place an index finger on the high point of the hip bone on each side. If the fingers are not level, you have a leg-length difference. Of course, the higher hip is connected to the longer leg.

Former Olympic coach Eddie Borysewicz, writing in his book *Bicycle Road Racing*, suggests another way. Lie on your back with bare feet. Have a friend lift both legs by the heels, shake them gently to loosen them, pull them gently to stretch them, and then lay them down together. Your friend can then see how your ankle bones align with each other. Eddie says that if they're off by more than a centimeter, corrective measures are in order.

For cyclists, the fix must occur at the front of the shoe, because that's the part on the pedal (as opposed to runners, who make corrections at the heel). The solution is to shim between the cleat and sole of the short leg with a piece of hard rubber or plastic. The amount doesn't have to be exact. In fact, Andy Pruitt, who has worked with many cyclists at his Boulder Center for Sports Medicine in Colorado, says that making up about half the difference should be enough to remedy the physical problems caused by a large discrepancy, while avoiding a rash of new discomforts with a wholesale change to your body's geometry. You can help the equalization by moving the longer leg's cleat rearward.

Once your cycling shoes are remedied, fix your running and dress

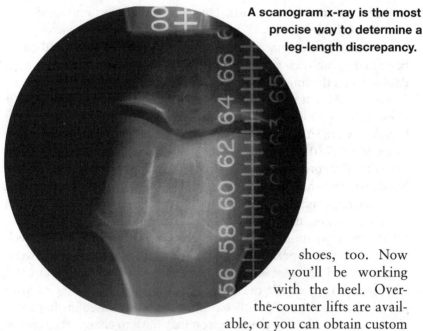

A scanogram x-ray is the most precise way to determine a leg-length discrepancy.

shoes, too. Now you'll be working with the heel. Over-the-counter lifts are available, or you can obtain custom orthotics from your podiatrist or orthopedist. These will be especially helpful if you have pronation or supination problems, too. If you do need orthotics made for your running and dress shoes, be sure to get some made for cycling, too.

You should notice improvement within a month after the discrepancy has been corrected. But if pain persists, visit an osteopath, podiatrist, chiropractor, or orthopedist for professional help. Otherwise, the chances of a chronic, debilitating injury increase. For want of a quarter-inch correction, a cycling career could be lost.

Neck and Shoulders

The longer the distances ridden, the harder cycling is on the muscles of the neck and shoulders. The reason is simple: The neck is held in an extended position for hours at a time. This makes it the weak link in the Race Across America, for example, where numerous riders have dropped out with neck pain or fatigue, unable to hold their head high enough to see the road. In fact, this condition has even been given a name, "Shermer Neck," in honor of RAAM cofounder Michael Shermer, who suffered this debilitating problem in more than one race. He and others have tried various emergency solutions, including wearing plastic neck braces or hooking a bungee cord from the back of their helmets to their shorts. One year, Paul Solon's neck miseries kept him off the bike for 12 hours and nearly cost him a victory. His crew wound up devising a harness with a headband at one end and a belt fixed to a crotch support at the other. Wearing this contraption, Paul reached the finish in the then-record time of 8 days, 8 hours.

Most of us will never experience this level of neck fatigue. But it doesn't take a 3000-mile ride to cause serious discomfort. Riders have been known to suffer nagging pain in events ranging from double centuries to the 750-mile Boston-Montreal-Boston. Some are forced to drop out. Others are seen crossing the finish line with one hand on the handlebar and the other propping up their chin. In shorter events, a sore neck might not be a ride stopper, but it will remove a lot of the fun.

In most cases, neck problems stem from poor conditioning or a faulty riding position. The primary muscle used to support the neck and head is the trapezius, which you can feel by squeezing between your neck and shoulder. Several other muscles lend minor support and are used to turn or tilt the head. Reducing the strain begins with proper stem length and handlebar position, as discussed in chapter 3. If adjustments don't do the trick, you may have to change the stem or bar, or even switch to a frame with more suitable dimensions.

Once your position is right, neck comfort becomes a matter of riding technique. First, don't hold your head in a static position for long periods. Change your hand location to alter your posture and the angle of your neck. Keep your elbows bent and loose, especially on rough surfaces. Don't hold the bar more tightly than necessary to prevent slipping on bumps. Riding with a death grip and stiff arms transmits shock to your upper back and neck, causing aches and fatigue while sapping energy. Ride with your shoulders relaxed, not pressed toward your ears. We see lots of riders making this mistake, hunching and jutting their necks like a turtle.

Tilt your head side to side on occasion, holding it a few degrees from vertical. This helps relax and stretch neck muscles, and prevents you from locking into the dead-center position. When you stop briefly, say, while waiting for a light to change, drop your chin to your chest, then rotate your head in a circle, once in each direction. At the first sign of soreness or stiffness, use a hand to massage the back of your neck and trapezius. Another effective way that you can relax neck muscles is first to tighten them by pulling your shoulders to your ears for several seconds. Then let your shoulders drop, and you'll feel the tension disappear.

Interestingly, a sunny day can be a pain in the neck. Squinting tenses

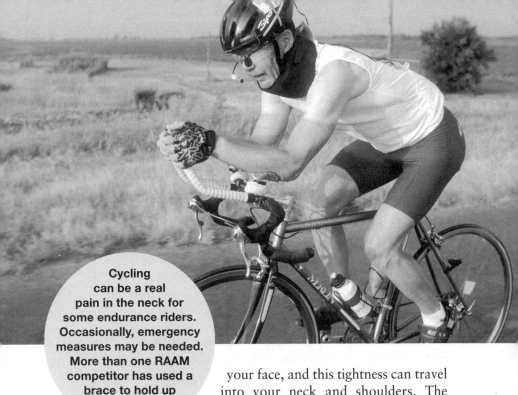

Cycling can be a real pain in the neck for some endurance riders. Occasionally, emergency measures may be needed. More than one RAAM competitor has used a brace to hold up their heads.

your face, and this tightness can travel into your neck and shoulders. The muscle soreness this causes could even produce a headache. The solution is to wear sunglasses that are dark enough to prevent eyestrain. As discussed in chapter 13, for all-around protection they should also block sunlight's harmful ultraviolet rays.

AERO BARS

Elsewhere we discuss the important comfort and speed advantages of using aero bars. But there can be drawbacks, too. Chief among them is the strain that a low, aerodynamic position puts on your neck as your head tilts back to see down the road. (There's relatively little danger of this when using bar-ends on a mountain bike. Your torso won't be nearly as horizontal, nor will your position be as static.)

To limit the stress, raise the stem or use riser pegs (if your aero bar offers them) to elevate the armrests. For a short, fast, time trial, you want to be as low as possible, even if this means craning your neck. But, for long rides, you must find a compromise between aerodynamics and neck comfort. The place to start is with the armrests at saddle height. As you grow accustomed to using an aero bar, you may be able to gradually lower it to improve speed without causing strain or soreness. Remember our tip about cocking your head slightly to one side or the other. The lower you go, the more it helps if your neck isn't locked straight back.

Flexibility and strength are the other keys to aero comfort. Condition your neck and shoulders with off-bike stretches and exercises. Rotate your neck gently and slowly through its full range. Do isometric strengthening by holding your head with your hands to resist movement as you try to tilt it forward, backward, and to either side. Push for 10 seconds in one direction, relax, and then push in another direction. Or use the neck apparatus you may find at health clubs. To strengthen the trapezius muscle, stand with a barbell or dumbbell in each hand, slowly raise your shoulders toward your ears, pause, and then lower. Use a weight that allows at least 20 repetitions, or reps. As your strength improves, build muscle endurance by increasing the reps instead of the weight.

COLD WEATHER

Cold air on a poorly protected neck can result in muscle stiffness or even a sore throat. Don't forget the effect of windchill on moist skin. Even on a calm winter day, your riding speed creates an icy breeze. For protection, wear a turtleneck undershirt or a jersey or jacket with a high collar. To cover skin entirely, use a balaclava under your helmet and tuck it in well to prevent air leaks. This can keep your neck from getting cranky even in subfreezing air. By the way, you needn't worry about the inside of your throat. Frigid air is instantly warmed by the body heat generated by exercise. In fact, it's been found that air breathed in at –40°F is warmed to more than 100°F before it reaches the lungs, even if you're breathing through the mouth.

In extreme conditions, or if breathing cold air is a particular problem for you, check into a balaclava or mask that fits over your mouth and nose. These retain heat and moisture to protect your face, and boost the temperature of the air being breathed in.

Back

The first twinges of back pain can be the start of a long, unhappy ordeal that makes it difficult or impossible to ride. It disrupts off-the-bike life, too. This is why it pays to understand back injuries and know how to deal with them.

The usual culprits are overexertion or—especially for new cyclists—a faulty riding position. In either case, pain occurs when nerve endings are abnormally stimulated. Muscles may go into spasm to hold the back immobile so that discomfort is reduced. Because the back's disks, ligaments, and muscles have so many nerve endings, it's a complex problem.

Stress, fatigue, and even the anxieties of daily life also play a role.

Before you get the wrong idea, we should emphasize that cycling is good exercise for your back—if you don't make the physical mistakes we've mentioned—because it enhances the circulation of blood and nutrients. Although back muscles are not directly involved in turning the pedals, they help stabilize your body and enhance the energy transfer from your hips and legs. To get down the road or trail efficiently and comfortably, your position must first meet the parameters established in chapter 3, and then you need to build strength and endurance through smart training. To keep yourself under control, obey the rule that says to increase your mileage (or time on the bike) by no more than 10 percent per week. Be equally sane about increases in speed, gearing, rides into hilly terrain, or going hard right after making an equipment or position change.

Whether you're on a road bike with a drop handlebar or on a mountain bike with bar-ends, you can help back comfort a lot by making full use of the various hand positions. This is the way, too, to maximize the leverage and power generated by back muscles, especially when climbing. For instance, sit up and slide back on the saddle to increase the force of each pedal stroke. On extended climbs, stand periodically with your hands gripping the brake lever hoods or bar-ends. Let your arms, body weight, and back muscles combine to help you turn the pedals. Alternating between sitting and standing lets you use your back muscles differently, avoiding stiffness and delaying fatigue. Even on flat ground, you'll benefit from getting out of the saddle occasionally to stretch your back and legs.

SUSPENSION AND STRETCHING

Cyclists who have a back injury from any source, or simply can't find lasting comfort on the bike, may benefit from suspension. Shock-absorbing seatposts, flexible seat beams, or frames with built-in rear suspension effectively reduce the jolts that make pain receptors fire. For the full treatment, check into a suspension fork or stem, too. They can be added to road bikes as well as mountain bikes. To take the edge off vibration and smaller impacts, try a more padded saddle or one with shock-reducing rubber inserts between the rails and plastic shell. A similar benefit comes from using wider tires with lower inflation pressure. This, however, costs some speed because of increased rolling resistance. Finally, it may help to violate some rules of ideal bike setup by raising the handlebar to seat level (or higher) or bringing it closer with a shorter stem. If this is what it takes to make your back happy, go for it.

Oh, That Painful Prostate

Fortunate is the man who makes it through his cycling career without at least one bout of prostate problems. The prostate's potential for trouble is related to its location. This walnut-size gland, which produces the fluid portion of semen, surrounds the neck of the urinary bladder. Infection or enlargement can make sitting on a bike seat very uncomfortable.

Prostatitis, or inflammation of the prostate, causes swelling and tenderness. This condition can be acute or chronic. The acute version, usually caused by bacteria, is marked by fever, pain at the base of the penis, and painful, frequent urination. Sitting on a bike seat, or any firm surface, hurts. Treatment includes antibiotics, bed rest, and extra fluids. Because dehydration can aggravate prostatitis, be certain to drink a lot if you are able to ride.

The chronic version is usually more difficult to treat. Often no bacteria can be identified as a certain cause, so a broad-spectrum antibiotic is used. Some physicians prescribe tranquilizers, contending that emotions and stress play a role. Hot sitz baths may help alleviate the tenderness.

As you pass through middle age, you may slowly develop a condition known as benign prostatic enlargement. This is thought to be related to hormonal changes associated with getting older. About 10 percent of men have some prostate enlargement by age 40; by age 60, the condition is almost universal. It impinges the urethra, thereby narrowing the passageway through which urine flows. This set of symptoms, known as prostatism, makes it difficult to begin urinating even as the need increases. Surgery to alleviate the blockage is the usual solution. Anyone who has this operation should not return to cycling until the doctor gives permission. When riding is out of the question, try sports such as running, swimming, skating, or hiking to maintain fitness. In some cases, a recumbent bike or ergometer may let you pedal pain-free and maintain cycling's specific muscle tone.

For mild prostatitis, try raising your handlebar to reduce your forward lean and lessen pressure on the tender gland. Switching to your mountain bike, even for road riding, may be more comfortable thanks to the higher bar position. Use a seat that's wide enough to support your weight on your butt. You may want to add a saddle pad for extra width and softness. You won't need a reminder to stand frequently.

Stretching can help remedy a tight, sore back—or prevent discomfort in the first place. Taut back muscles limit your range of motion and increase the chance of pulls and strains. See chapter 17 for recommended stretches both on and off the bike. In addition, many riders have found that a daily set of abdominal crunches effectively stretches their lower back and tones their midsection. It sounds paradoxical, but one key to a healthy back is a strong stomach. The reason for this is that weak abdominal muscles allow the lower back to curve inward, increasing the strain on its muscles, ligaments, and discs. Ed Pavelka, once a victim of frustrating lower-back pain, has kept the problem at bay for years by doing up to 200 crunches after every ride. Many other long-distance riders follow a similar regimen.

If you have back pain that doesn't subside with position changes, better riding techniques, the addition of suspension, or stretching and strengthening, take some time off. A 7- to 10-day break could be the answer. If not, visit a sports medicine clinic for evaluation by a specialist who is familiar with the demands of cycling. The problem could be bone-related, such as a compressed or herniated disc. Or it could result from a leg-length discrepancy, a condition that Andy Pruitt says he often finds in riders with chronic lower-back pain. Extensive treatment may be necessary to prevent the pain from affecting not just your cycling, but also your routine daily activities.

Finally, when riding in chilly weather, make sure your lower back is covered by your jersey and windbreaker. We've seen cyclists with their clothing riding up and exposing their skin to cool air. It's a good bet they'll be stiff the next day. One of Ed Pavelka's winter tricks is to wear a small fanny pack that keeps his jacket in place and holds more body heat on his lower back. It's also a handy way to carry food when jersey pockets are covered.

Sore Muscles

"My legs feel so sore and heavy that I can hardly walk, let alone pedal a bike. I need to take the day off."

If you've said this, it was probably after a long ride with plenty of hills. But why? What makes our muscles so tight and tender? How could our finely trained bodies fail like this? After all, we've worked on climbing and have plenty of miles in our legs. Our muscle tone is top-notch, isn't it?

Well, maybe—but there's still such a thing as doing too much. Each of us has a limit. When it's exceeded, the day after is almost sure to bring an athletic hangover. In more formal terms, it's called "delayed onset of muscle soreness," or DOMS for short. Long-distance riders are especially susceptible, because our events almost always exceed training distances and intensities. This is why DOMS is the dominant complaint during the days after big-time events such as Paris-Brest-Paris or Boston-Montreal-Boston. No one can train sufficiently for rides that cover 750 miles with 35,000 feet of climbing. For a couple of days after the finish, climbing a flight of stairs seems as tough as taking the final steps up Mt. Everest.

The cause of this discomfort is deep fatigue due to overuse, plus minor strains in individual muscle fibers. What doesn't cause it (despite what high school coaches may have told you) is lactic acid, even though this nasty stuff is abundant during a hard, hilly ride.

Lactic acid is produced during intense exercise when the muscles' demand for oxygen increases beyond the amount that the blood can deliver. To generate enough energy, the body begins a different process, which works in the absence of oxygen. Lactic acid is a by-product of this anaerobic activity. And because it is an acid, it causes muscles to burn and seize up. We've all felt this painful effect when pedaling hard on a steep climb.

But lactic acid is completely washed out of muscles within 60 minutes after a ride. Because the worst of muscle soreness doesn't show up till 24 to 36 hours later, scientists have been exercising their brains to come up with another explanation. The most popular theory says that when you overdo cycling, weight training, or any other intense activity, it actually tears the membranes of muscle fibers. During the next 24 hours, they become swollen with blood. Chemical irritants are released, and these do a number on pain receptors. Instead of moving freely, muscle fibers are bloated, fatigued, and sore. Nerves perceive this abnormal state and send pain signals to the brain as soon as you move your legs the next morning. Although movement is what it takes to restore muscles to a normal state, you can't exercise at your full potential because damaged muscles aren't at full strength.

Help the healing process by stretching, massaging, applying an analgesic sports balm, or sitting in a hot tub or sauna. To relieve pain, over-the-counter anti-inflammatories such as aspirin or ibuprofen are effective. They make it more comfortable to begin riding again.

To avoid DOMS in the first place, train sensibly to gradually increase the strength and endurance of your muscles. Stretch and warm up properly for each ride. Remember that intense cycling and activities such as weight training use certain muscle cells that aren't used regularly in normal riding or your daily life. It all comes down to what's known as the specificity of training, where your muscles, tendons, and ligaments adapt to the demands of a particular sport.

In addition, as we grow older, our muscles and surrounding tissues have less elasticity. We tend to feel more tightness and soreness than we did in our teens or twenties. But if you stay in shape, you should be able to ride just as hard right through your thirties and into your forties, with few bouts of serious muscle strain. You may feel some stiffness after a real tough ride or weight session, but stretching and an easy warmup will chase it away the next day.

Don't forget, though, that sore muscles are damaged muscles. As with any injury, they must be given time to heal. This may require several days of easy spinning. You'll sense when it's okay to start pushing harder again. Until then, have self-control so you won't develop a more serious injury—or the deep fatigue that marks the downward spiral into overtraining.

Cramps

We know what a muscle cramp is—an out-of-control contraction that won't stop without quick action—but no one knows for sure why cramps happen. What is certain is that they can disable even the fittest cyclist. They strike suddenly in long, hard events, giving their victims a few seconds of excruciating pain. Even worse, after a muscle cramps, it often feels ready to do it again unless you ride gently for a while—perhaps even the rest of the distance. There goes your chance for a top performance.

Several factors are involved with cramping. Included are muscle exhaustion, dehydration, electrolyte imbalance, and low blood glucose. Even a change in equipment or position can be the spark. Here's a good example. During an attempt to break the 277-mile New York cross-state record, Ed Pavelka began instinctively clawing the pedals upward with extra force to maintain his speed. He didn't know it, but the brake pads were dragging on the rear rim. It seems that his right brake lever had loosened just enough to slide farther around the handlebar curve, pulling the cable tighter as though the brake were being applied. What Ed did know was that the bike was getting darn hard to pedal. Mystified, he switched to his backup bike just before reaching the route's biggest climbs. The first time he stood, one of his overworked hamstrings cramped. Ed managed to squeeze out the knot and avoid toppling over, but the twinging threat of another seizure kept him in the saddle and riding hills gingerly for the remaining 140 miles. He made it, but then paid big-time when both hamstrings wadded up like a bad test paper as he dismounted. All that yelling was not exactly in celebration of getting the record.

Of all the cramp contributors, dehydration is probably the most common. Cyclists can sweat out as much as a quart of fluid per hour when working hard in hot weather. Because this loss lowers blood volume, there's less blood going to muscles to deliver oxygen, and cramps can result.

Another possible cause, related to dehydration, involves electrolytes. These are positively or negatively charged ions that are necessary for nerve transmission and muscle function. The minerals sodium and potassium, together with calcium and magnesium, serve as electrolytes that help regulate muscle contraction and relaxation. Because sodium is lost during sweating, dehydration can contribute to an electrolyte imbalance. This, in turn, may cause muscles to contract involuntarily. People who are unusually susceptible to cramps may have inherently low electrolyte levels.

Cramps may also strike more often when muscles are overworked and fatigued. This may be why cyclists who aren't well trained tend to get more cramps. Cold weather also seems to increase cramping in some people. Other, less-common factors include diabetes and circulatory or neurological disorders. Think about any medications you're taking, too. Some drugs, such as diuretics and bronchial dilators, are thought to play a role. If you're on any kind of medication and have persistent cramps, check with your doctor or pharmacist about a possible connection.

QUICK RELIEF

Regardless of the cause, the way to get immediate relief is the same for any cramp. Straighten and stretch the muscle as best you can. At the same time, squeeze or knead it to help unlock the knot. Stroke toward the heart to get blood passing through. The relief that this brings may last only a short time, however, if the underlying cause isn't identified and corrected.

If a cramp occurs while you're riding, try to stretch out the affected muscle if you can do so without jeopardizing bike control. Otherwise, stop so that you can massage the area and swig some sports drink that has electrolytes (most do). You may have to stay off the bike for 10 to 20 minutes until the muscle relaxes. Then spin easily before gradually rebuilding your intensity. Continue to stretch and massage the muscle, especially if it begins twinging again. Chapter 17 describes a number of effective on-bike stretches.

Here's an interesting trick to try. The next time you feel a cramp coming on, grab your upper lip and pinch it firmly. This provides immediate relief for some people. We're not sure of the physiological reason. Maybe there's some alteration of the neurotransmission to the muscle. But who cares, as long as it works? Also effective is eating antacid tablets high in calcium as soon as twinges begin. We learned this trick from Furnace Creek 508 champion Dan McGehee, who once handed Ed Pavelka a couple of Tums to save him on a hilly 85-mile ride in Arizona.

To lessen the chance of cramping in the first place, start each ride well hydrated, and then keep pumping in fluids while on the bike. Remember, don't rely on thirst as a guide. By the time you feel thirsty, you may already be at the point where dehydration is hurting performance—and about to hurt your muscles with cramps. You'll probably have to force yourself to drink more than you think you need, because thirst is usually quenched before fluid needs are met.

A sports drink is the best anticramp fluid. It replenishes blood sugar and electrolytes as well as water. Avoid any drink with caffeine, including coffee, tea, and some soft drinks, because it makes your body excrete fluid, working against your efforts to stay hydrated. To boost cramp prevention, also make sure your diet includes ample levels of potassium (bananas and oranges are good sources), plus calcium and magnesium (fat-free milk and yogurt, whole-grain breads and cereals, leafy green vegetables, and beans). You may wish to salt your food to ensure adequate sodium, especially in hot weather, but be cautious about using salt tablets unless you know they agree with your system. They could cause stomach irritation and draw water from the bloodstream into your intestines.

In a study conducted for several years at the Hotter'n Hell Hundred century ride in the heat of Texas, it was determined that magnesium is what separated the riders who cramped from those who didn't. The crampers had less of this mineral. If you're the victim of chronic cramping, you might want to copy what they did in Texas and have a blood test immediately after a ride that makes your muscles seize. This can tell you if a low level of one or more electrolytes may be at fault.

Finally, stretching before and after riding usually reduces cramping. If nighttime cramps are a problem, you should try stretching before going to bed.

15

Battling Your Body and the Elements

In the 1999 Furnace Creek 508, 43
solo riders battled temperatures that were extreme even for Death
Valley in mid-October. At one point, the mercury reached 107°F. More
than half of these brave athletes abandoned the race and, as is the
custom in ultramarathon events, the reasons for their ill fortune were
recorded. "Exhaustion," said one. "My body shut down," explained
another. "I wasn't ready to meet God," commented a third. The over-
riding reason, however—cited by a third of all nonfinishers—was
simply "stomach." This is why we say in chapter 6 that eating and digesting food while riding is the most difficult challenge for many long-
distance cyclists.

Endurance athletes in any sport routinely complain of gastrointestinal problems. An estimated one-quarter of them even experience
diarrhea during or after long events. Let's look into the causes of and
solutions for this potential showstopper, as well as several other
common medical and environmental roadblocks that long-distance
cyclists may run into.

Gastrointestinal Distress

It seems as if nearly every person who rides long distances will eventually encounter GI grief. In fact, it may be unavoidable due to how
our bodies work. Gastrointestinal functioning requires an ample blood
supply to deliver oxygen and carry away water and nutrients. As you
ride, however, less blood is available for your intestines. Instead, it's
directed to your heart and working muscles. Low blood sugar and dehydration further aggravate the situation as a ride wears on. Then add
a few hills. Bloodflow to the GI tract may decrease by as much as 80

percent during strenuous climbing. Without adequate blood, cells starve for oxygen and water pools in the large intestine. The first symptoms are abdominal pain and cramping. Then diarrhea. Then internal bleeding and loss of tissue.

Sounds nasty, and it is. Here are some things you can do to reduce the risk.

Avoid bowel-stimulating substances. Caffeine ranks as the most common intestinal irritant. Some people can't handle certain sugars, such as lactose or fructose. The former is found in dairy foods, while the latter is derived from fruit and used as a sweetener in processed foods, including many energy bars and sports drinks. If you think that caffeine, lactose, or fructose may be causing stomach distress, simply avoid it before and during rides to see if there is improvement. If lactose is the culprit, the Lactaid line of products lets you get the nutritional benefits of dairy foods without the GI risk.

Eat light. Try low-fiber carbohydrate foods such as bananas, oatmeal (without added sugar), and toast before a ride. Bananas are a popular on-bike food because they're high in nutrients and easily digested.

Establish a preride bathroom routine. Give yourself enough time between waking up and starting a morning ride. A light meal can trigger a bowel movement. So can a cup of coffee, but too much caffeine can cause trouble during the ride. You may want to see if a cup of green tea (lower in caffeine than coffee) or herbal tea does the trick.

Consider a new training time. If morning rides often stimulate bothersome bathroom calls, ride later in the day.

Avoid highly concentrated beverages. Use sports drinks that have no more than 10 percent carbohydrate. Most bottled brands have the right carbo content, but be careful if you mix your own from powder. Beverages that are more concentrated than 10 percent can delay stomach-emptying and draw water into your intestinal tract, causing diarrhea. Also, beware of drinks that use fructose as the primary sweetener. (This is the case if fructose is the first or only sugar on the ingredients list.) Fructose is known to cause GI upset in some people.

Gradually boost your exercise level. When you're in top condition, your muscles use oxygen efficiently. This allows them to share more blood with your intestines. If you're having stomach problems, insufficient blood supply may be the reason. Reduce your effort until continued training brings you to a higher level of fitness. Increases in your distance, time, or exertion on the bike should not exceed 10 percent per week.

Stay hydrated. Make sure to drink plenty before every training ride or event. Get in the habit of carrying a water bottle during your daily activities so that you can sip frequently.

Calm down. Pre-event anxiety is notorious for causing a queasy stomach or diarrhea. You can reduce this risk by establishing a routine and sticking to it.

Avoid surprises. Don't eat or drink anything in an important event that you haven't tested in training. A couple of weeks before, contact the organizer to find out which specific foods and drinks will be provided at rest stops. If there are things new to you, try them during a couple of long training rides. Still not confident? Stick to the things you normally eat and drink, even if you have to load your pockets before the start or arrange for someone to supply you along the route.

Use medication. Try products such as Pepto Bismol or Immodium AD to curb diarrhea. Follow the directions. Antacids and products such as Pepcid AC may alleviate indigestion or even stop it from beginning. Ultramarathon champion John Stamstad takes capsules of activated charcoal, available at drugstores, to combat an upset stomach.

Preseason Physical

Do you need a medical examination every year? Yes! Even if you feel perfectly healthy, it's smart to get checked if you're planning a full season of training and tough events. If there are any irregularities in your body's cardiovascular, neurological, orthopedic, or respiratory functions, you certainly want them found and treated before the season begins. Otherwise, there's the risk of a problem revealing itself right when training stresses are mounting, setting you back at a time you should be making big gains.

Schedule your annual physical for February or March, allowing time to treat any problems before serious training begins. Be sure your doctor has your complete medical history (including injuries). Also be certain to mention any symptoms related to exercise, such as wheezing or lightheadedness. Don't overlook anything. The exam should include a blood test to determine your red cell, white cell, hemoglobin, and hematocrit counts, which together establish your general state of health. These are especially useful if you're having chronic problems with fatigue or strength. A blood test also provides a baseline for reference in case of illness or injury.

Experiment with these and other products to find what works for your unique digestive system.

If you have habitual bowel discomfort, or if you notice blood in your stools (fresh bleeding looks red, while blood from higher in the GI tract may appear black), see a doctor right away. You could have an infection or bowel disease unrelated to cycling.

Heat and Hydration

The best way to beat the heat is to ride in it. This is called acclimation. If you'll be traveling to an event in a place that's much warmer than where you live, try to go a week early and then follow the upcoming advice. These tips also are useful when your own area is smothered by an extended heat wave.

Reduce your cycling intensity and duration. Then gradually build back up. It's hard to give specific guidelines, because everyone adapts differently to heat stress. Be cautious and do a bit less than you can handle rather than push your limits.

Ride early to beat the heat. In the first few days of acclimation,

A complete preseason physical should discover the following:

- Any medical or orthopedic problems that would be aggravated by cycling or complementary activities such as weight training

- Any medical or orthopedic problems that require further evaluation or therapy before you begin serious training

- Any structural features that predispose you to injury or may require corrective measures such as orthotics

- Your percentage of body fat and overall physical fitness, and whether any specific conditioning programs are needed

Done with the doc? Now visit your dentist and optometrist. Schedule all annual exams at the same time in late winter, so you'll go into the season with all systems in top shape.

train first thing in the morning when the air is cooler and cleaner. The event will probably have you riding right through midday, though, so on the final 2 or 3 days, go out between noon and 3:00 P.M. Don't ride hard and compound the stress.

Prehydrate. Drink at least 16 ounces of fluid during the 90 minutes before riding. Then start drinking as early as 15 minutes into the ride. Don't wait until you feel thirsty. Also, don't gulp a lot at a time, which could upset your stomach. Instead, sip small amounts (one or two mouthfuls) frequently.

Drink, drink, and drink some more. When riding at a strong pace in extreme heat, you can sweat as much as 2 quarts per hour. The formula is simple: If your fluid loss through sweating and urination exceeds your fluid intake, you'll experience a deficit. That's dehydration. When this loss exceeds 3 percent of body weight, one result is an impaired ability to efficiently use oxygen. That spells fatigue. When it exceeds 6 percent, your power will deteriorate tremendously. Remember, even during nonathletic activities in hot and humid conditions, your fluid loss may approach 10 quarts every 24 hours.

Use a carbohydrate-electrolyte drink. During a ride, fluid that contains 6 to 10 percent carbohydrate may improve your endurance by delaying the point of exhaustion. Research has also shown that a postexercise carbohydrate-electrolyte beverage replaces lost fluid in the blood faster than pure water. To get these benefits, use a carbo-rich sports drink that contains minerals such as sodium, chloride, and potassium.

Get enough salt. Cyclists who ride for hours in hot and humid conditions, or who tend to sweat heavily, run the risk of dangerously depleting their sodium level. A pound of sweat contains 400 to 700 milligrams (mg) of sodium, so during a strenuous 3-hour ride in the heat, as much as 5,700 milligrams could be lost. The more acclimated to the heat you become, the less sodium you'll lose in your sweat. But if a deficit does occur, the effects can include poor fluid absorption from the stomach, muscle cramps, and general fatigue. The best treatment is prevention—be sure your sports drink contains sodium, and eat salty foods. Three or four pretzels or a slice of bread provide around 200 milligrams of sodium, a bagel contains about 320, and a small salt packet that you can mooch from a fast-food place has 500. For long rides in sultry weather, you also can take a sodium chloride tablet (available at drugstores) every 4 hours. One tablet typically provides 250 to 400 milligrams.

Of course, it's a lot easier to know what to drink than it is to actu-

During Team RAAM '96, Skip Hamilton battled midsummer heat between each 30-minute riding shift. Note the ice bag behind his neck and the cold soda can under his arm.

ally drink it after your liquids become as hot as shimmering asphalt. The trick is to keep them cool so they stay palatable. Studies have found that cool fluids (45° to 55°F) actually empty quicker from the stomach and help reduce body temperature.

Standard water bottles baking in the sun won't stay cold for long. One solution is to freeze a sports drink in your bottles and swig the melting fluid. Or, you can use insulated bottles. In either case, however, the amount of cold liquid you can carry is limited by the bottles' relatively small capacity. For long rides in hot conditions, ensure enough cold liquid by using a backpack-style hydration system. Fill the reservoir with ice cubes made from your sports drink, then top it off with more of the drink before starting. The contents will stay cold for the 2 hours or so that it takes to drink down the reservoir. Then you can stop at a convenience store to refill it with ice and whatever sports drink is available. (Often you can avoid buying a bag of ice—much of which will go to waste unless you're riding with friends—by using the self-serve soda station. Fill the largest cup with ice and set it on the counter with the drink you're buying. It's the rare cashier who'll try to charge for the ice when face-to-face with a poor, hot, sweaty cyclist.)

Judge your state of hydration by weighing yourself each morning right after you visit the bathroom. Record the number in your training diary. If you should see a weight loss of 1 percent or more from the previous day, don't ride until you're rehydrated. Do this by drinking 16 ounces of fluid for each pound of body weight that you're down. Even better, weigh yourself in the buff immediately before and after riding to learn how much you should be drinking on the bike to stay fully hydrated. Ideally, you will finish hot-weather rides within a pound of your starting weight.

The status of your body's fluid level also can be judged by how much you are urinating. An average adult will excrete about 1.2 quarts every 24 hours. If your volume is less, it's a sign that your body is conserving fluid. You're not drinking enough. Dark yellow urine is another sign of dehydration. When you're properly hydrated, your urine will be almost clear.

HEAT ILLNESS

You might find it valuable to monitor your core body temperature during and immediately after riding. It should stay below 102°F. Unfortunately, we're talking about your rectal temperature, because an oral reading isn't accurate for this measurement. Should your core temperature reach 104°F, you're on the verge of heatstroke, a serious, potentially fatal medical emergency.

Heatstroke is the ultimate hot-weather hazard. It occurs when the body's temperature-regulating processes simply stop functioning. Sweating ceases and skin becomes hot and dry. Other symptoms include disorientation, headache, vomiting, and unconsciousness. Death could be just minutes away, so immediate action is required, even before emergency medical help arrives. Lower the victim's body temperature by any means possible. Get him into an air-conditioned building or at least into the shade. Immerse him in cool water (a pond or stream, for example) or apply ice if it's available. Even rubbing alcohol poured on the skin will help.

Three lesser forms of heat illness are more common: muscle cramps, heat syncope (fainting), and heat exhaustion. Cramps usually can be prevented by drinking enough fluid that contains electrolytes such as sodium and potassium. Most sports drinks do. In extreme conditions, you should also eat foods high in sodium (check the label) or take salt tablets. Fainting is most likely to occur when you stop rather than when you're riding. So beware of this at rest areas, especially if they come right after a hard effort. Also, don't get off to recover at the top of a long climb. Wait till after the descent, when your body has cooled and your heart rate is down. Heat exhaustion is just what it says—the inability to continue physical activity due to the effects of high temperatures. This condition is readily reversed by replacing fluids and electrolytes. Unheeded, however, it can escalate to headache, dizziness, and nausea—all the way to heatstroke.

Factors that increase your risk of developing these heat-related maladies include insufficient sleep, glycogen depletion, certain medications such as diuretics, a cold or other illness, and a sudden increase in training volume or intensity. The potential for fainting and exhaustion is reduced by two key factors already discussed—acclimation and sufficient hydration.

Cold-Weather Survival

Ed Burke is on his mountain bike in Alaska's 100-mile Iditabike, riding the famous Iditarod dogsled trail. It's a clear night with a three-quarter moon. No lights are needed. The snow glows silver, the trees are black. There are no other colors and no other riders within miles. The only sound is Ed's tires crunching the snow. It's –30°F.

The Iditabike course winds through wild, desolate terrain and frozen rivers on the way to the remote Eagle Song Lodge on the shores of Trail Lake. That's the halfway point. The route isn't a problem during the day, but because this is a race, the riders don't stop when the long February night begins. To make it a bit easier, there are supply tents along the way. Each rider has to find the pace that lets him or her reach the next fuel stop before becoming exhausted.

Ed completed this arctic adventure in 21 hours and 52 minutes, during which he was off the bike for only about 4 hours to thaw, eat, and refill his CamelBak hydration system. The sense of achievement he felt had nothing to do with his placing in the race, and everything to do with successfully completing the distance in such challenging conditions. "Even if you're not interested in long-distance winter racing," he says, "winter doesn't have to be a time for hibernation. It can actually be the most fulfilling season, considering the rare beauty and crisp, clean air that you will experience while everyone else is cooped up inside complaining about the weather."

For those of us who live in northern climates, being a cyclist means that the season doesn't start and stop with warm weather. In fact, as both of your authors know well, winter can be a fun and productive time to ride a bike and enjoy complementary sports. We discuss this in detail in chapter 18. But there's no denying that along with low temperatures come certain risks.

To become accustomed to the cold, you must exercise in the cold. This is the same well-known concept called acclimation that also applies to the heat. For example, one study found that after 6 weeks of outdoor winter activity, test subjects suffered less loss of bloodflow and numbness in their fingers during 4 hours of exposure. **Never push yourself to exhaustion on a winter ride.** You need to pedal intensely enough to maintain your core temperature, but don't overdo it. If you should run low on energy way out on the route, you'll be in for a long, chilly slog home. Also, riding too hard increases sweating, which dampens clothes, makes you feel colder, and opens the door for a dangerous medical condition known as hypothermia. In winter, always save some energy for the unexpected—changes in weather, or delays caused by a flat tire or other mechanical problem.

Watch the wind. One of the oldest tenets in cycling is still one of the wisest: Ride into the wind during the first half of the ride so that it will be at your back on the way home. It's better to tackle a headwind when you're fresh, rather than have it batter you for miles as your energy is waning. Also, it's uncomfortable and even dangerous to have an icy wind against you after you've become damp with sweat. A tailwind seems almost balmy by comparison.

Ride at midday. Any sunlight will be at its most intense around noon, adding some warmth and helping drivers see you, just as it helps you see road hazards. Be cautious when riding into shadows, because they may be hiding icy spots or potholes. Also, realize that your winter head protection may reduce your hearing or vision. Stay alert for cars approaching from behind, especially on roads narrowed by snowbanks. In winter, you need to ride even more defensively.

DRESS FOR DURESS

During cycling, your body generates 8 to 15 times more heat than it does at rest. This is more than enough to maintain its core temperature. By dressing properly, even the subzero temperatures that result from windchill will have minimal effect on your ability to stay warm.

A useful mnemonic for winter cycling is VIP: ventilate, insulate, protect.

Ventilate to reduce heat buildup. The best way is to wear a lightweight outer jacket with a windproof front, breathable back, and full-length front zipper. When climbing or riding with a tailwind, zip down to let excess body heat escape. Then zip up on descents or headwind sections. For one-hand operation, hold the jacket down by strapping a belt or fanny pack around your waist. A fanny pack has the added advantages of trapping heat on your lower back and allowing you to carry extra items.

Insulate by dressing your upper body in layers. This technique helps to trap body heat much better than a single thick jacket. In

Winter doesn't need to be a time for hibernation if you have the right equipment, clothing, and adventurous attitude.

addition, wear fabrics that are designed to draw moisture away from your skin to keep it drier and warmer. Polypropylene is a generic fiber that does this well. You'll find various proprietary brand-name materials, too. Ideally, each layer will perform this wicking action to keep sweat moving away from your skin.

Protect your head, hands, and feet. A balaclava works great for preventing excessive heat loss through your head and neck. Mittens or three-finger "lobster" mitts are warmer than gloves because they trap hand heat in compartments instead of isolating each finger. Whatever type you choose, be sure it has a high, stretchy cuff that overlaps your long sleeves by a couple of inches to prevent air leaks. Protect feet with wool socks and insulated booties, as discussed in chapter 5.

Feet that perspire excessively will feel clammy and cold. You may find it effective to apply an underarm antiperspirant to your feet before you put on your heavy socks. Another way to shut down sweat ducts is to soak your feet in a bucket of warm water with a tablespoon or two of boric acid the night before a long, cold ride. To generate more heat, sprinkle some cayenne pepper in the toe area of your socks. This encourages bloodflow in the capillaries. After the ride, rinse off the pepper with cool water before your shower, or the hot water may burn your skin. Also available are battery-heated socks and insoles. These products aren't specifically for cyclists but do work well, especially on long rides that eventually sap body heat no matter how well insulated you are.

All of these tips will help you avoid hypothermia, a potentially fatal condition in which the body's core temperature drops far below normal. Contributors are fatigue, damp clothing, and windchill. It needn't be very cold for hypothermia to set in. In fact, it can occur in midsummer, particularly in mountainous regions where cyclists get caught in high-altitude thunderstorms. Early signs are shivering, muscle weakness, and loss of coordination. When you experience these symptoms, it's best to continue riding and get the wind at your back. Don't stop unless you can go into someplace warm. At the first opportunity, have something hot to drink. Take a warm shower or bath, and put on dry clothes.

NUTRITIONAL NEEDS

Riding in the cold usually requires more calories because you and your bike are heavier. First there's the extra weight of winter clothes. Simply adding 100 to 200 grams to each foot by wearing heavier socks and booties causes a measurable increase in oxygen consumption. Your winter bike may be heavier because it has lights, fenders, and a rear rack with a trunk on top. It may have relatively heavy, more durable wheels and tires, too. Overall, these things create more air and rolling resistance that increases energy cost.

There's no need to significantly increase your caloric intake during cold weather, but you may want to have a snack before you ride. Digesting it will add some heat to your body via metabolism, sort of like putting another log on the fire. It's a good idea, too, to carry food on every winter ride in case you need emergency energy. Make sure it isn't something that will freeze and be difficult to eat. Energy gels are a good choice if stored inside the warmth of your jacket.

As in summer, you must keep drinking during rides. Remember the three times to take another sip: when you're thirsty, when you're not thirsty, and in between. Don't be fooled because it's cold and you don't feel like you need to drink. Obviously, you still sweat on winter rides, and considerably more fluid is used during breathing than in balmy temperatures. Inhaled air must be warmed and moistened in your throat and lungs. Then, as you exhale, lots of fluid is lost in that cloud of steam you see with each breath. To make matters worse, you also lose fluid through increased urine production in low temperatures, an effect called cold dieresis.

Keep up with fluid demands by drinking plenty both on and off the bike. If you allow yourself to become dehydrated, the resulting decrease in blood volume will mean less blood flowing to your skin and extremities. This, in turn, raises the risk of hypothermia and even frostbite.

There is a potential problem with winter hydration, though—the temperature of an on-bike drink will quickly sink to the air temperature. If this is near freezing, it actually takes energy for your body to warm the liquid and assimilate it (about 35 calories per liter). This isn't a concern in most situations, when there is adequate heat production from exercise, but if you're feeling chilled, it might be best to reduce drinking to avoid additional caloric drain. Don't stop completely, though, if you still have a ways to ride. When the choice is between cold fluid and no fluid, drink the cold fluid.

To prevent your drinks from freezing, use insulated bottles or carry them under your jacket where they will be warmed by body heat. Do the same with a backpack-style hydration system. Use an insulated cover for the hose, or tuck it inside your jacket between sips. Heating your drinks before riding will negate the caloric cost just mentioned and add warmth under your jacket, at least for a while.

As in summer, it's best to use a sports drink that does double duty by replacing calories and electrolytes as well as fluid. Drink 8 to 12 ounces before starting, then 4 to 8 ounces every 15 to 20 minutes during the ride. Avoid beverages that contain caffeine, because they promote urine production, which increases annoying pit stops. The airflow created by riding always feels colder after you've stopped even for just a minute.

Finally, if you're prone to exercise-induced asthma (see below), breathing cold, dry, winter air could cause an attack. Wear a lightweight balaclava, scarf, or ski mask over your mouth and nose to warm incoming air.

Crash Rash

It begins to rain. The road becomes slicker than you expect. As you lean through a turn, your wheels slip out from under you, and a layer of precious skin is left on the asphalt. Welcome to the world of "road rash" or, because most mountain bike wrecks happen on trails rather than pavement, the all-inclusive "crash rash." But whatever it's called, the result is the same—a wound that breaks the skin's protective barrier, damages the soft tissue underneath, and opens the door to bacteria.

If it isn't treated properly, what seems like a minor abrasion can lead to infection and fever. This in turn may result in several days off the bike and a setback in your progress. For this reason, even the most superficial skin damage must be treated with respect. Consider every wound contaminated, then clean it and dress it properly. Here's how. The products mentioned can be found at any drugstore.

First, thoroughly clean the wound. If it contains any dirt, gravel, or other foreign matter, these things must be removed. Scrub with a medical brush or a washcloth until all that's left is raw skin. Sure, this hurts. But if you don't do it, the chance of infection and delayed healing skyrockets. Use regular soap if it's the only thing available. Better still is an antibacterial cleanser from the drugstore. (Mountain bikers, especially, are smart to keep a bottle of this at home to clean nicks and scrapes.) Then apply hydrogen peroxide as a second step in cleaning and disinfection.

Blot dry with sterile gauze, then apply a topical antibiotic ointment. Use one that contains two or more antibiotics, a "shotgun" approach that does a better job of preventing infection by fighting a range of bacteria. You don't want anything growing but new skin. Cover with a nonstick bandage. This has several benefits, including protection from germs and from bumps that could reopen the wound. It also provides a moist environment that encourages healing. Depending on the wound's location, a bandage can also limit or prevent movement that interferes with healing. And it keeps the wound from sticking to clothing or sheets. To keep everything in place on a leg or arm, you may want to cover the bandage with a medical "fishnet" material that pulls on like a sock. Compared with tape, this allows freer movement and ventilation.

Change the bandage every 24 to 48 hours or as soon as it becomes soiled by sweat or dirt from more riding. Continue using a bandage and ointment as long as it takes the wound to heal from the inside out. You might be tempted to quit this routine once the thing stops oozing, but then a scab will form. Although this is nature's way of protecting a wound, a scab has three disadvantages: It blocks oxygen, and in doing so actually slows healing; it might crack and bleed; and it's likely to leave a worse scar.

Alternatively, you can apply a semipermeable dressing such as Spenco Second Skin. This clear material provides a moist environment that lets skin cells form rapidly. Several studies have found that when a semipermeable dressing is used on a clean wound, and when the dressing is changed at 24-hour intervals or as needed, most abrasions heal in 4 to 8 days. Use fishnet to hold the stuff in place, and be careful when changing it to avoid reinjuring the wound. It's not necessary to remove all traces. Rinse the wound with hydrogen peroxide, saline, or water, and then apply fresh dressing.

If your fall was hard, there also may be internal bleeding. As soon as the wound is properly dressed, apply an ice bag to reduce swelling and pain. For best results, you must do this right away. Hold the ice in place with an elastic bandage, which also helps reduce swelling by providing compression.

These procedures should let you successfully self-treat most abrasions. But, as with any wound, if you develop a fever and the area feels warm to the touch, or the borders turn red, this means infection is present and you must get medical help quickly. Also, be aware of the danger of tetanus infection from any cut or abrasion. Tetanus is caused by a bacterium that's found as a dry spore nearly anywhere— including on roads and trails. Once it enters a wound and starts to grow, a very potent toxin begins to damage nerve and muscle cells. The first sign is stiffness in the jaw and neck, which gives tetanus the common name "lockjaw." If untreated, this disease results in high temperature, great pain, and even death from asphyxiation or exhaustion. Fortunately, tetanus can be prevented with a shot that provides immunity for 10 years at a time. Any cyclist who hasn't had this vaccination in the last decade should get it as soon as possible.

Common Cold

It never seems to fail. A big ride that you've had circled on your calendar for months is coming right up, and suddenly you feel the telltale sore throat that means a cold is coming on. Within a couple of days it's full-blown—runny nose, sneezing, stuffed head, fatigue. Your training schedule is calling for plenty of miles in final preparation for the event. Now you're faced with a real dilemma: Do you ride or not?

Many people think that weather factors cause colds—the sudden onset of chilly temperatures, catching a draft, getting caught in the rain—but none of these has been proven guilty through research. In fact, more people catch colds in winter not because of the outdoor environment, but because of what's indoors: lots of people with viruses. If you catch a cold, it's because you've been unlucky enough to encounter someone with one, not because you got chilly while fixing that flat tire.

Almost deceitfully, this seemingly minor ailment transforms a strong cyclist into someone with the endurance of a weekend cul-de-sac pedaler. Indeed, a week of inactivity can cost you about 25 percent of your fitness. The good news is that it takes only 2 to 3 weeks to recoup the loss. But what if your big event is coming up before then?

Training through a cold can be disheartening, but if it's done properly, you should still be able to achieve a good workout. Keep in mind, however, that an illness makes it easier for you to push your body beyond its ability to repair itself. If you break down your defense mechanisms, get ready to be sicker for longer.

In general, if your cold is not accompanied by fever and the symptoms are located from the neck up (head congestion, runny nose, sneezing, scratchy throat), you should be able to continue training without danger of making yourself worse. Some athletes say that they actually feel better if they work out. This makes sense, because exercise can increase mucus flow, relieving congestion and pressure. Remember the standard admonition about drinking plenty of fluids to encourage the movement of mucus and combat that "dried up" feeling. A humidifier in your bedroom may also help. Also, take a pain reliever to relieve the mild head- and muscle aches that a cold usually causes.

To determine if a head cold is really a mild one, take a 15-minute test ride. Just cruise at an easy speed. If your head seems to clear a bit and you feel pretty peppy, then go ahead and do your ride, though you'd be smart to avoid anything strenuous like climbing or interval training. But if every bump makes your head pound and it feels like you're pedaling through water, there's no benefit in continuing.

When you have a fever or the cold's main symptoms are below the neck—chest congestion, hacking cough, muscle aches, loss of appetite—it's a different story. Don't even think about riding. A fever means that your body is combating an infection. Help the fight by increasing rest, not stress. We recommend waiting 24 hours after a fever breaks and your body temperature returns to normal before you attempt a workout. Then, start with a 15-minute test ride as just described. By waiting until the fever is completely gone, you'll reduce the risk of dehydration. As soon as you're over the hump and feeling better, any remaining chest congestion shouldn't be a problem. In fact, the deeper breathing that results from riding may help you expel it.

Although a cure for the common cold has yet to be found (chiefly because it can be caused by some 200 different viruses), there are plenty of over-the-counter products than can make the symptoms more tolerable. They may help you resume training several days sooner than if you simply let the cold run its typical 7- to 10-day course. You'll find that most cold products contain several ingredients, each aimed at one of the several symptoms that may be present. Check labels to get a product that contains only the medication you need.

Of course, the best way to combat a cold is to avoid catching it in the first place. You'll reduce the risk if you follow these tips.

- Don't share water bottles, towels, or other personal items.

- Avoid stress, get enough sleep, and drink lots of fluids (Mom was right).

- Use disposable tissues instead of handkerchiefs.

- Avoid people with colds as much as you can.

- Wash your hands frequently.

- Don't touch your eyes, nose, or mouth when you're in public. Researchers have found that we often give colds to ourselves after picking up germs from a doorknob or other object that a person with a cold has used.

Asthma and Allergies

Cyclists who don't normally suffer from asthma or allergies can still develop symptoms that are brought on by unaccustomed changes in temperature or humidity. This is known as exercise-induced asthma. It can occur during or immediately after a ride, causing breathlessness that may be accompanied by chest pain or tightness. Breathing is labored and may be accompanied by wheezing.

Exercise-induced asthma develops when air passages are cooled, typically by breathing dry air. When you ride in a place where the humidity is low, increased amounts of body moisture evaporate from these passages. The resulting congestion's effect on performance can be devastating, as budding ultramarathon rider Harv Kulka learned in a recent Furnace Creek 508. Harv, 40, lives and trains in Michigan, a far cry from the race's Death Valley environment. Despite training as well as possible, he had no way to prepare for the desert's dryness and its wide temperature range between day and night.

Harv stayed near the leaders for 200 miles, until beginning the course's biggest climb, Towne Pass, late at night. About halfway up, he says, "My legs just gave out. I felt great mentally and physically, but I just couldn't turn the pedals over. My muscles felt like Jell-O. It was so frustrating. I decided to go down for a rest. An hour later, I sat up and couldn't breathe. I coughed up huge amounts of phlegm in a fit that lasted 5 minutes. I thought that if I lay back down for 30 minutes, it might clear up, but it only got worse. With nearly 300 miles left, there was no use in continuing."

This is a classic case of exercise-induced asthma. While riding hard for 12 hours, Harv had experienced a 50° temperature swing from the desert floor's dry high of more than 100°F. The lung congestion this produced prevented enough oxygen from fueling his working muscles. This is why he could feel strong right up to the point of losing his legs. Within minutes, his race was over.

What could Harv do next time to prevent a recurrence? Here are several guidelines if you're asthmatic, have allergies, or will be riding in conditions conducive to causing exercise-induced asthma.

- Use medications or inhalants before cycling to prevent an attack, and carry them with you for emergency use.

- If you know that certain things may cause an allergic reaction, go out of your way to avoid them.

- Drink plenty, to help your body cope with fluid loss through respiration as well as perspiration.

- Lessen the danger of cold, dry air. Many asthmatic athletes find that wearing a surgical mask or other covering for their mouth and nose prevents cold air from reaching their lungs and triggering a reaction. Carry a bandanna if you expect the temperature to drop during the ride. When riding indoors on a resistance trainer, run a humidifier nearby.

- Take plenty of time to warm up. Don't immediately charge up a steep hill. First, let your heart and lungs adjust. Riders who suffer from asthma or allergies must learn their tolerances and respect them, pacing themselves and taking medication when necessary.

Women's Issues

A lot is known about the physiological changes caused by cycling and other sports, but the same can't be said of all of the medical changes. This is especially true for the effect of exercise on a woman's reproductive system. Chances are good that if you're a woman who is interested in riding long distances, you have questions about cycling's impact. Let's have a look at several key issues.

Menstrual Cycle

Studies have found a higher rate of menstrual irregularity in female athletes than in sedentary women. This is particularly true for women in sports such as cycling that emphasize large volumes of exercise and a lean physique. Irregularity shouldn't result in lasting harm if it's caused solely by physical activity, but it's a different story if a hormonal imbalance is involved. When this is the case, there could be a loss of bone mass leading to irreversible damage.

A woman is said to be eumenorrheic if she has regular menstrual cycles. A cycle normally occurs every 24 to 35 days, but its length isn't as important as its regularity. When the cycle is irregular, the condition is called oligomenorrhea. A woman may have several normal periods, go more than 40 days without one, start menstruating again, then miss a month. The final level is amenorrhea, in which menstruation stops completely.

Let's assume that you're well experienced with the signs and symptoms of your menstrual cycle, but aren't quite as up on the underlying physiology. A quick explanation will help you to understand what happens if periods become irregular.

Your monthly cycle is orchestrated by two pituitary hormones—LH (luteinizing hormone) and FSH (follicle-stimulating hormone). A part of the brain called the hypothalamus regulates their release. The hypothalamus is also an emotion center, which explains why strong feelings can affect your menstrual cycle.

During the cycle's first half, the pituitary hormones direct the maturation of the egg to prepare for ovulation (release of the egg from the ovary). The egg matures in a special section of the ovary called the follicle, which secretes the female hormone we know as estrogen. Estrogen stimulates the lining of the uterus to prepare for pregnancy if the egg actually gets fertilized.

About halfway through the menstrual cycle, LH levels rise and cause the egg to be released. During the cycle's second half, the egg takes over production of estrogen and the other female hormone, progesterone. If pregnancy does not occur, the egg dies, the levels of these hormones suddenly drop, and menstrual bleeding begins.

Okay, now what effect should this process have on your cycling performance? Very little (if any), according to every study we've seen. Certain phases of the cycle may put some women in a condition more conducive to efficient performance, but the differences are so slight for most women that they're virtually unnoticeable.

However, if the menstrual cycle becomes irregular and there is a decline in estrogen levels, it's time to be concerned. When lack of bleeding is accompanied by lack of ovulation, then a significant source of estrogen production is absent. Problems arise, because estrogen has several important health effects in addition to its role in reproduction. One of these, as you probably know, involves estrogen's role in bone density and retention of calcium. Lack of estrogen after menopause is why many older women are susceptible to osteoporosis.

For younger women, menstruation and its discomforts are normal functions and needn't interfere with training or events. However, if things change—for example, you have greater pain, prolonged or heavy flow, or bleeding between periods—then a trip to the gynecologist is in order. There's no need to stop riding unless the doctor demands it. Cycling may not always be the culprit, even though some menstrual problems are linked to exercise. Almost always, the benefits of cycling far outweigh the drawbacks.

If you are also very thin, consider gaining a few pounds—especially if you're riding a lot. Or, cut back your mileage a bit. On the other hand, if you feel good at your present weight and exercise level, there's no need to make any changes. What is important is that you are knowledgeable and comfortable about what you're doing.

During rides while menstruating, use a tampon to deal with the flow. Don't leave the string outside where it can cause irritation. If your flow is heavy, try using two tampons. This will probably be more effective and comfortable than using a tampon and a pad.

Amenorrhea

Surveys of women athletes have found a higher incidence of menstrual irregularity and amenorrhea (cessation of periods) than occurs in the general population. While some people put the blame on exercise, it's not that simple.

As every female endurance cyclist knows, a training program involves a host of variables. Included are changes in body weight, percentage of body fat, diet, sleep, and physical and emotional stress. It's very hard to isolate and study any one of these factors. It's been well established, however, that exercise has both an immediate and long-term effect on the concentration of various hormones. So do emotions. A woman putting in many miles on her bike is likely to experience hormonal changes not only in response to the physical stress but also due to the anxiety that occurs while trying to coordinate cycling with a busy schedule. Her social and professional activities also may produce stress and confuse the picture.

Personality is another factor. Long-distance cyclists tend to be intelligent, educated, ambitious, and disciplined. The type of woman who is inspired to become an endurance athlete may be more likely to experience menstrual irregularity simply because she is a highly motivated person, driven toward stressful patterns of achievement.

Amenorrhea can develop in women who lose a significant amount of body fat. This is true for athletic women as well as for those who lead a much less active lifestyle. Amenorrhea also can occur in women suffering from anorexia nervosa or other psychiatric problems. Such disorders are accompanied by hormone alterations beyond those that are found in simple cases of thinness or weight loss. It's also known that some hormones, including estrogen, are produced and metabolized differently in thin women. The net result of these factors can easily be menstrual disturbances.

In addition, it appears that exercise itself, independent of other factors, may have immediate and long-term effects on menstruation. Recently, it was found that endorphins may decrease the concentration of the hormones needed for normal menstrual function. The fact that these natural narcotics are present explains both the "high" and the "addiction" experienced by many female endurance cyclists. Because the chemical pleasure keeps them coming back for more, exercise escalates and the hormonal imbalance grows greater. At least, that's the theory.

There is no evidence, however, that exercise itself causes amenorrhea. It should be fine for a woman who is experiencing this condition to continue riding while being evaluated. It's not possible to know whether amenorrhea is being caused by a serious medical condition without a thorough gynecologic exam and endocrine test. An athlete's amenorrhea should never be dismissed as simply the result of exercise. She should demand the same thorough evaluation that would be given to a nonathlete.

After a medical disorder has been ruled out, an amenorrheic cyclist can simply be monitored during the season. Often, menstruation will return to normal when training is decreased in the fall and winter.

On the other hand, recent research has found reasons for concern if women continue to go without menstruating. This ties back to the estrogen deficit discussed above and its role in low bone density. Amenorrheic athletes have a much higher incidence of bone stress fractures, tendinitis, and muscle strains. In fact, it's been found that some of them have the bone density of people twice their age.

Aside from avoiding amenorrhea, bone loss may be slowed or prevented by taking calcium supplements or an estrogen-progesterone replacement or both. The American Academy of Pediatrics recommends a low-dose oral contraceptive (less than 50 micrograms of estrogen per day) to protect against bone loss in amenorrheic females over the age of 16. It would be better to fend off the problem before it results in measures like this. The key is to get medical care at the first signs of menstrual irregularity.

By the way, don't consider amenorrhea as a form of birth control. Just as your period may stop, it can just as easily return. Female athletes have become pregnant when they thought they weren't ovulating.

Menstrual Cramps

These are caused by contraction of the muscles making up the uterus. The trigger is pain-provoking compounds called prostaglandins, which are produced by various parts of the body in many situations. The fact that uterine cramps result is unfortunate and unpleasant, but it's not abnormal.

Several drugs can prevent the formation of prostaglandins. These products are safe and can be prescribed by a gynecologist. For many women, they work miraculously to prevent menstrual cramps. A side benefit is less menstrual blood loss, an advantage in cycling or any endurance sport.

You may find that menstrual cramps become less severe after you begin a regular cycling program (or any consistent exercise). One

Crotch Comfort

Here's a quick checklist for women who are having trouble getting comfortable on their bikes.

Saddle type. Every body is different, which makes saddle selection highly individual. In general, though, most women do better with a wider saddle because they typically have wider pelvises than men. The key to comfort is having your sit bones supported on top of the seat. Some seats are anatomically designed for women, and certain models have padding or cutouts to reduce contact and pressure on tender tissue. If your present saddle leaves a lot to be desired, test-ride some of these special ones.

Saddle position. In addition to proper height in relation to the pedals (see chapter 3), check your seat's tilt. The top should be level, but if this still seems to cause uncomfortable pressure or irritation to the urethra, angle the nose down slightly. Just a degree or two can make a big difference. Don't go farther or you'll tend to slide forward, putting more stress on your hands and arms as you hold yourself in place.

Shorts. A well-stocked bike shop or mail-order company is likely to have cycling shorts anatomically designed for women. The cut will help them fit and stay up better than men's shorts. In addition, the absorbent liner (chamois) will be ideally positioned and sewn without seams in potentially uncomfortable places. Women should avoid any liner with a central seam. Instead, choose a one-piece liner or one that's sewn of three pieces in "baseball" fashion so the center section is seam-free.

Riding technique. Stand frequently, change your hand location, and sit on different areas of the saddle to prevent constant, numbing pressure. A low, aerodynamic riding position on the nose of the saddle is the worst for many women. Fortunately, this posture isn't necessary for most long-distance riding, though it's a help when bucking a headwind. By improving your flexibility, you may be able to keep your pelvis relatively upright to reduce pressure on your pubic area while you bend into an aero position.

reason may be the effect of endorphins and other natural painkillers that are generated by physical activity. It's also plausible that endurance cyclists perceive less pain because they are able to tolerate more—a result of self-disciplined training. In any event, if you experience some relief from menstrual cramps due to cycling, be grateful. But if cramps are a significant problem that inhibits your riding, see your gynecologist about a prescription for a prostaglandins inhibitor. Because menstrual cramps can be caused by diseases, you should have a gynecological exam before drug treatment begins.

Vaginitis

Vaginitis, an infection of the vagina, is usually caused by one of three organisms: *Candida vaginalis, Trichomonas vaginalis,* or *Gardnerella vaginalis.* The most common symptoms are itching, discharge, and odor. Cycling doesn't cause any of these infections, but the discomfort of vaginitis can certainly interfere with sitting on the saddle.

Myth has it that a moist chamois or even tight shorts make a woman more likely to develop vaginitis. We have found no studies that support this. A vagina is naturally moist, so if you use a lubricant on your skin or chamois, apply it sparingly and keep it in the sit bone area.

A woman experiencing the symptoms of vaginitis should visit her gynecologist for a "wet prep" exam. The discharge will be checked with a microscope to determine the responsible organism and the appropriate medication.

Candida is a yeast infection that usually causes itching. Some women are particularly susceptible, including those who are diabetic or pregnant, or are taking birth control pills or antibiotics. *Candida* grows in a high-sugar environment, which puts diabetics at risk because they tend to have more sugar in all of their cells, including those of their vagina. Women who are pregnant or taking birth control pills have high levels of estrogen and progesterone, another factor that raises the sugar

CHAMOIS
Many women find more comfort on a shorts liner (chamois) made without a center seam.

content of vagina cells. Antibiotics that kill harmful bacteria anywhere in the body also kill the good bacteria that live in the vagina, thus permitting the growth of *Candida* and other fungi. If you tend to get *Candida* infections frequently and aren't in one of the high-risk categories, your doctor should check to see if your immunity is abnormal. If you get *Candida* only when you take antibiotics, you can supplement them with medicated suppositories that prevent infections.

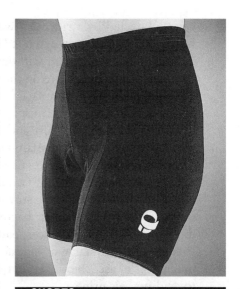

SHORTS

Women's shorts have a smaller waist and leg openings for a gender-specific fit. Shorter legs than traditional shorts raise the tan line.

Trichomonas usually causes a profuse discharge with a pungent odor. *Gardnerella* typically causes a sharp odor, but there may not be a discharge. These infections are transmitted sexually, so your partner should be treated, too. Less common sources include a contaminated toilet seat, towel, tub, and so on.

To reduce the risk of vaginitis, wash your shorts after every ride and never wear a soiled pair. It may also help to change into fresh shorts once or twice during a ride that has you in the saddle all day. Should you develop an infection, use an over-the-counter medicated cream that controls itching and discharge. A cortisone cream will reduce irritation. These products can help you continue to ride in relative comfort while the infection is clearing up. Of course, if self-treatment doesn't seem to be working, see your doctor.

Bladder Infections

Most women have experienced the burning and frequent urination that results from a bladder infection. This ailment is usually caused by *E. coli,* a bacterium commonly found in feces. Because a woman's urethra (the tube through which the bladder empties) is close to the anus, wiping in the wrong direction may give *E. coli* easy access. In addition, a woman's urethra is very short, increasing the bladder's vulnerability. For cyclists who do not clean themselves properly, the *E. coli* can spread through the chamois to the urethra. In this way, a bladder can be infected by a rider not wearing clean shorts for each ride, or not changing shorts on extended rides.

Similar symptoms (but without the *E. coli* colonization) can result from chafing and pressure on the urethra from the chamois or saddle, or a faulty riding position. The resulting irritation is similar to the "honeymoon" condition caused by an overload of sexual activity. Like a worn-out bride, a cyclist should forgo sexual intercourse for the couple of weeks it takes inflammation to subside.

Antibiotics are effective against bladder infections, but as we've noted, they raise the risk of *Candida*. You can help prevent an *E. coli* attack in the first place by staying well hydrated, which causes frequent urination that expels bacteria to keep it at a safer level. In addition, acidic urine reduces bacterial growth. Some women have lessened the frequency of bladder infections by taking 500 to 1,000 milligrams of ascorbic acid (vitamin C) or a couple of aspirin each day to acidify their urine.

If a bladder infection occurs during a multiday ride, drink a lot to help wash away bacteria with urine. Make it cranberry juice when you can—it's a good urine-acidifier. For urethra irritation, tilt the saddle's nose down just a bit. If this doesn't help enough, stop at the next bike shop you pass and install a seat with a hole through the top. This may relieve the pressure and rubbing.

Pregnancy

Physically fit women usually withstand the rigors of labor better than sedentary ones. In addition, we haven't come across any studies that claim to have found any harmful effects of exercise during pregnancy. Even so, if you have a baby on the way, you should stay in close communication with your obstetrician and be ready to make intelligent modifications to your cycling program.

Common sense says that training intensity should be reduced during pregnancy. How much depends on how far along you are, and whether any special medical concerns have developed. Be especially sensitive to unusual pain or bleeding. Ride within your limits, and be smart about stress. For example, ride early in the day to avoid summer heat. Your body temperature should not exceed 101°F while you are pregnant. Heat has been implicated in premature labor as well as in certain birth defects.

You can continue cycling right up to your delivery day, comfort allowing, but it's wise to stop riding long distances after the fifth or sixth month. At that point, you need to be concerned about any increased metabolic effort and the corresponding boost in body temperature. You also don't want to put yourself at risk of crashing, so be cautious when riding with others and consider staying off trails altogether. Indoor cycling is the safest option, as long as the room is cool, a fan is blowing to keep your body temperature under control, and you drink plenty.

There's no rule for when you can return to cycling after delivering your baby. Much depends on any complications that may have developed, as well as your overall energy level. Again, stationary cycling may be the best way to retain some fitness without undue stress as you build back up.

(17)

Stay Loose

As mentioned throughout, you need to stretch before and after cycling or other exercise. We know, we know—stretching is about as exciting as fixing a flat in the rain. To a go-go cyclist, it seems so slow and tedious. Besides, riding time is precious enough without wasting any of it lying on the floor. Instead of stretching, you can just pedal easily for a few minutes to loosen your legs, right? That's been the tradition in cycling since the days of the highwheeler.

But—you knew this was coming—as healthful an exercise as cycling is, it is far from complete. When you ride, the muscles involved in pedaling become stronger but also shorter and tighter, due to their limited range of movement. The more you ride, the greater this effect. Often described as a "midrange" activity, cycling rarely causes legs to be fully bent or straightened, so their muscles almost never fully contract or extend. This simple fact, played out during countless pedal strokes, can lead to a host of minor but aggravating injuries marked by pain in the lower back, hamstrings, and knees.

Cyclists who put in long hours on the bike are prone to what we call "muscular rigor mortis." This is an unfortunate drawback of endurance riding—a gradual loss of muscle elasticity and decrease in joint flexibility. It's what John Howard was referring to when he switched to the triathlon after his multichampionship road racing career and found that his body had "turned to concrete." After so many years of nothing but high-mileage cycling, he didn't have the flexibility to swim or run well. John knew this was unhealthy, so he dedicated his training to conditioning his whole body. It worked, and he became the first cyclist to win Hawaii's famed Ironman triathlon. It wouldn't have been possible if John hadn't made stretching a key part of his training.

We encourage you to follow John's example even though long-distance cycling, not multisport events, is your main goal. Here's a quick rundown on several cycling-specific benefits of greater flexibility.

- **More speed.** With improved flexibility and range of motion, stress on muscles and joints is reduced. This, in turn, helps you ride longer at a faster pace. Flexibility in the lower back and hamstrings lets you stay in a more efficient aerodynamic position.

- **Improved workload.** Your muscles can absorb more stress before tightening up if they're stretched before you get on the bike. Then, stretching during the ride reduces the muscle soreness and stiffness that develops from strenuous efforts such as climbing.

- **Faster recovery.** By stretching after riding, you can reduce or even eliminate stiffness.

- **Greater comfort and control.** When your body is supple and movements are fluid, you simply feel more at home on the bike. On the other hand, tight muscles or joints may eliminate certain riding positions, reducing the variety that's key to long-distance comfort. A stiff body can't flow with the bike, a problem that hurts performance in technical off-road terrain.

- **Injury prevention.** Stretching is a form of preventive medicine. A daily dose will go a long way toward making you immune to nagging aches and pains.

Technique

The way to create greater flexibility is called static stretching. It's a simple technique. Stretch slowly and gently until a mild amount of tension (not pain) is felt in the muscle. Hold the position for 20 to 30 seconds, concentrating on letting the muscle relax. If it doesn't, back off a bit. If it does, move slightly farther into the stretch to create mild tension again. This second phase is called the developmental stretch. It should be held for another 15 seconds or so. Tension should stay constant or slightly diminish. Pain tells you that you are overstretching and need to ease off. The purpose of the developmental stretch is to safely create flexibility. Your breathing throughout should be slow and deep.

The wrong technique is called ballistic stretching. This is when you "bounce," or repeatedly push against muscle tension and back off. This is ineffective and can lead to injury. As you bounce, the muscle responds by contracting to protect itself from overstretching. Tension develops and prevents it from being fully stretched. Bouncing may also cause tiny tears in the muscle, resulting in scar tissue that makes it less flexible than it would be without any stretching at all.

By the way, stretching and warming up are not the same thing. Stretching comes first to gently loosen muscles and joints so they're ready to begin cycling. Then, a few minutes of easy pedaling will warm up your body by increasing heart rate and circulation. As you spin along, you can do some more stretching on the bike by standing, lowering each heel for a few seconds as you coast, and arching your back. Climb an easy hill out of the saddle to loosen your lower back and hips.

When to Stretch

Before and after riding. In addition to your preride stretch, do a 5-minute routine as soon as you get off the bike. This helps eliminate the tightness you may develop from cycling's relatively fixed position. It also helps lessen the soreness in a muscle that may have cramped.

While riding. As hours pass during a long ride, certain muscles will become tired and tight. When this happens (or, even better, before it happens), ease up when terrain and traffic allow so that you can do several on-bike stretches. Or, if conditions aren't right, stop briefly and do them off the bike. These stretches are described below. The key is not to wait till you're in discomfort and slowing down. It's amazing how well a few seconds of stretching can invigorate a fatiguing body.

During the day. Just a couple of minutes of stretching several times a day will keep muscle tension at bay, helping your general recovery from training. If your company recommends a short break from work every couple of hours, that's a good stretching opportunity, as is your lunch hour. At home, plop on the floor in the evening and stretch while watching TV or listening to music. In fact, this can be an ideal time to go through a complete stretching routine. Ned Overend uses this technique, gaining beneficial flexibility instead of watching his favorite programs from the couch. When half of your mind is on something enjoyable, the other half won't think of stretching as just another chore. This is also a good time to elevate and massage your legs to reduce tightness and fatigue after a hard ride.

Posture Protection

At this point, you have plenty of good reasons to stretch. But there also are benefits beyond what it does to improve your cycling. These relate to your general appearance.

Lack of flexibility can put you on the fast track to poor posture. This begins with mechanical imbalances in the hips, back, shoulders, and neck. Next, body segments are pulled out of line. The resulting muscular tension can put tremendous strain on ligaments and tendons. Inflexibility in the shoulders and upper back can lead to a hump-backed spine and may reduce lung capacity. Tight muscles in the hips, hamstrings, and lower back can rotate the pelvis forward, resulting in

Get Back

If your back complains as the miles pile up, use these additional stretching exercises to improve its strength and flexibility. Should pain increase or result in tingling or numbness in either leg, don't mess around—see your doctor.

Pelvic tilt. Lie on your back with your knees bent, feet flat, and arms at your side. Tighten your stomach muscles to flatten the small of your back against the floor without pushing down with the legs. Hold for 5 seconds, then relax. Repeat 10 times.

Crunches. Lie on your back with your knees bent and feet flat. Cross your arms on your chest. While keeping your chin tucked, curl your upper back off the floor several inches. Hold for 3 seconds, then return slowly. Repeat up to 20 times. It might help to tuck your feet under something that will hold them down.

Cat. On your hands and knees, relax your midsection so that your back sags downward. Then arch your back like a cat and hold briefly. Repeat up to 10 times.

Back extension. Relax on your stomach with your hands under your shoulders. Push your upper body up, while keeping your hips and thighs on the floor. This arches your back. Hold for 3 seconds, then slowly lower. Repeat five times. Eventually, you may be able to lock your elbows with your hips still touching the floor.

Side stretch. While standing, hold a broom across your shoulders behind your neck, with your arms fully extended on it. Slowly bend to the right side, then to the left. Repeat 20 times. If no broom is handy, do this with your hands atop your head.

lower-back curvature and pain in the butt and thighs (sciatica). Tight calf muscles can place undue stress on the foot, leading to several orthopedic problems, including painful Achilles tendinitis.

The bottom line: Flexibility isn't just for helping you ride more comfortably. It also safeguards your posture by relieving chronic muscle tension and stiffness.

At-Home Stretches

Using the static technique described above, include these 10 stretches in your daily routine. Establish each stretch for at least 20 seconds, relax, extend the stretch slightly, then hold for another 15 seconds. Breathe slowly and deeply.

Groin. Sit on the floor, bend your knees outward, put the soles of your feet together, and hold your toes. Gently lean forward by bending at the hips.

Calf. Stand about 2 feet from a wall with your feet together. Lean on the wall with your forearms, head resting on your hands. Move your right foot forward with the knee bent and weight removed. Slowly push your hips forward until you feel the stretch in your left calf. Keep your left heel flat, with your toes pointed straight at the wall. Switch legs and repeat.

Quadriceps. Stand near the wall and use your left hand for support. Bend your left leg behind and reach back to grasp your foot with your right hand. Pull the foot toward your butt. Repeat, using the right leg with your left hand.

Lower back and hips. Take a big step forward with your left leg and position its knee directly over your ankle. Kneel on your right knee. Let your hips sink forward to feel the stretch. Switch legs and repeat.

Hamstrings. Lie on your back and bend your right knee upward, keeping your foot flat. Lift your straight left leg from the hip, then grip behind the knee to gently pull the leg more vertical. Keep your lower back flat on the floor. Switch legs and repeat.

Lower back, hips, hamstrings. Lie on your back with legs straight. Bend your left leg, grip below the knee, and pull it toward your chest. Switch legs and repeat.

Shoulders. Stand and interlace your fingers on top of your head, palms facing up. Extend your arms upward and slightly backward, holding the stretch at the top.

Triceps and torso. Stand or sit with your arms extended overhead.

Calf and ankle stretch.

Quadriceps stretch.

Bend your left elbow so that your forearm goes behind your head. Grasp the left elbow with your right hand and pull it to the right as you lean toward that side. Switch arms and repeat.

Midback. Stand with your hands on hips and knees slightly bent. Gently rotate your torso clockwise. Repeat, going counterclockwise.

Full-body stretch. Lie on your back with your legs straight and arms extended past your head. Cross your left leg over your right leg and your right arm over your left arm. Extend the fingers and toes of the crossing limbs to elongate your body. Switch limbs and repeat.

Rest-Stop Stretches

Use these stretches during breaks from riding. Be careful when wearing cleated shoes, because they may slip and cause you to stretch too far. Also, they can intensify some stretches (particularly those involving the calf) because they elevate the ball of the foot.

Quadriceps. Face the left side of the bike (the side without the chain) and put your right hand on the seat for balance. Reach behind with your left hand and grab your right foot, then pull it toward your butt. Grasp the handlebar stem with your left hand and reverse the procedure to stretch your left quad.

Calf and ankle. Face the left side of the bike with one hand on the seat and the other on the handlebar stem. Slightly bend your left knee and step 18 inches back with your right foot. Keeping your right heel

Arms, back, shoulders stretch.

on the ground, slowly bend your right knee. Switch legs and repeat.

Arms, back, shoulders. Stand 3 to 4 feet from either side of the bike, one hand on the seat and the other on the stem. Keeping your knees slightly bent and your hips directly over your feet, slowly lower your upper body and move your chin toward your chest until you feel the stretch.

Knees. Stand about 2 feet from the left side of the bike with your feet shoulder-width apart and toes pointed slightly outward. Grasp the middle of the seat tube and down tube. Slowly squat, keeping your heels on the ground and your knees in line with your feet. Be cautious if you're prone to knee injuries. Stop this stretch if you feel pain.

Hamstrings. Face the side of the bike, and lift one leg to place its ankle atop the seat or the rear tire while holding the back edge of the seat or top tube with one hand and the stem with the other. Keep the other leg slightly bent, with the foot pointed straight at the bike. Relax the quads of the elevated leg and slowly bend forward until you feel a stretch in its hamstring. Switch legs and repeat.

Groin. Face the left side of the bike, and grasp the seat and handlebar stem. Spread your legs to twice shoulder width. Slightly bend your left knee, then move your hips to the right (parallel to the bike) and down till you feel the stretch along the inside of your left thigh. Move to the left to stretch the right thigh.

Shoulders. Set the bike aside or lean it against you. Interlace your fingers behind your butt. Slowly lower your hands to straighten your arms, then gently rotate your arms backward and upward until you feel a stretch through the front of the shoulders.

Neck. Sit in a comfortable position. Keep your back straight and slowly roll your head in five clockwise circles. Repeat, going counterclockwise.

Hamstrings stretch.

On-Bike Stretches

Even when you faithfully follow a stretching program, you'll still feel cycling rigor mortis setting in during long rides. Here's how to prevent or at least limit this gradual buildup of tightness in your muscles and joints.

First, change your hand location frequently so your arms and upper body don't lock into a fixed position. Second, stand every few minutes to alter everything from the pressure on your feet to the action of your shoulders. These techniques will do a lot to ward off stiffness, but it also helps to perform some on-bike stretches when conditions allow. Don't do this when riding in a group, unless you are at the back with no one behind.

As in other stretching, the key is to relax and concentrate on the muscles you're trying to loosen. Maintain the stretch for up to 15 seconds, and repeat if necessary after pedaling briefly to get your speed back up. For safety, maintain a straight line and stay aware of what's going on around you.

Shoulders and neck. Shrug both shoulders toward your ears until you feel muscle tightness. Hold for 5 seconds, then slowly lower as you consciously release tension. For a related stretch that emphasizes the neck, turn your head toward one shoulder and then the other during the shrug.

Face. Facial tension develops from clenching your teeth during hard efforts or even from squinting into the sun. Relax the muscles by turning your chin toward one shoulder, opening your mouth as if making the "O" sound, and then moving your chin farther to the side. Then turn and do the same toward the other shoulder.

Back. While sitting in your normal riding position, round your back as you lower your head slightly. Hold for 5 seconds, then straighten your back by lifting from your chest and looking slightly upward to extend your spine. Hold for 5 seconds more.

Lower back. Grip the handlebar next to the stem with one hand. Reach behind with the other hand and place your forearm across your lower back. Twist your upper body toward the arm that's behind you. Hold for 5 seconds, then repeat for the other side. You might want to do this twice for best results.

Fingers and forearms. Place one hand on your hip with the fingers pointing upward. Gradually straighten that arm until a stretch is felt. Hold for 10 seconds, then do the other arm. This is especially helpful in terrain that causes hand fatigue and stiffness from lots of braking or shifting.

Calf and achilles tendon. While standing, coast and put one foot at the bottom of the pedal circle. Then move your hips toward the handlebar. Keep your knee straight as you drop the heel below the ball of the foot. Hold for 10 seconds, then do the other leg.

Triceps. Hold on to the bar with one hand. The most stable position is next to the stem, but for this stretch it's less awkward to grip closer to the brake lever. With your free hand, reach across your chest and up over the shoulder. Extend till you feel a good stretch. Repeat with the other arm.

Hamstrings and butt. With the crankarms horizontal, stand, straighten your legs, and drop your heels. Rotate the crankset 180 degrees and repeat.

Massage

Another effective way to keep muscles loose and healthy is with daily massage. Massage is traditional in cycling, and for good reason—it helps riders recover faster from training, which in turn increases training potential.

Technically, massage aids the venous and lymphatic return and prevents stasis in muscle capillaries. This means that it increases blood flow as well as the interchange of substances between blood and tissue. A key result is less swelling in muscle cells. Tension is released, circulation is improved, and muscles feel more limber. In fact, they are healthier.

Massage after hard training or an event goes a long way toward eliminating the effects of fatigue. As soreness is reduced, the flexibility and elasticity in muscles, tendons, and ligaments is increased. Studies have found that postride massage speeds muscle recovery two to three times faster than passive rest. It may even help remove lactic acid if the massage occurs within 20 minutes of the end of a hard ride.

A massage session should include deep, long strokes to stimulate bloodflow, jostling or shaking to relax the muscle, and cross-fiber kneading. The last prevents the buildup of adhesions that can cause stiffness and "trigger points" of pain. A complete massage for legs and upper body takes at least 30 minutes and will leave you feeling physically and psychologically improved. It's best done in the evening, about 90 minutes after dinner. This allows time for the meal to partially digest so more blood can be in circulation.

Self-massage. Now that we've sold you on the benefits of massage, let's get real. Not many of us have a massage therapist standing by. Even if we did, paying for a daily professional massage would be expensive (although very beneficial). We recommend one weekly fullbody session with a pro when you're riding big miles, and lower-body self-massage on other days. Just 5 minutes on each leg will cause a reduction in fatigue that you can feel on your next ride.

The technique is easy. Start by finding a regular time so self-massage blends seamlessly into your routine. It may be just before bedtime. Or take a tip from Ned Overend and use evening TV time to stretch and work on your legs. The key is to be relaxed and comfortable. You don't need to use massage oil, which would have to be washed off afterward.

Lie on your back on the floor or bed. Put both legs up the wall or on a chair for about 3 minutes. They should be elevated at least 45 degrees. This lets gravity drain blood and give your legs a lighter feeling. Then sit up with your back against the wall, headboard, or chair. Bend one leg and massage it completely, starting with the foot, and proceeding to the ankle, calf, knee, quadriceps, and hamstring. Always stroke toward the heart, because this is the direction in which you want the blood to flow. After about 5 minutes on one leg, do the same to the other. A variation is to remain on your back with your legs still elevated on the chair or wall. Place a large pillow under your head and shoulders to help you reach and massage one bent leg, then the other. This effectively combines stroking and gravity.

After massaging both legs, return to spots that still feel tight. Work on them for another minute or so. However, don't dwell on any area that is painfully sore. You may have muscle damage, and extra massage might make it worse. In this case, apply ice and take aspirin or ibuprofen to reduce pain and swelling.

Finish by elevating your legs again and relaxing for several minutes. Then sit up and do your stretching, now that your muscles are limber.

18

Year-Round Fitness

You've trained well throughout spring, summer, and fall. It has paid off with some of your best-ever performances in long rides. Now the air is chilly, the sun is setting early, and the thought of putting more miles on your bike has become less exciting. You're ready to hang it up for a while, literally and figuratively. You'll get 2 or 3 months of rest and start again in the spring. Okay? Not exactly.

Yes, you do need a break, which is necessary for your body and brain to recover from the stresses of a long season. But unlike in the past, when cyclists traditionally would rest during winter, it's much smarter to keep your hard-earned fitness by switching to enjoyable cross-training activities. These include other forms of cycling, such as cyclocross, mountain biking (for roadies), riding on a stationary trainer, or joining a spin class or other aerobic program. In addition, there are numerous noncycling recreations that can help you retain cardiovascular fitness, muscle tone, and endurance. Favorites include running, swimming, inline skating, cross-country skiing, and snow-shoeing. Any of these, combined with strength training, will help you start the next cycling season from a higher physical foundation. This, in turn, gives you the chance to have even better results on the bike.

Most of us have busy daily schedules that are pushed to the limit during the cycling season. We don't need this madness to extend year-round. To keep off-season conditioning sane as well as effective, our guiding principle is "efficiency of effort." This means getting maximum gains for the time spent, and keeping time spent to a minimum. It helps to base as much activity as possible at your home. This makes it easier to fit workouts in, especially during winter's limited daylight, and it avoids using time for traveling to a gym or health club.

Using our tips and your creativity, you can make an off-season program fun as well as effective. This dual benefit is most likely when you combine different activities and vary the workouts. Don't let yourself get into a rut. Your body will enjoy the variety, and so will your head.

Mountain Biking

It's a safe bet that most of you are roadies. Traditionally, long-distance cycling has meant long-distance road riding. If you've spent the whole season (or your entire career) pounding the pavement, winter is the time to swap your skinny tires for knobbies. Yes, you'll still be on a bike, but the freshness of riding off road makes it seem like a whole new sport. Pedaling keeps your legs honed, while the demands of trail riding give your upper body a workout unlike anything you've been experiencing. In addition, it's well documented that the bike-handling skills developed by mountain biking enhance control and confidence on the road, too. We don't have the space in this book to go into all of the essential trail-riding techniques, but we can refer you to an excellent book that does: *Mountain Bike like a Champion,* by off-road legend (and sometimes roadie) Ned Overend.

One special type of winter cycling has captured the fancy of Ed Burke—snow biking. It's a hoot if you live where the white stuff is plentiful, as Ed does in Colorado. "Cycling in the cold and snow seems difficult—until you do it," he says. "Winter isn't a frigid torture chamber. It's just another season in a yearly training program. For most of us, cycling isn't a fair-weather-only activity in summer, so you have to look at it that way in winter, too.

"You need to be tough, though. It's certainly easier to stay inside and ride the rollers while watching an old movie or football game. But if you embrace the winter, you'll see that it's a beautiful time for riding. It's fun and challenging, and the sights and sounds are completely different from when you ride the same trails in summer."

Jeep trails, ski area access roads, fire roads, old mining roads, snowmobile trails—all are great for snow cycling. Stay off groomed cross-country ski trails, though. Your wheels will ruin the parallel tracks, which annoys skiers to no end. Hard-packed snow is ideal; packed powder is second best. If you try to pedal in more than half a foot of powder, you'll sink like you're in quicksand. But if you find hardpack topped by a couple of inches of powder, you'll think you're cruising on clouds.

The secret to riding on snow is flotation. To limit sinking or plowing, always make smooth, gradual movements. Maintain a slow and steady pedaling rhythm by using slightly higher gears than usual.

Get out of the saddle gingerly when you need to climb or accelerate. Make wide turns, and go with the flow if the wheels start to slide. To improve traction on icy surfaces, you can install chains similar to those made for car tires, or use bike tires with metal studs. Snow Cat double-wide rims increase the size of the tires' "footprint" on the snow, as does a low inflation pressure of just 10 to 15 pounds per square inch. For more about cold-weather clothing and equipment, as well as safety in low temperatures, see chapters 5 and 15.

Cyclocross

This form of off-road cycling experienced a boom in the late 1990s. A favorite winter sport in Europe for decades, cyclocross combines riding in tricky terrain with jumping off to carry the bike over obstacles and up or down hills that are too steep to ride. This is done on a short course that's covered several times in a typical 'cross event. You can imagine the great all-round workout this provides, combining cycling with running and even a bit of weight lifting. It develops strength, power, agility, and bike-handling skills.

Cyclocross can be done using a mountain bike, which is fine for low-key club racing or for a training loop you set up. But for more serious competition, a cyclocross bike is a better choice. It looks much like a road bike at first glance, but there are special features, such as wider tires and greater wheel clearances, that help it handle muddy conditions. Perhaps the biggest advantage is its weight, which is several pounds lighter than that of the typical mountain bike and makes it easier to hoist and carry.

You could also convert an old road bike by installing lower gearing, bar-end shifters, mountain bike pedals, and knobby tires. (This won't work if there isn't enough tire/frame clearance to prevent mud from jamming the wheels.) Raise the stem a centimeter, lower the saddle by the same amount, and move the brake levers a bit higher on the curve for a more upright riding position.

Running is integral to cyclocross, but it's not something you'll be accustomed to after a long season on your bike. Break in with easy jogs on flat ground, preferably on trails or in fields rather than on unyielding pavement. Your legs will probably be plenty sore initially, so go easy until this passes and you can start jumping rocks and logs and sprinting up hills. Then, begin doing it with your bike. Carry it on your right shoulder so the drivetrain won't bang against your body. Put your right arm through the frame's triangle, then reach up

Cyclocross is gaining popularity because it's fun, different, and a terrific workout. It lets you combine cycling with running and even throw in some weight lifting.

and grasp the handlebar. This keeps your left arm free for balance or catching yourself when you stumble. Improve your technique and get some great conditioning by running uphill this way in a series of 30- to 60-second intervals.

Cyclocross is a sport full of unique skills. The best way to learn is to watch good 'crossers, then practice what you see. Everything revolves around two basic rules: First, maintain momentum. This means picking the correct line, gear, and pedaling force to get the best combination of traction and speed. Second, be smooth. This applies to mounting, dismounting, and every move involved with negotiating the riding sections, running sections, and obstacles. But even if your skill never rises past the novice level, the fun and fitness you'll get from cyclocross makes it one of the best winter activities.

Indoor Cycling

The good news about indoor cycling is that you can get a load of training benefits while minimizing workout time. This is a really good deal if you're pressed for time because of work or family commitments that gobble up winter's brief daylight hours. But even though it's effective, indoor cycling produces too much physical and mental discomfort for many people. Their enthusiasm flows away like the sweat dripping from every pore. The lack of visual stimulation makes time nearly come to a standstill, turning an hour workout into an or-

Before each session on a nowhere bike, set up fluids and a fan to counteract heavy sweating.

deal that seems to have no end. It doesn't have to be this way, though. It's possible to make riding inside fun as well as productive. Grinding away in front of the television while watching MTV won't do it. Your mind will mutiny if you don't increase the challenge, so let's see how.

TECHNIQUES

Organize your area. You're going to sweat buckets, so have something underneath to protect the floor. Likewise, drape a hand towel over the front of the bike. Put another towel, a spare sweatband, and at least two full water bottles on a table or shelf that you can easily reach from the saddle. Wear a sweatband, absorbent wristbands, and a T-shirt or jersey to hold the perspiration. Crack a window to let in fresh air. Position a large fan where it can make a cooling headwind. You may want to use an unheated part of your home, such as a garage or basement.

Allow time for a warmup and cooldown. As with any workout, you should devote at least 5 minutes to each.

Avoid marathon sessions. Yes, you're interested in endurance, but indoors is not the best place to work on it. Instead of droning away for a couple of hours, you'll get much more fitness from 45 minutes of intervals. The time will go faster, too.

Record each workout. Monitor your performance with a bike computer, then write the results in your training log. Keep track of things like time, distance, average speed, max speed, and heart rate, depending on what's important for a particular workout. This will help you see improvement and spot deficiencies.

Spinning the Winter Away

Ed Burke admits to being skeptical when he first heard about Spinning, the exercise program in which an instructor leads a roomful of people pedaling furiously on special stationary bikes. Then Ed gave Spinning a try. Even better, the opportunity came with Spinning's founder, the flamboyant Johnny G, leading the session. Ed tells what happened.

"I warmed up at a steady pace with my Polar heart rate monitor reading about 60 percent of my max. Then the real ride started, with Johnny having us increase the pedaling resistance as we increased our cadence. Next, I pedaled while standing out of the saddle, alternating a rocking side-to-side motion with a crouched position just over the saddle. We sat down and increased resistance as if climbing a hill. We did jumps—four counts standing, four counts sitting, and so on. We never stopped pedaling throughout the 40-minute workout, and the thumping music never ceased. When finished, I was exhausted but exhilarated. After downloading my Polar, I found that my heart rate had ranged from 65 to 93 percent of maximum, much as it would have on a hilly road or trail.

"As Johnny says, the essence of spinning is fluidity. Resistance is changed throughout the workout simply by turning a knob. In this way, you simulate intervals, hills, and sprints. The experience left me convinced that Spinning is an excellent form of indoor training, especially if you don't have the equipment or self-motivation to ride in your own home."

Most metropolitan areas have a Spinning facility or something similar run by one of several competitors. Check at your local health club.

Use your ears. Make training tapes that include your favorite songs. Avoid falling into a steady rhythm by mixing hard-driving rock with easy-tempo tunes so your effort varies with the beat. Use headphones to hear the music better and avoid bothering others.

Don't overdo it. Former pro road racer Chris Carmichael, who has coached several top cyclists including Lance Armstrong, recommends a maximum of 2 hours indoors per day for his elite riders. Most of us can't last that long—nor do we need to, for our purposes. Shoot for 45 to 60 minutes per session, including the warmup and cooldown. Go longer only if you have the desire and an effective workout that keeps it from becoming a drawn-out slog.

Ride every other day. That's plenty. Leave time for the other off-season activities that give you a beneficial physical and mental break from cycling.

WORKOUTS

If the following workouts seem too tough at first, simply shorten them. Build up to where you're able to ride for at least 45 minutes. Remember, each session must include a warmup and cooldown. "Hard" and "easy" efforts depend on the gears and cadence that make them so for you. In general, maintain a cadence of at least 90 rpm. Indoor training also is a great time to develop smoothness at pedaling speeds of 110 revolutions per minute or higher.

Descending ladder. Do a 10-minute hard effort followed by 2 minutes of easy spinning for recovery. Then do 8 minutes hard, 2 minutes easy. Then 6 and 2, 4 and 2, and 2 and 2. As the hard efforts get shorter, try to increase their intensity with bigger gears or a faster cadence or both. This pattern allows you to maintain the fitness benefits of intense efforts despite the fact that you're getting tired.

Pyramid. Do 1 minute hard, then 1 easy; 2 minutes hard, then 2 easy. Continue this pattern till you reach 5 minutes hard and 5 easy, then work your way back down to 1 and 1.

A variation is done by changing gears instead of time. Choose a cadence to maintain (at least 90 rpm), then pedal in a moderate gear that combines the big chainring with one of the larger cogs. After 2 minutes, shift to the next smaller cog and keep your cadence the same. Two minutes later, do it again. Continue this pattern till you reach your smallest cog (highest gear), and then work your way back to the gear you started in. If this seems too difficult, use 90- or 60-second intervals instead of 2 minutes. It helps to have a metronome or a cyclecomputer with a cadence function. This workout is great for teaching your body to tolerate fatigue, such as when you climb a long hill that gets steeper and steeper.

Rapid recovery. Ride 5 minutes in a hard gear, using your normal flat-terrain riding position. Then switch to your seated climbing position for 3 minutes, using an easier gear but a faster cadence so that your speed stays nearly the same. This keeps you working, but also gives lactic acid a chance to leave your leg muscles. Finish the set by returning to your standard position for 3 minutes of hard pedaling. Rest by spinning easily till you feel fully recovered for another set. Try for three sets. This workout helps you maintain speed while recuperating quickly from tough efforts, such as when catching up to other riders or pumping over short hills.

Pace maker. This workout improves your sustainable pace, which pays off during climbs and long headwind stretches. Here's the pattern: Pedal 1 minute in a moderate gear, using your middle chainring (or small ring if you have only two) with a cadence of about 110 rpm and heart rate that's 65 to 80 percent of your maximum. Then shift to the large ring but stay on the same cog. Go for 1 minute at a cadence of about 90 rpm with a heart rate of 75 to 90 percent of maximum. When time is up, shift back to the middle ring for 1 minute. Continue this pattern. Start with a 20-minute set and work up to 30 minutes, then switch to a pair of 20-minute sets. The gear changes let you push up your heart rate without fatiguing your muscles. You should not feel a burn if you are doing these intervals correctly. As you continue to improve, you can choose to increase the duration past a minute or increase the gear, or both.

King of the hill. Here's the way to simulate climbing on a trainer. Select a gear big enough to slow your normal cadence by 15 to 20 rpm. Slide back on the saddle, and imagine yourself going up a long hill. Maintain this workload until your cadence falls off due to leg fatigue or the fact that you're gasping like a fish out of water. Then shift to a lower gear, and spin easily to recover completely before another bout at the high resistance. This workout develops leg strength, lung power, and climbing technique, improving your ability to handle real hills. For a more lifelike climbing simulation, raise the front of the bike by setting the front wheel on a block.

Isolated leg. Here's a great workout for learning to pedal in full circles. Simply unclip one foot and rest it on a stool beside the bike, or hook it over the trainer beside the rear hub. Pedal with the other leg in a moderate gear, concentrating on making smooth revolutions. You might find this very difficult at first, but that's the point—it's proof that you haven't been getting the most out of your pedal strokes. It'll teach you what it feels like to use your muscles through the complete circle. Keep at it until you're able to ride for at least 5 minutes with each leg. Then you could even try one-leg variations of the above workouts. Pedal this way twice a week to imprint the feeling.

These indoor workouts only begin to describe the variety that's possible. Also do them on rollers if you have a set. Anything goes, as long as it boosts your cadence and heart rate and challenges your muscles. Vary each session to keep workouts as fresh as possible. Stay with it. You'll see the benefits when daylight lengthens and you start getting out for your first long rides of the season.

Winter Sports

Cross-country skiing. When max VO2 and other physiological benchmarks are compared among aerobic athletes, it's the cross-country skiers who come out on top. Why? Because theirs is a complete activity, exercising the upper body as strenuously as it works the legs. This is also why skiing is an ideal off-season sport for cyclists, a fact backed by many European riders as well as Americans ranging from roadie Greg LeMond to mountain biker Ned Overend. Besides improving all-around muscle tone, skiing is a great way to maintain or increase cardiovascular fitness throughout the winter.

The other advantage of skiing is psychological. It gets you away from the same old routine and provides different terrain to explore. Especially for road riders, skiing puts you into the peaceful quiet of the forest—a fresh change from yet another indoor cycling workout or from dodging cars on snow-lined roads.

Of course, don't think of skiing (or any other activity) as the only thing you need to do in winter. You still need to pedal and spend time in the weight room. Sure, when the snow is ideal, go ahead and ski all you can. Make maximum use of the opportunity. In a few days, once conditions deteriorate, return to different activities.

Skip Hamilton, a national-class masters cyclist and cross-country skier who lives in Aspen, Colorado, coaches a number of riders. In winter, he recommends two skiing workouts per week, with other training devoted mainly to cycling. The skiing should include one endurance workout and one that's more intense, raising your heart rate to your lactate threshold for at least 30 minutes. A course with some long hills should do the trick. As for cycling, Skip suggests two

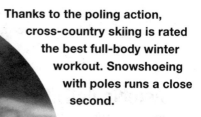

Thanks to the poling action, cross-country skiing is rated the best full-body winter workout. Snowshoeing with poles runs a close second.

steady road rides per week (conditions permitting) to maintain endurance, plus a couple of hilly mountain bike rides for strength and power. If it's not possible to ride outside, use an indoor trainer.

Snowshoeing. This is an excellent complement (or alternative) to skiing that you already know how to do because it's this simple: If you can walk, you can snowshoe. It doesn't require perfect snow or groomed trails. In fact, you can do it anywhere there's a few inches of the white stuff.

Snowshoeing develops strength, power, and aerobic capacity. It's similar to mountain biking in that it gives you all-terrain capability. It lets you travel through areas that would be too difficult or dangerous to ski. Even so, no special technique is needed. You'll find that the lower-body range of motion is similar to that of cycling. Cross-country ski poles help provide balance and thrust in deep snow or hilly terrain. As in skiing, using them also conditions upper-body muscles.

This is a deceptive sport. It looks easy, yet the cardiovascular intensity is anything but. On climbs, newcomers will get sore in their hip flexors, quadriceps, and butt just as they would when cycling hard in hilly terrain. Going down is a blast. The snow cushions each step to protect your knees—and everything else—if you take a tumble. Snowshoe racers train with intervals, hill work, and long, steady distance—the same tools used in cycling. You can do formal workouts like these, or just go out for a power hike. Hills or deep snow will ensure a good workout without the need to force it. Compared with running at the same speed, snowshoeing requires more effort and burns more calories.

Aerobic Activities

Inline skating. Okay, now let's suppose you live in an area where usable snow is rare or nonexistent. You'll miss the fun of skiing and snowshoeing, but you can still get similar fitness benefits if you lace on a pair of inline skates. Skating is especially good for developing the quadriceps, hamstrings, and powerful gluteal muscles of the butt. For decades before inline skates were invented, a traditional winter sport for cyclists was speed skating on frozen lakes and ice rinks. Conversely, numerous world-class speed skaters used cycling as their summer sport and became stars on the bike, too. The list includes Connie Carpenter, Sheila Young, and Eric and Beth Heiden.

"Precision heart rate training is the key to improving your fitness with inline skating," says cycling coach Tom Schuler, himself a former speed skater. "Get scientific about your workouts. Use a heart rate monitor to ensure that you are getting your heart rate into the 70- to 80-percent target range that develops your cardiovascular system. Do a combination of steady-state skating to increase your aerobic capacity and burn fat, and higher intensity hill workouts to push yourself to your anaerobic threshold and build strength and power."

Here's an example of an inline skating workout that will give you these benefits. Newcomers to the sport should begin with simple 30-minute steady-state skates, then switch to interval workouts like this one as skill improves.

1. Stretch and warm up by skating for 5 to 10 minutes at a heart rate that's 50 to 60 percent of your maximum.

2. For the next 20 to 30 minutes, alternate 3 minutes at a heart rate that's 80 to 90 percent of max with 3 minutes at 60 to 70 percent of max.

3. Cool down for 5 minutes by decreasing intensity to 50 to 60 percent of max.

Always wear protective gear when skating. You're almost certain to take a tumble now and then, especially when learning. Knee pads, elbow pads, and hand/wrist guards will help you avoid needless injury. And always wear your cycling helmet, just in case.

Running. Regardless of what you might hear, running is not detrimental to cyclists. It's a fine cardiovascular conditioner and a good addition to your off-season program. It's also one of the least expensive and most versatile forms of exercise. The only thing you need to buy is a high-quality pair of running shoes. Then you can run virtually any place at any time.

There are some drawbacks, however, which is why running was frowned upon by cycling traditionalists until quite recently. The main one is the leg and hip soreness that a bike rider is almost certain to experience because of running's weight-bearing nature. Unlike a cyclist making light and fluid pedal strokes, each stride a runner takes produces an impact greater than body weight. The result can be nearly catatonic soreness or actual injury if you don't ease into a running program (or any other sport that involves running, for that matter).

Once you have the shoes, start stretching your legs well and taking fast walks that include some jogging intervals. You'll probably still get sore, but this gradual approach will reduce the danger of injury to your muscles or joints. Do this every other day, alternating with workouts such as indoor cycling or swimming that are relatively easy on the legs. Soon you'll be jogging more of the time, as soreness becomes a thing of the past. It helps to stretch following the workout, too. Once you're up and running, be sure to begin and end each session with several minutes of stretching and easy jogging for warming up and cooling down.

As in the previous activities, workouts can range from steady-state efforts to intervals. Uphill running may have the best carryover to cycling, because it emphasizes short strides and quadriceps power, and it produces a redline heart rate. Lots of bike racers who live in hilly terrain will either do repeats up a tough section or run on an undulating loop. Be very cautious on the downhills. It's easy to get going too fast and give your knees and hips a dangerous pounding. Remove the risk by walking the descents, using them to recover fully for the next uphill effort.

Avoid pavement whenever possible. The relative softness of natural surfaces, combined with the cushioning and support of good shoes, will reduce the chance of injuries. But if you do develop pain or nagging soreness, back off running rather than risk a chronic problem that will carry over to cycling. Usually a few days away will heal you up, and then you can ease into it again. In the meantime, switch to non-weight-bearing activities such as cycling or swimming.

Remember, you're a cyclist first and a runner second (or third or fourth). There's plenty else you can do to stay fit in the off-season if running doesn't agree with you. Don't force it.

Swimming. Most cyclists who swim do so because they enjoy the activity, not because they think it will help them ride better. Swimming helps cardiovascular fitness and teaches breath control, but in terms of the muscles used, there's little carryover to pedaling a bike. In a way this is good, because the muscles you do use to swim are primarily in the chest, shoulders, and back—areas not conditioned by cycling.

The first requirement is finding a pool that isn't too crowded and has convenient hours. For effective lap swimming, it should be at least 25 yards long and have lane buoys. Check with your local YMCA, college, or health club to see if they have fitness swimming programs. Any triathlete in the area will know where the pools are. Then, of course, you need to know how to swim reasonably well in order to get effective workouts. The freestyle (crawl) stroke is all but mandatory for lap swimming, especially when sharing a lane with other people. It requires about 80 percent upper-body strength and 20 percent leg strength, improving your range of motion in the shoulders while loosening your hamstrings and hip flexors—tight, injury-prone areas in most cyclists.

As with any of the off-season sports, you need to maintain a heart rate in your training zone in order to get fitness benefits. Some heart rate monitors work in the water, or you can stop occasionally to check your pulse manually. Be aware that your heart may beat 13 to 15 fewer times per minute for the same perceived effort you have in other activities, owing to the water's coolness and pressure. Help make up this difference by kicking steadily instead of just dragging your legs behind you.

If your freestyle technique needs help, have a good swimmer or coach watch you for a few laps and explain what you need to work on. An excellent source for how-to information and effective workouts is Rodale's *Fitness Swimmer,* a bimonthly magazine. Steady swims of up to a mile will help you maintain a fitness base and possibly improve your endurance, but workout after workout of lap after lap may eventually sink your enthusiasm. It's better to mix distance swims with interval workouts in which you push the pace and try techniques such as kicking with a kickboard or pulling only with your arms.

Weight Training

We've made the case throughout this book that success in long-distance cycling requires speed and power, not just endurance. The last we get best through on-bike training, while the strength that's needed to push big gears, climb steep hills, bore through headwinds, and tame technical trails can be developed very well with weight training. Winter is the ideal time to make these gains. As a bonus, greater strength also improves endurance by reducing the overall body fatigue you feel after hours on the bike. Here's an example: Think about what hurts during your first long rides of the spring. For many cyclists, their triceps lead the list. These arm muscles, which are used in holding the upper body in position, will gradually be conditioned by lots of miles, but most of the soreness can be avoided in the first place by a winter weight program that includes a simple exercise called triceps extensions.

Studies have found that weight training boosts both absolute strength and time to exhaustion, and it does so without an increase in maximal oxygen consumption. In addition, researchers at the University of Maryland investigated the effects of weight training on lactate threshold and endurance. Eighteen men were randomly assigned to either a strength training group for 12 weeks or to a control group that did no strength training. Despite no difference in maximal oxygen consumption after 3 months, the strength-trained men had a 33 percent increase in cycling time to exhaustion when pedaling at 75 percent of their peak oxygen consumption. There also was a significant reduction in their blood lactate concentrations at exercise intensities between 55 and 75 percent of peak oxygen consumption. In fact, their lactate thresholds averaged 12 percent higher.

Okay, now exactly what does this mean for all of us who want to ride longer and stronger? Sports physiologist Steve Fleck, Ph.D., who has worked with various Olympic athletes, explains it this way: "A higher lactate threshold means that a cyclist can ride at a higher intensity before fatigue sets in and causes a reduction in speed. The Maryland study indicates that strength training improves endurance performance independently of changes in oxygen consumption. This improvement appears to be related to increases in lactate threshold and leg strength." The bottom line is that strength training and endurance training are not mutually exclusive. Combined, they produce improved performance.

Now, before you move into the weight room, remember that strength training is supplemental training for cycling. Yes, it can improve performance, but it's not meant to substitute for actually pedaling a bike. In addition, we're not talking heavy lifting here. Perhaps it's best to think in terms of *resistance* training rather than *weight* training. It's as important to condition tendons and ligaments as it is muscles, and this won't happen safely when pushing heavy weights. Never lose sight of the fact that we are cyclists, not bodybuilders or powerlifters.

EXERCISES

Here are Ed Burke's recommendations for a simple-yet-effective strength-training program. It's adapted to endurance cyclists from the routines used by the Olympic-caliber racers Ed has worked with. Some of the exercises don't require equipment—your body weight is sufficient. Others can be done using a basic barbell/dumbbell set, bench, and squat rack; a multigym; or the specialized machinery at a health club. If you have any doubt about the proper way to do an exercise, ask a professional trainer in your town. Always stretch before starting a workout. A good way to warm muscles and get blood flowing is to hop on a stationary bike for a few minutes.

Back extensions. Lie facedown on the floor, arms at your sides. Contract your lower back muscles to raise your upper torso. Relax to return to the floor. Repeat. To increase the resistance, put your hands behind your head. Hold a light weight there if necessary. This exercise also can be done on a back extension machine at a health club. Cycling benefit: strengthens lower back to improve riding comfort and stabilize the torso when climbing.

Bent rows. Using a barbell, bend forward till your upper body is nearly parallel to the floor. Keep your knees slightly bent. Grip the barbell at shoulder width and pull it to your lower chest, then lower it slowly. Repeat. Using a machine, sit facing it with your knees slightly bent and feet braced. Keep your back straight as you pull the bar toward your lower chest, then return it slowly till your arms are straight. Repeat. Cycling benefit: strengthens shoulders and upper back to pull on the handlebar when climbing or sprinting. Rows are particularly beneficial for mountain bikers who ride technical trails. In fact, former world champ Ned Overend calls this his favorite exercise.

Bench press. Lie on the bench with your feet flat on the floor. Slowly lower the bar to your upper chest (nipple level), then push it up to full arm extension. Don't arch your back. Repeat. If you're using a barbell rather than a machine, you must have a spotter to help you in case you can't finish the last rep. Pushups are a good substitute exercise. Cycling benefit: aids upper-body support by strengthening the chest, shoulders, and triceps.

Triceps extensions. Raise a barbell overhead, then bend your elbows to slowly lower it behind your neck. Keeping your arms against your ears, push the barbell to full extension. Repeat. This also can be done with one arm at a time using a dumbbell, or on a machine by pushing the bar downward from your shoulders to upper thighs while keeping your elbows by your sides. Cycling benefit: strengthens the arm muscles that support your upper body on the handlebar.

Crunches. Lie on your back with your feet flat on the floor. Even better, bend your hips and knees 90 degrees to hold your feet in the air. Put your hands on your chest or behind your head (but don't pull). Tuck your chin, and slowly contract your abdominal muscles to curl your shoulders off the floor. Pause, lower slowly, and repeat. You're doing it right when there are just 6 to 8 inches of movement, and only your abdominal muscles are used. Cycling benefit: remedies one of the weakest body parts for cyclists (and most other people), the abdominal muscles. Strong abs are key to transferring your power to the pedals when climbing, and to providing the muscle balance that reduces the risk of lower-back injury.

Squats. This is one of the best exercises for cyclists, but it's also potentially dangerous. Never do squats without a spotter or a rack that will catch the bar should you lose balance or not be able to complete the last rep. Leg presses on a machine eliminate the risks and are nearly as effective. When squatting, keep your head up, back straight, and feet flat, and do not go lower than the point where your thighs are parallel to the floor. Cycling benefit: increased strength in the lower back and the powerful pedaling muscles of the thighs and butt.

Lunges. Place a barbell across your shoulders behind your neck as when squatting, or hold a dumbbell in each hand by your sides. Step forward about 30 inches with one leg. That foot should be flat for stability as you pivot to the toes of the rear foot. Stop when your forward thigh is parallel to the floor. Push back to the starting position, and then step forward with the other leg. Cycling benefit: strengthens the upper thigh, hips, butt, and lower back.

Heel raises. Stand with toes on a two-by-four or other raised surface. Hold a barbell across your shoulders, or a dumbbell in each hand. Slowly rise onto your toes, then return your heels to the floor. Repeat. Cycling benefit: strengthens the calves and Achilles tendon for a more powerful pedal stroke, especially during seated climbing.

Step ups. Face a 16- to 18-inch-high bench (or box) with a barbell across your shoulders or a dumbbell in each hand. With one leg, step onto the bench, pause while standing tall on that foot, then step down. Repeat with the same leg till the set is complete, then do the other leg.

Cycling benefit: strengthens the thighs and lower back to improve the power portion of the pedal stroke.

YEARLY SCHEDULE

There's no one mandatory way to strength-train. Use our exercise suggestions and the equipment that's available to set up a program that fits your schedule, objectives, and ambition. In general, we recommend using lighter weights that allow more reps. Higher reps may have some endurance value, and they tend to build strength without bulk. Plus, there's less risk of injury or burnout when you steer clear of heavy metal. If every set ends in maximum strain and pain, you might start looking for less brutal ways to spend your time. It's better when you can do up to 15 repetitions before nearing your limit, and then stop one rep short of maximum.

Here's a basic schedule. It's okay to stop lifting when the cycling season begins in earnest—many riders do—but maintain your hard-won muscle tone with crunches and pushups at least every other day.

October through February: Do 1 to 3 sets of 10 to 15 reps of each exercise every other day. If you're in a time bind, it's been found that one set done to maximum reps is nearly as effective as multiple sets.

March and April: On 2 days per week, do 1 or 2 sets of the upper-body exercises (crunches, back extensions, triceps extensions, rows, bench press), and do 1 set of lower-body exercises (squats, lunges, heel raises, step ups). Do 10 to 15 reps of each exercise.

May through September. If you want to continue working with weights, do a 1-set, 8- to 12-rep maintenance program that includes all of the upper-body exercises. Once or twice a week is enough. Don't worry about your legs, which will be getting all of the work they need on the bike.

GLOSSARY

A

Aerobic: Exercise at an intensity that allows the body's need for oxygen to be continually met. This intensity can be sustained for long periods.

Anaerobic: Exercise above the intensity at which the body's need for oxygen can be met. This intensity can be sustained only briefly.

B

BMB: Boston-Montreal-Boston, North America's version of Paris-Brest-Paris. Held every year that PBP does not occur.

Bonk: To run out of energy, usually because the cyclist has failed to eat or drink enough.

BPM: Beats per minute, in reference to heart rate.

Brevet: A qualification ride of 200, 300, 400, 600, or 1000 kilometers for PBP or BMB. All distances must be completed in order and within prescribed time limits.

C

Cadence: The number of times during 1 minute that a pedal stroke is completed. Also called "pedal rpm."

Carbohydrate: In the diet it is broken down to glucose, the body's principal energy source, through digestion and metabolism. Carbo can be simple (sugars) or complex (bread, pasta, grains, fruits, vegetables); the latter contains additional nutrients. One gram of carbohydrate supplies four calories.

Cardiovascular: Pertaining to the heart and blood vessels.

Century: A ride of 100 miles.

Chondromalacia: A serious knee injury in which there is disintegration of cartilage surfaces due to improper tracking of the kneecap. Symptoms start with deep knee pain and a crunching sensation during bending of the afflicted leg.

Criterium: A short-course road race featuring numerous laps with tight turns that put a premium on cornering and sprinting ability.

Cross-training: Combining sports for mental refreshment and physical conditioning, especially during cycling's off-season.

Cue sheet: A list of turn-by-turn directions.

Cyclocross: A fall or winter event contested mostly or entirely off pavement. Courses include such things as barricades, steps, steep hills, or other obstacles that force riders to dismount and run with their bikes.

D

Draft: The slipstream created by a moving cyclist. Another rider close behind can keep the same pace while using about 20 percent less energy.

Drops: The bottom, horizontal portion of a road bike's handlebar.

Dualie: A bike with front and rear suspension. Short for "dual suspension."

E

Electrolytes: Substances such as sodium, potassium, and chloride that are necessary for muscle contraction and maintenance of fluid levels.

Ergogenic: Something that increases a person's potential for exercise performance.

Ergometer: A stationary, bicycle-like device with adjustable pedal resistance used for physiological testing or indoor training.

F

Fat: In the diet, it is the most concentrated source of food energy, supplying nine calories per gram. Stored fat provides about half the energy required for low-intensity exercise. It is also necessary for insulation and vitamin storage.

G

Glucose: A sugar, glucose is used for energy by muscles and is the only fuel that can be used by the brain and nervous system. Also called "blood glucose."

Glutes: The gluteal muscles of the butt. They are key to pedaling power.

Glycogen: A fuel derived as glucose (sugar) from carbohydrate and stored in the muscles and liver. It's the primary energy source for high-intensity cycling. Reserves are normally depleted after about 2½ hours of riding.

H

Hamstrings: The muscle on the back of the thigh, not well developed by cycling.

Hardtail: A mountain bike with no rear suspension.

HRM: Heart rate monitor.

Hybrid: A bike that combines features of road and mountain bikes. Also called a "cross-bike."

I

Interval training: A type of workout in which periods of intense effort are alternated with periods of easy effort for recovery.

ITB: Iliotibial band, which extends along the outside of the leg from the hip to the knee.

L

Lactate threshold (LT): Also called "anaerobic threshold." The exertion level beyond which the body can no longer produce energy aerobically, resulting in the buildup of lactic acid. This is marked by muscle fatigue, pain, and shallow, rapid breathing.

Lactic acid: A substance formed during anaerobic metabolism when there is incomplete breakdown of glucose. It rapidly produces muscle fatigue and pain. Also called "lactate."

M

Maximum (max) VO2: The maximum amount of oxygen that can be consumed during all-out exertion. This is a key indicator of a person's potential in cycling and other aerobic sports. It's largely genetically determined, but can be improved somewhat by training.

Metabolism: The physical and chemical processes through which energy is made available.

Metric century: A 100-kilometer ride (62 miles).

Mitrochondria: Microscopic filaments that are the source of energy in cells.

O

Orthotics: Custom-made supports worn in shoes to help neutralize biomechanical imbalances in the feet or legs.

OTC: Olympic Training Center. The main one for cyclists is in Colorado Springs.

Overtraining: Deep-seated fatigue, both physical and mental, caused by training at an intensity or volume too great for adaptation.

P

Paceline: A single-file group formation in which each rider takes a turn breaking the wind at the front before pulling off, dropping to the rear position, and riding the others' draft until at the front once again.

PAC Tour: A company that holds endurance training camps and rapid transcontinental tours that average between 110 and 140 miles per day. Its Web site is at www.pactour.com.

Panniers: Large bike bags used by touring cyclists or commuters. Panniers attach to racks that place them low on each side of the rear wheel, and sometimes the front wheel.

Patella: Kneecap.

PBP: Paris-Brest-Paris, cycling's oldest event, first conducted in 1891 and now held every 4 years. Riders must cover the 1200-

kilometer (744-mile) course in 90 hours or less, meeting time limits at checkpoints along the way.

Power: The combination of speed and strength.

PR: Personal record.

Protein: In the diet, it is required for tissue growth and repair. Composed of structural units called amino acids. Protein is not a significant energy source unless not enough calories and carbohydrate are consumed. One gram of protein equals four calories.

PSI: Pounds per square inch, the unit of measure for tire inflation and air pressure in some suspensions.

Q

Quadriceps: The muscle group on the front of the thigh, well developed by cycling. "Quads" for short.

R

RAAM: Race Across America, an annual event for individuals and teams first run in 1982.

Randonnée: A long-distance event in which cyclists must ride an exact course and reach checkpoints within prescribed times. The riders are called "randonneurs."

Randonneurs USA: The organization in charge of qualifying American cyclists to ride in PBP and BMB. Its Web site is at www.rusa.org.

RDA: "Recommended dietary allowance," the amount of a given nutrient that should be consumed during a day.

Repetition: Also called a "rep." In weight or interval training, each individual exertion. For example, if you press a barbell five times or do a series of five sprints, you are doing five reps.

Resistance trainer: A stationary training device into which the bike is clamped. Pedaling resistance increases with pedaling speed to simulate actual riding. Also known as an "indoor," "wind," "mag," or "fluid" trainer (the last three names derived from the fan, magnet, or liquid that creates resistance for the rear wheel).

Rollers: A stationary cycling device consisting of a low frame with three long cylinders connected by a belt. Both bike wheels roll on these cylinders so that balancing is much like actual riding.

S

Saddle sores: Skin problems in the crotch that develop from chafing caused by pedaling action. Sores can range from tender raw spots to boil-like lesions if infection occurs.

Set: In weight or interval training, one group of repetitions. For example, if you do eight reps three times, you are doing three sets.

Singletrack: A trail too narrow for two cyclists to ride side by side.

Speed: The ability to accelerate quickly or maintain a fast pace.

Speedwork: A general term for intervals and other high-velocity training, such as sprints and time trials.

Spinning: Pedaling with a fast cadence using low to moderate gears. Also, the brand name of an indoor exercise regimen that uses ergometer-like bikes.

U

Ultra: Term used for cycling events of extreme length.

UltraMarathon Cycling Association: UMCA, the rule-making and race-sanctioning organization for RAAM and other ultra events. Visit it at www.ultracycling.com.

W

Windchill: The effect of air moving across the skin, making the temperature seem colder than it actually is. A cyclist creates a windchill even on a calm day, a situation that must be considered when dressing for winter rides.

ABOUT THE AUTHORS

Edmund R. Burke, Ph.D., is a professor in and director of the Exercise Science Program at the University of Colorado at Colorado Springs. He received his doctorate in exercise physiology from Ohio State University, and his master's degree in exercise physiology from Ball State University in Muncie, Indiana. He also is a fellow of the American College of Sports Medicine. He was director of the Center of Science and Technology for the U.S. Cycling Team in Colorado Springs from 1982 to 1987. He also was a staff member for the 1980 and 1984 Olympic Cycling Teams. He has written several books on cycling physiology, health, and nutrition, and writes for several cycling magazines and Web sites.

Ed enjoys riding his road, mountain, and tandem bikes with friends and his wife, Kathleen. He has participated in such events as the Leadville 100, 24 Hours of Moab, and Iditasport. He rides several centuries and other ultra events every year.

Ed Pavelka has served as editor of *VeloNews,* the journal of competitive cycling, and as executive editor of *Bicycling* magazine. He also has produced 24 books about cycling, including the acclaimed *Bicycle Road Racing,* coauthored with U.S. Olympic cycling coach Eddie Borysewicz. His most recent work is *Mountain Bike Like a Champion,* with former world champion Ned Overend. Ed currently writes about cycling as director of content for PerformanceBike.com, the country's largest Internet cycling retailer. He is a graduate of the University of Florida's College of Journalism.

On the bike, Ed has emphasized long distances for more than 10 years. He has ridden two transcontinental PAC Tours, and in 1996 helped set the senior record of 5 days, 11 hours in the Team Race Across America. He has ridden Paris-Brest-Paris twice, with a best time of 57 hours, 35 minutes. He also holds the New York cross-state record. His personal solo records include 228 miles in 12 hours, 414 miles in 24 hours, and 100 miles in 3 hours, 59 minutes—all accomplished over age 50.

PHOTO CREDITS

© Gregg Adams, p. 225
Courtesy of BrikoUSA, p. 195
Courtesy of Ed Burke, p. 63 (right)
Courtesy of Co-Motion, p. 66
Courtesy of CompuTrainer by RacerMate, p. 82
© Chuck Haney, pp. 1, 65, 67
Courtesy of John Hughes, p. 143
© Peter Kain/Stone, p. 119
© Jeff Kausch, p. 132
© John Kelly, p. 25
© Anne Krause, p. 261
© Mel Lindstrom, p. 56
Mitch Mandel/Rodale Images, pp. 9, 202, 247, 248, 249, 256
© Scott Markewitz, pp. 5, 163
© Bryan Moody/Courtesy of Granny Gear Productions, p. 161
© David Nelson, pp. 165, 171, 181, 191, 207
Courtesy of Ed Pavelka, pp. 11, 13, 29, 69, 103, 158, 169, 221
Courtesy of Performance, pp. 63 (left), 72, 78, 80, 85, 87, 89, 97, 176, 238, 239
Courtesy of Peter White Cycles, p. 84
© Todd Powell, p. 136
© Beth Schneider, p. 255
© Paul Schraub, pp. 32–33, 40–41
© James Stratt, p. 45
Courtesy of Tourmalet, p. 60

INDEX

Underscored page references indicate boxed text. **Boldface** references indicate photographs.

A

Abrasions, 227–29
Achilles tendon, stretching, 250
Accutane, for saddle sores, 189
Adaptation, to long-distance cycling, 4
Adventure Cycling Association, touring advice from, 56
Aero bars
advantages of, 47–48, 73
avoiding, when sleepy, 159, 162
for preventing hand discomfort, 170–71, **171**
preventing neck pain from, 207–8
for touring rides, 55
Aerobic activities, for off-season conditioning, 262–64
Aerodynamics, 47–48
Aging, effect of, on cycling performance, 12–13
Air resistance, decreasing, 47–48
Allergies, 231–32
Amenorrhea, in women cyclists, 235–36
Anaerobic metabolism threshold, 150, 151

Analgesics, for muscle soreness, 193–94
Ankle, stretching, 247–48, **247**
Antibiotics, for saddle sores, 189
Antioxidants, for preventing free radical damage, 105
Arms
positioning
for mountain bike, **41**, 42
for road bike, 31, **33**
stretching, 248, **248**
Arousal
achieving adequate level of, 114–16
ranges of, 115, **115**
Asthma, exercise-induced, 231–32

B

Back
positioning
for mountain bike, **40**, 42
for road bike, **32**, 35
stretching, 246, 247, 248, **248**, 250
Back extensions
for back pain, 245
for strength training, 266

Back pain
  causes of, 208–9
  preventing, 183, 209
  treating, with
    stretching, 211, 245
    suspension, 183, 209
Bag Balm, for skin irritation, 74,
    189
Balaclava, 89, **89**, 208, 225
Bar-ends
  choosing, 73
  for mountain bike position,
    39
  for touring rides, 55
Battery lights, 83
Ben-Gay, analgesic effect of, 193,
    194
Bench press, for strength training,
    266
Benign prostatic enlargement,
    210
Bent rows, for strength training,
    266
Beverages
  carbohydrate-protein, 26–27,
    106
  sports. *See* Sports drinks
Bib shorts, 85, **85**
Bicycles
  for bad weather, 26
  calculating weight of, 61
  cleaning, after riding in rain, 53
  frame materials for, 61
  maintenance on, 27
  types of
    hybrids, 37
    mountain bikes, 64–65, **65**
    road bikes, 30–31, **32–33**,
      34–38
    sport bikes, 59–60
    tandems, 28, 65–67, **66**

touring bikes, 37, 61, 64
travel bikes, 68–70, **69**
for women, 62–63
Bike Friday, 68–69, **69**
Bike trailer, for transporting child,
    28–29
Bladder infections, in women
    cyclists, 239–40
Blisters, foot, 178–79
Boil Ease, for saddle sores, 188
Bone loss, from amenorrhea, 236
Bone mass, effect of aging on,
    12–13
Bonking
  causes of, 91, 98–99
  preventing, 98–99, 99–100
    in half-century, 126–27
Booties, 88, 89, 225
Brake levers
  for road bike position, **33**, 34
  on women's bikes, 63
Braking
  in rain, 53
  during touring rides, 55–56
Breathing, during climbing, 50
Butt
  positioning, for road bike, **32**,
    36
  stretching, 250
BYCUE cue-sheet holder, 75

C

Cadence, for climbing, 50
Caffeine
  avoiding, in winter riding, 227
  benefits of, 104–5
  gastrointestinal distress from,
    217
  for night riding, 162
Calf, stretching, 246, 247–48,
    247, 250

Calluses, foot, 179
CamelBak Razor hydration
    system, 71
Camps, cycling, 28
Candida infections, in women
    cyclists, 238–39, 240
Carbohydrate loading
  before century, 127
  classical regimen of, 92–93
  modified regimen of, 93–94, 93
  at 70 percent, 94
  when to use, 94
Carbohydrates
  consuming, during ride, 95, 98,
    99–100
  depletion of, bonking from,
    98–99
  as fuel source, 91, 92
  low-fiber, for preventing gas-
    trointestinal distress, 217
  postride consumption of,
    102–3, 106, 107
  protein taken with, 106
  in sports drink, 101–2
  storage of, 7
Cat stretch, for back pain, 245
Century
  double. *See* Double century
  nutrition for, 127–28
  off-road, preparing for, 134–35
  popularity of, 121
  preparation before, 128–31,
    130
  recovery after, 136
  strategy for, 131–33
  tapering before, 125–26
  training for, 123–25, 124, 125
Chafing, preventing, 74
Chain lube, 27
Chamois
  for comfort, 183–84, 188

lubricants for, 74
  for women, 237, 238
Chamois Butt'r
  for preventing saddle sores, 186
  for skin irritation, 74
Checklist, pre-event, 130
Chondromalacia, 199
Cleat covers, 75
Cleats, checking, after crash, 201
Climbing
  techniques for, 48–51
  during touring rides, 56
  during training, 25–26
Clipless systems, for preventing
    foot discomfort, 176–77
Clothing
  balaclava, 89, 89, 208
  bib shorts, 85, 85
  care of, 26
  foot covers, 89
  gloves, 86
  Illuminite fabric for, 87, 87, 89
  for preventing knee problems,
    201
  rainwear, 26–27, 53, 86–87
  streamlining, 48
  undershirt, 85
  vests, 86
  for winter riding, 26–27, 85,
    86, 88, 89, 224–26
Coaches, hiring, 28
CO_2 cartridges, for inflating tires,
    77
Colds
  preventing, 231
  training with, 229–30
  treating, 230–31
Cold weather
  clothing for, 85, 86, 88, 89,
    224–26
  nutritional needs in, 226–27

Cold weather *(cont.)*
  preventing neck problems from,
    208
  reducing risks from, 223–24
Commitment
  developing, 109–10
  for reaching goals, 112
Commuting, training during,
    24
CompuTrainer, 82–83, **82**
Concentration, maintaining,
    116–17
Cornering, in rain, 52
Corns, 179
Cramps, menstrual, 236–38
Cramps, muscle
  causes of, 213–14, 222–23
  quick relief for, 214–15
Crank Brothers Speed Lever,
    76–77
Crankarm length
  for mountain bike position, **41**,
    42
  for road bike position, **32**, 38
Crankarms
  checking, after crash, 201
  on women's bikes, <u>63</u>
Crash, correcting bike damage
    after, 201
Crash rash, 227–29
Cross-bikes, features of, <u>37</u>
Cross-country skiing, for off-
    season conditioning,
    260–61, **261**
Crosswinds, 46
Crotch discomfort, preventing,
    179–84, <u>237</u>
Crunches
  for back pain, 211, <u>245</u>
  for strength training, 267
Cue-sheet holder, 75

Cyclecomputers
  choosing, 79
  purpose of, 7–8
Cycling performance, effect of
    aging on, <u>12–13</u>
Cycling shorts
  choosing, 183–84, 188
  for women, <u>237</u>, **238**, **239**
Cyclocross, for off-season
    conditioning, 254–55, **255**

D

Dehydration
  muscle cramps from, 214,
    222
  preventing, 96–97
    in century, 128
    in half-century, 126
  weight loss as sign of, 107
Delayed onset of muscle soreness
    (DOMS), 212–13
Diarrhea, preventing, 216–19
Discomfort. *See also* Pain;
    Soreness
  preventing, in
    crotch, 179–84
    feet, 173–79
    hands, 168–73
Distance, increasing, 15–16
Dogs, repelling, <u>52</u>
DOMS, 212–13
Double century
  experience benefiting, 138
  expert advice on, 140
  fast, training for, <u>150–52</u>
  nutrition for, 147–49
  preventing injury from, 138–39
  tips for, 149, 152–53
  training phases for
    building base, 144–45
    creating peak, 145–46

increasing intensity, 145
tapering, 146–47
training programs for, 141–44,
   <u>142</u>
Drafting, 43–44
Drawing salve, for saddle sores,
   188
Drinking fluids. *See* Fluid
   consumption
Drinks
   carbohydrate-protein, 26–27, 106
   sports. *See* Sports drinks
Drop bar positions, for preventing
   hand discomfort, 168–69

E

Eating. *See* Food
Endurance, effect of aging on, <u>12</u>
Equipment. *See also specific*
   equipment
   care of, <u>26–27</u>
Erythromycin Topical Gel, for
   saddle sores, 188
Examination, annual physical,
   <u>218–19</u>
Exercise. *See also specific types*
   for delaying aging, <u>13</u>
Eyewear
   choosing, 70–71, 195–97, **195**
   prescription lenses for, <u>196</u>
   for preventing neck and
      shoulder pain, 206–7
   for riding in rain, 53

F

Face, stretching, 249
Fainting, from heat, 222–23
Fat, dietary
   avoiding, during ride, 95
   for double century, 149
   as fuel source, 91, **100**

Feet
   cold-weather protection for, 225
   maladies of
      blisters, 178–79
      corns and calluses, 179
      hot feet, 177–78
      ingrown toenails, 179
   positioning, for road bike, **33,**
      36–37
   preventing discomfort in, with
      clipless systems, 176–77
      orthotics, 179
      shoe selection, 173, 174–76
Fenders, 74–75
Fiber, avoiding, during ride, 96
50-mile rides. *See* Half-century
Fingers, stretching, 250
Flexibility
   benefits of, 243
   effect of aging on, <u>13</u>
   problems from lack of, 242,
      245–46
Fluid consumption
   for century, 128
   for half-century, 126
   in hot weather, 220, 221–22
   postride, 106–7
   pre-event, 96
   for preventing
      dehydration, 96–97
      gastrointestinal distress, 218
   during ride, 99–100, 101–2
   for winter riding, 226–27
Food
   for century, 127–28
   difficulty in choosing, 90
   for double century, 147–48
   drinks as, 26–27
   for half-century, 126–27
   liquid meals, 148
   postride nutrition, 102–3

Food *(cont.)*
  preride nutrition, 91–94, 95–96
    carbohydrate loading, 92–94,
      <u>93</u>
    fuel sources, 91–92
    glycogen limits, 92
  during ride, 96, <u>98–99</u>, 99–100
  for touring rides, 55
  for winter riding, 226
Foot covers, 89
Foot position, for preventing knee
      injury, 201
Fore/aft saddle location
  for mountain bike position, 39,
      40
  for road bike position, **32**, 36
Forearms, stretching, 250
Frame
  materials for, 61
  for mountain bike position, **41**,
      42
  for road bike position, **32**, 38
  on women's bikes, <u>62</u>
Free radical damage, antioxidants
      for preventing, <u>105</u>
Fructose, gastrointestinal distress
      from, 96, 217
Fuel sources, 91–92, **100**
Full-body stretch, 247

G

Gardnerella infections, in women
      cyclists, 239
Gastrointestinal distress,
      preventing, 96, 216–19
Generator lights, 83–84, **84**
Gloves
  choosing, 86, <u>88</u>
  for preventing hand discomfort,
      172–73
  for touring rides, 55

Glucose, as fuel source, **100**
Glycogen
  depletion of, 92
  in endurance training, 7
  as fuel source, 91, **100**
  replenishment of
      postride, 102–3, 106, 107
      pre-event, 95
Glycogen supercompensation. *See*
      Carbohydrate loading
Goal-setting
  realistic, 111–12
  strategy for, 112–13
  training diary for, 117–18
Graduated stress test, for
      determining maximum
      heart rate, 8–9
Grips, for preventing hand
      discomfort, 172–73
Groin, stretching, 246, 248

H

Half-century
  nutrition for, 126–27
  preparation before, 128–31,
      <u>130</u>
  tapering before, 125–26
  training for, 122–23
Hamstrings, stretching, 246, 248,
      249, 250
Handlebar covers, for cold
      weather, <u>88</u>
Handlebar palsy, 172
Handlebars
  for mountain bike position, 39,
      41
  for road bike position, **33**, 34
  on women's bikes, <u>63</u>
Hands
  cold-weather protection for,
      225

positioning
  for mountain bike, **41**, 42
  for road bike, 31, **33**, 34
  preventing discomfort in, 168
    aero bars for, 170–71, **171**
    drop bar positions for,
      168–69
    gloves for, <u>88</u>, 172–73
    grips for, 173
    mittens for, <u>88</u>, 225
    mountain bike bars for,
      170
Head
  cold-weather protection for,
    225
  positioning
    for mountain bike, **41**, 42
    for road bike, 31, **33**
Headwinds, 46
Heart rate
  elevated, as sign of overtraining,
    18
  measuring, 19
Heart rate monitor (HRM)
  purpose of, 7–8
  selecting, 10, 80
Heart rate zones, 9–10
Heat
  dehydration from, 96–97
  riding in, 219–22
Heat exhaustion, 222–23
Heatstroke, 222–23
Heat syncope, 222–23
Heel raises, for strength training,
  267
Helmet, choosing, 70
Helmet light, 83
Hips, stretching, 246
HRM. *See* Heart rate monitor
  (HRM)
Hybrids, features of, <u>37</u>

Hydration. *See* Fluid
  consumption
Hydration systems, 71, **97**, <u>99</u>
Hypothermia, symptoms of, 226

I

Iliotibial-band (ITB) syndrome,
  200, 202
Illness, training after, 16
Illuminite fabric, 77, 87, **87**, 89, 163
Indoor cycling
  disadvantages of, 255–56
  techniques for, 256–58, **256**
  workouts for, 258–60
Indoor trainer
  choosing, 81–83
  training on, 27
Infections
  bladder, 239–40
  yeast, 238–39
Ingrown toenails, 179
Injury(ies)
  knee, 198–200
    preventing, 200–201
    therapy for, 202–3
  preventing, from double
    century, 138–39
  training after, 16
Inline skating, for off-season
  conditioning, 262
Insulin, in glycogen formation,
  103, 106
Intensity
  in endurance training, 10–11,
    143
  increasing, for double century,
    145
ITB syndrome, 200, 202

J

Jacket, for winter riding, 224

K

Knee injuries, 198–200
  frontal, 199–200, 202
  medial, 200, 202–3
  preventing, 200–201
  therapy for, 202–3
Knees
  anatomy of, **199**
  stretching, 248
Kodiak Barrier vests, 86
Kool Kovers, for cleats, 75

L

LAB, 56–57
Lactate threshold
  for century, 131–32
  for fast double century,
    150–51
  testing for, 11, 14
  training at, 14–15, **15**
Lactose, gastrointestinal distress
    from, 217
Lance Armstrong Cycling Plan
    from PC Coach, as training
    software, 28
League of American Bicyclists
    (LAB), touring advice from,
    56–57
Leg-length discrepancy
  determining, 203, 204, **205**
  injuries caused by, 203–5
Legs, self-massage for, 251
Lights
  for night riding, 83–85, 153,
    163–64
  types of
    battery light, 83
    generator light, 83–84, **84**
    helmet light, 83
    Photon micro-light, 84–85
Lips, sun protection for, 192

Liquid meals, for double century,
    148
Long, slow distance (LSD)
    training, problems with, 6
Lube, chain, 27
Lunges, for strength training, 267

M

Massage
  benefits of, 250–51
  self-, 251
Maximum heart rate, determining,
    8–9
Menstrual cramps, in women
    cyclists, 236–38
Menstruation, 233–35
  cessation of, 235–36
Mental edge
  from arousal, 114–16
  for century, 133
  from concentration, 116–17
  goal-setting for, 111–13
  importance of commitment in,
    109–10, 112
  for touring rides, 54
  for training, 110–11
  training diary for, 117–18
  visualization for, 113–14
Menthol, in analgesics, 194
Methyl salicylate, in analgesics,
    194
Mirrors, rearview, 74
Mittens, 88, 225
Moleskin, for saddle sores, 189
Mountain bike
  advantages of, 64–65, **65**
  for off-season conditioning,
    253–54
Mountain bike bars, for
    preventing hand
    discomfort, 170

Mountain bike position, 38–39, **40–41**, 42
Mouth soreness, 192–93
Mudguards, 74–75
Multi tools, 73–74
Muscle cramps
  causes of, 213–14, 222–23
  quick relief for, 214–15
Muscle fibers, effect of training on, 6–7, 143
Muscle soreness
  causes of, 211–12
  preventing, 212–13
  relieving, 212
    with analgesics, 193–94
    with massage, 250–51
Muscular rigor mortis, 242

N

Neck
  positioning, for road bike, 31, **33**
  stretching, 248, 249
Neck pain
  causes of, 205–6
  preventing, 206–7
    with aero bars, 207–8
    in cold weather, 208
    with neck brace, **207**
Negative split, during century, 133
Night riding
  Illuminite fabric for, 77, 87, **87**, 89, 163
  lighting for, 83–85, 153, 163–64
  during 200-mile-plus rides, 157–59
  safety for, 163–64
Nutrition
  for century, 127–28
  for double century, 147–49

for half-century, 126–27
on-bike, 96
postride, 102–3
preride, 91–94, 95–96
  carbohydrate loading, 92–94, <u>93</u>
  fuel sources, 91–92
  glycogen limits, 92

O

Off-road century, preparing for, <u>134–35</u>
Off-road ultras, <u>160–61</u>
Off-season conditioning, activities for
  cross-country skiing, 260–61, **261**
  cyclocross, 254–55, **255**
  indoor cycling, 255–60, **256**
  inline skating, 262
  mountain biking, 253–54
  running, 263–64
  snow cycling, 253–54
  snowshoeing, 261–62
  spinning, <u>257</u>
  swimming, 264
  weight training, 264–68
100-mile rides. *See* Century
100 to 200 mile rides. *See* Double century
Orthotics
  choosing, 179
  for leg-length discrepancy, **202**, 205
Osteoporosis, <u>12–13</u>
Overtraining
  danger of, 5, 16–17
  emotional signs of, 18
  physical signs of, 17, 18
  preventing, 18–20

P

Paceline
  in century, 131
  drafting in, 43–44, **45**
  pointers for, 44–46
Packing, for touring rides, 55, 56,
    57–58
Pain. *See also* Discomfort;
    Soreness
  back, 208–9, 211, <u>245</u>
  knee, 198–203
  from leg-length discrepancy,
    203–5
  from muscle cramps, 213–15,
    222–23
  neck, 205–8
  prostate, <u>210</u>
  saddle, preventing, 180–82,
    183–84
Panniers
  choosing, 78, **78**
  for touring rides, **56**, 57, 58
Patella tendinitis, 199, 202
Pedaling, for climbing, 50
Pedals
  checking, after crash, 201
  for cold weather, <u>88</u>
Pelvic tilt, for back pain, <u>245</u>
Photon micro-light, 84–85
Physical examination, annual,
    <u>218–19</u>
Plateaus, for increasing mileage,
    16
Position, riding
  on mountain bike, 38–39,
    40–41, 42
  on road bike, 30–31, **32–33**,
    34–38
  for women, <u>237</u>
Posture protection, from
    stretching, 245–46

PowerTap, for watts
    measurement, 80–81
Pregnancy, 240–41
Profile Air Stryke ZB aero bar,
    73
Prostate problems, <u>210</u>
Prostatitis, <u>210</u>
Protein
  avoiding, during ride, 95
  for double century, 149
  as fuel source, 92, **100**
  taken with carbohydrates, 106
  taken with sports drink, 102
Pulse, counting, 19
Pump, for inflating tires, 77

Q

Quadriceps, stretching, 246, 247,
    247

R

Racks, rear, 79
Rain, riding in, 51–53
Rainwear, 86–87
Randonneurs USA, as ultraride
    resource, 155
Rearview mirrors, 74
Recovery
  after century, 136
  importance of, 144
Recumbents, 67–68, **67**
Repairs, multi tools for, 73–74
Retinaculum, medial, thickening
    of, 200
Riding position. *See* Position,
    riding
Road bike position, 30–31,
    32–33, 34–38
Road rash, 227–29
Running, for off-season
    conditioning, 263–64

S

Saddle height
  for mountain bike position, 38, 40
  for preventing knee injury, 200–201
  for road bike position, **32**, 35–36
Saddle pain, 179–80
  preventing, with
    cycling shorts, 183–84
    saddle features, 180–82
Saddle sores
  causes of, 185–86
  preventing, 74, 186, <u>187</u>, 188
  treating, 188–89
Saddle tilt
  for mountain bike position, 38, 40
  for road bike position, **32**, 36
Saddles
  choosing, 70, 180–82, 186
  position of, for preventing discomfort, 186, <u>237</u>
  for touring rides, 55
  on women's bikes, <u>63</u>, 63, <u>237</u>
Safety, for night riding, 163–64
Salt loss, in heat, 220
Salve, drawing, for saddle sores, 188
Seatpacks
  choosing, 77
  for double century, 153
Seatposts, shock-absorbing, 71–72, **72**
Shifting
  for climbing, 50
  during touring rides, 55
Shoe/pedal system, for touring rides, 55

Shoes
  for leg-length discrepancy, 204–5
  road vs. mountain bike, **176**
  selecting, 174–76
Shorts
  bib, 85, **85**
  cycling
    choosing, 183–84, 188
    for women, <u>237</u>, **238**, **239**
  for preventing saddle sores, 188
Shoulders
  positioning
    for mountain bike, **41**, 42
    for road bike, 31, **32**
  sore, 205, 207
  stretching, 246, 248, **248**, 249
Side stretch, for back pain, <u>245</u>
Skating, inline, for off-season conditioning, 262
Skiing, cross-country, for off-season conditioning, 260–61, **261**
Skin
  functions of, 190
  irritated, preventing, 74, 185–89
  sun protection for, 190–92
Sleep, during 200-mile-plus rides, 157–58
Sleep deprivation, from 200-mile-plus rides, 155–57
Snow cycling, for off-season conditioning, 253–54
Snowshoeing, for off-season conditioning, 261–62
Socks, <u>88</u>, 89, 225
Sodium loss, in heat, 220
Software, training, 28

Soreness. *See also* Discomfort; Pain
    mouth, 192–93
    muscle
        analgesics for, 193–94
        causes of, 211–12
        massage for, 250–51
        preventing, 212–13
Sores, saddle. *See* Saddle sores
Specialized Body Geometry
        saddle, 70
Spinning, for indoor training, <u>257</u>
Sport bikes, for one-day rides,
        59–60
Sports drinks
    for century, 128
    choosing, 101–2
    for half-century, 126
    for hot weather, 220
    for muscle cramps, 215
    postride consumption of, 106–7
    for preventing
        bonking, 99–100
        heat illness, 222
    preventing gastrointestinal
        distress from, 217
    for winter riding, 227
Squats, for strength training, 267
Stem
    for mountain bike position, 39,
        41
    for road bike position, **33**,
        34–35
    on women's bikes, <u>63</u>
Step ups, for strength training,
        267–68
Stomach problems, preventing,
        216–19
Strength, effect of aging on, <u>12</u>
Strength training, for
    climbing, 51
    delaying aging, <u>12</u>, <u>13</u>

double century, 145
neck, 208
off-season conditioning
    benefits of, 264–66
    exercises for, 266–68
    yearly schedule for, 268
Stretching
    at-home, 246–47
    for back pain, 211, <u>245</u>
    benefits of, 243, 245–46
    before century, 130
    during century, 133
    importance of, 242
    for muscle cramps, 214, 215
    on-bike, 249–50
    rest-stop, 247–48, **247**, **248**,
        249
    technique for, 243–44
    when to perform, 244
Sun protection, 190–92
Sunburn, treating, 192
Sunglasses
    choosing, 70–71, 195–97, **195**
    prescription lenses for, <u>196</u>
    for preventing neck and
        shoulder pain, 206–7
Sunscreen, 191, 192
Supplements
    antioxidants, <u>105</u>
    caffeine, <u>104–5</u>
Suspension
    benefits of, <u>182–83</u>
    front, 72–73
    rear, 71–72
    for treating back pain, 209
Swimming, for off-season
        conditioning, 264

T

Tailwinds, 46
Tandems, 28, 65–67, **66**

Tapering
  before century, 125–26
  before double century, 146–47
Tetanus, from abrasions, 229
Time management, for scheduling
    long-distance cycling,
    22–29
Tire levers, choosing, 76–77
Tires
  choosing, 75–76
  deflating, for riding in rain,
    52–53
  flat, preventing, <u>26</u>
  inflating, 77
Toenails, ingrown, 179
Tools, multi, 73–74
Top tube and stem lengths, for
    road bike position, **33**, 35
Torso, stretching, 246–47
Touring, loading bike for, 54–58
Touring bikes, <u>37</u>, 61, 64
Trailer, bike, for transporting
    child, 28–29
Training
  adaptation in, 4
  building foundation for, 5–7
  carbohydrate storage and, 7
  for century, 123–25, **124**, **125**
  cyclecomputer for, 7–8
  desire and, 5
  for double century, 141–47,
    <u>142</u>, <u>150–52</u>
  effects of, 6–7
  finding time for, 22–29
  for half-century, 122–23
  heart rate monitor for, 7–8
  increasing mileage in, 15–16
  intensity in, 10–11, 143
  lactate threshold for (*see*
    Lactate threshold)
  long, slow distance, 6

  mental attitude for, 110–11
  personal style for, 4–5
  quantity vs. quality in, 3–4
  for touring rides, 54
Training diary
  for increasing training, 16
  information included in,
    20–21
  mental, 117–18
  for preventing overtraining,
    19–20
  recording century in, 136
  for reminiscing, 21
Transportation, riding for,
    24–25
Travel bikes, 68–70, **69**
Travel cases, 79
Triceps, stretching, 246–47, 250
Triceps extensions, for strength
    training, 266–67
Trichomonas infections, in women
    cyclists, 239
Trico Split-Rail saddle, 70
Trunks, rack, 77–78, **78**
Tubes, <u>26</u>
24-hour races, off-road, <u>160–61</u>
200-mile-plus rides
  essentials for, 154–55
  handling sleep deprivation
    from, 155–57
  night-riding strategies for,
    157–59
  safety equipment for, 163–64
  techniques for staying awake in,
    159, 162

U

Ultra rides, 137–38. *See also*
    Double century; 200-mile-
    plus rides
  off-road, <u>160–61</u>

UltraMarathon Cycling
    Association
    as resource for coaches, 28
    as ultra rides resource, 137, 155
Undershirt, 85
Upper body, positioning
    for climbing, 50–51
    for mountain bike, 40, 42
    for road bike, 31, 32

V

Vaginitis, in women cyclists,
    238–39
Vests, 86
Visualization, for improving
    performance, 113–14

W

Water drinking
    for half-century, 126
    during ride, 100
Weight loss
    for double century, 145
    as sign of dehydration, 107
Weight training. *See* Strength
    training
Wheels, choosing, 76
Wind, riding in, 46–47

Winter conditioning. *See* Off-
    season conditioning
Winter riding
    dressing for, 224–26
    nutrition for, 226–27
    preventing neck problems from,
        208
    reducing risks from, 223–24
Women
    bicycles for, 62–63
    health issues affecting
        amenorrhea, 235–36
        bladder infections, 239–40
        menstrual cramps, 236–38
        menstrual cycle, 233–35
        pregnancy, 240–41
        vaginitis, 238–39
    riding comfort for, 237
Wrists, positioning, for mountain
    bike, 41, 42

Y

Yeast infections, in women
    cyclists, 238–39

Z

Zephrr Classic vests, 86
Zones, heart rate, 9–10